Network Corruption: When Social Capital Becomes Corrupted

Network Corruption: When Social Capital Becomes Corrupted

Its Meaning and Significance in Corruption and Network Theory and the Consequences for (EU) Policy and Law

Willeke Slingerland

eleven
international publishing

Published, sold and distributed by Eleven International Publishing
P.O. Box 85576
2508 CG The Hague
The Netherlands
Tel.: +31 70 33 070 33
Fax: +31 70 33 070 30
e-mail: sales@elevenpub.nl
www.elevenpub.com

Sold and distributed in USA and Canada
Independent Publishers Group
814 N. Franklin Street
Chicago, IL 60610
USA
Order Placement: (800) 888-4741
Fax: (312) 337-5985
orders@ipgbook.com
www.ipgbook.com

Eleven International Publishing is an imprint of Boom uitgevers Den Haag.

ISBN 978-94-6236-880-4
ISBN 978-94-6274-932-0 (E-book)

Preface

It was a mere case of coincidence which led me to do corruption research. I don't remember having heard anything about corruption during my master's study in Groningen, so when dr. Michel van Hulten and prof. dr. Johan Wempe invited me to a Saxion roundtable on corruption, I was keen to learn more about this phenomenon and its presence in our society. This meeting led to a collective read with some fellow researchers of Michael Johnston's book *Syndromes of Corruption*. This was actually the moment when I realised that corruption is an intangible crime but nevertheless the root cause of bad governance, poverty, inequality, pollution; major challenges lawyers, social scientists, decision-makers and others seek to solve. This triggered me to analyse corruption in greater depth to get an understanding of the mechanisms behind corruption.

The main international organisations such as the United Nations, the Council of Europe and the OECD have established their own conventions against corruption, but the fight against corruption remains a problematic one. One reason its eradication is problematic is the fact that there are ways in which decision-making is influenced, which some argue to be corruption, while others consider this to be part of normal politics. This observation triggered me to write a book on defining and measuring corruption. However, I soon found out that in the past many scholars had already attempted to come up with a universal definition of corruption and all of these attempts had failed. The main reason for this failure is that there is no consensus in the international community on any one definition which captures all the appearances of corruption.

I did not have the illusion of being able to solve this issue, so I abandoned the plan to qualify and quantify corruption. This decision was also prompted by three other realisations during the first years of my corruption research. One of the experiences, which also taught me the most about corruption, is the research I carried out as part of the pan-European project on the model National Integrity Systems by order of Transparency International. This model is built on the idea of the coherence of law and policies and practices among and within society's institutions. In order to get an objective and realistic picture of the National Integrity System (NIS) of the Netherlands, I carried out 42 interviews with key figures of these institutions. Doors remained closed when I made clear that I also wanted to talk about corruption in the Netherlands and doors were opened when I underlined that the interview would be about integrity. Nevertheless, I did touch upon the topic of corruption during these interviews, and nearly all interviewees had their own examples, concerns and dilemmas which lay at the heart of corruption, namely when does 'influence' become 'undue influence'?

The second experience which stimulated me to do research into the phenomenon, which I would later refer to as 'network corruption', is my work as the National Corruption Correspondent for the Netherlands, reporting to the European Commission. I report on corruption developments together with the 27 other correspondents, and during our informal talks I became aware that the other correspondents also observed the complexity of assessing issues related to networks, the elite, informal circuits and corruption in their countries. Many of these countries named, in particular those in the northwest of the EU, are praised for their low corruption levels in international rankings. So I started to wonder what concepts and notions of corruption are used in these rankings and whether they include these other contexts or whether they departed from the traditional concept of bribery.

Sometimes you look back and realise you learned more from the journey than the point of arrival itself. This is definitely true when I reflect on my experiences during the NIS project. Initially I thought that the Dutch government would be keen on hearing the conclusions of this report. Little did I know that the weaknesses in the overall well-performing Dutch NIS would cause such turmoil. The Minister of Security and Justice had expressed that he wanted to officially receive the report in the Dutch Parliamentary Press Centre Nieuwspoort. Nevertheless, a few weeks before the press presentation of the NIS, I received an email from his staff, indicating that I had to get rid of two of my conclusions; otherwise, not only would he refuse to accept the report, but my methodology, the report and I myself would also be discredited publicly. I did not censor the report and alternatively I handed it to the National Ombudsman. This third experience taught me that striving for specific interests can coincide with undue influencing. Six years after this personal experience, this practice would make the headlines, when current affairs programme Nieuwsuur reported that on several occasions senior justice officials of the Ministry of Security and Justice had directly interfered with independent research into the Ministry's own policies. Officials deleted research questions, made notes in the study and removed entire chapters with conclusions and recommendations on how government policy could be improved. The then Minister of Security and Justice, Opstelten, would later defend his policies before the House of Representatives to show these studies supported his policy (Meijer, 2017).

More interested than ever due to these experiences, I continued with the research and the questions which arose from these experiences offered a good starting point to conduct a study on the link between networks and corruption, to try to distinguish when influencing becomes undue influence. There is a large body of knowledge on individual corruption and corruption by companies, but the available literature on corruption by informal groups and associations is limited, even though society is asking for it. On the one hand, there is a clear attempt in most EU member states to regulate behaviour linked to connections, such as the rules on lobbying, the financing of political parties, asset declarations and conflicts of interest, as well as the cooling down periods for former ministers. On the other hand, these member states remain hesitant to criminalise the corrupt offence of 'trading in influence' because they consider networking, interest representation and lobbying to be fundamental in politics and democracy and, as such, believe it should not be regulated.

Nearly every person I spoke to during the eight years of my corruption research showed a keen interest in the topic of networks and corruption. It is clear that this subject matters to everybody. During these conversations, nearly everyone with whom I spoke deemed it impossible to distinguish 'influence' from 'undue influence' and some even advised me to refrain from my corruption research because corruption will always be present and most individuals will eventually go a long way to influence decision-making. I doubt whether this is true. My research has taught me that our current concepts of corruption are too limited and that there is too much focus on the individual acting, which hinders us from getting to the core of the corruption concept. With this book I aim to contribute, based on a conceptual and empirical analysis of networks and corruption, to alternative ways of preventing and combating corruption. I will explain how we could, and should, acknowledge the powerful context of networks and their great influence on our society.

This book is the result of more than eight years of research and I could not have written it without the support of my colleagues, friends and family. I owe a big thank-you to dr. Michel van Hulten for his inspiring stories and talks on corruption. I have good memories of our work on anti-corruption in Romania. Prof. dr. Johan Wempe has been my nestor from the beginning and his support, honest feedback and belief in a good end result kept me going. Johan, thank you so much for challenging me to broaden my horizon and jump into the deep and do things outside my comfort zone. I've learned so much from you. Prof. dr. Leo Huberts, a big thank-you for introducing me to the topic of Integrity Systems and supporting my research on networks and corruption. I would like to thank prof. dr. Paul Heywood for fact-checking the phone-hacking case and Bruce Searby from the US Department of Justice for fact-checking the FIFA case. Also a word of gratitude to prof. dr. Wouter Stam for reading my chapter on networks and prof. dr. Frank Anechiarico for his feedback on my chapter on corruption. Also a big thank-you to staff of the Rijksrecherche and investigative journalists for checking the facts of the Roermond case. I would also like to express my gratitude to all of you with whom I got the chance to write articles, speak at conferences and have informal talks about corruption. These moments offered valuable insights and ideas on how to set up and carry out my research.

Last but not least I want to thank my amazing family and friends. Especially during the last stage of my research, I often had to give my research priority over leisure time and time off to do great things with all of you. I hope we can catch up and finally pick days to get away.

Deventer, August 28, 2018

The leading counsel in the judicial Leveson Inquiry, Robert Jay QC, on the perception of influence between the Press and the Police, referred to the deterioration of networks as follows:

> "… As so often happens in human affairs, the difference between healthy and dysfunctional behaviours does not have to be vast. By this, I mean at least two things: first, that it does not necessarily take many rotten apples to undermine the whole body politic, and secondly, that very often it does not take many adjustments in behaviours, objectively measured, to turn what is good into what is bad and vice versa. More precisely, the potential for abuse on both sides of this bilateral equation is significant, leading to the risk, if not the reality, of unhealthy, over-cosy and overly close relations between the two … Ultimately, the vice here is lack of democratic accountability and the perception, if not the reality, of personal gain. The noun "gain" in this context needs, of course, to be broadly interpreted and should certainly be apt to accommodate the enhancement of an individual's professional or personal profile." (Honourable Lord Justice Leveson, 2012: 851).[1]

1 Quote from Case Study 2 of this study: United Kingdom's News of the World (NoW) International phone-hacking scandal.

Table of Contents

List of Abbreviations

ACR	Anti-Corruption Report
CFU	Caribbean Football Union
CoE	The Council of Europe
Concacaf	The Confederation of North, Central America and Caribbean Association
COSP	The Conference of the States Parties
ECJ	European Court of Justice
FBI	Federal Bureau of Investigation
FIFA	The Fédération Internationale de Football Association
GRECO	The Group of States against Corruption
ISCT	Integrative Social Contract Theory
ISL	International Sport and Leisure
LRCC	The network of local research correspondents on corruption
NIS	National Integrity System
NoW	News of the World
RICO	The US Racketeer Influenced and Corrupt Organisations Act
TFEU	The Treaty on the Functioning of the European Union
TI	Transparency International
UN	The United Nations
UNODC	The United Nations Office on Drugs and Crime
UNWCC	The United Nations War Crimes Commission

1. Introduction

1.1 Research Subject

In this introduction to my research I will claim that our society suffers from corruption, yet too little is known about the role networks play in the emergence of corruption. Networks generally have a positive connotation and are considered to make up the social capital which human beings depend on, but their unique characteristics not only contribute to positive outcomes but can also result in unforeseen behaviour which can have damaging social effects. I will argue that this research into 'network corruption' will make a phenomenon visible which our society has hitherto been unable to recognise, understand and deal with. This chapter provides an introduction into the research subject (paragraph 1.1), the purpose of the research (paragraph 1.2), the central question (paragraph 1.3), the relevance and implications of the research (paragraph 1.4), the research method (paragraph 1.5) and a guide to the subsequent chapters (paragraph 1.6).

1.1.1 Corruption Cases

Corruption cases continue to make the headlines in Europe. Some of these cases are straightforward corruption cases in which an individual bribed a civil servant or politician and in return received a favour. For instance, in July 2015 a Norwegian court sentenced four former top executives of the world's biggest nitrate fertiliser maker, Yara, to jail, for paying bribes (USD eight million) to Libyan and Indian officials and in return was allowed to establish joint ventures in their respective countries (Berglund, 2015). In that same month, ex-News of the World features editor, Jules Stenson, was given a prison sentence for plotting to hack phones in the UK phone-hacking scandal. He was the ninth journalist convicted of phone hacking. In 2014, his former colleague, Dan Evans, was sentenced to prison on grounds of phone hacking and making illegal payments to officials in return for access to more than a thousand hacked voicemail messages (BBC, 2015; The Guardian, 2014). In the Netherlands, a former provincial governor, Ton Hooijmaijers, was sentenced to a prison sentence of two and a half years because, among others, he accepted bribes from project developers and entrepreneurs and in return gave them the provincial contracts (ECLI:NL:GHAMS:2015: 1212). According to the judges, he maintained close ties with entrepreneurs from the real estate sector. Seven entrepreneurs and four companies settled with the public prosecutor to escape criminal prosecution (Openbaar Ministerie, 2015; Kreling, 2015). At the same time, multinationals such as Siemens, Philips, Petrobras and SBM Offshore were accused of bribery. Although all of the above examples are worrisome from a moral perspective, the laws and policies throughout most EU states are clear and provide clear-cut provisions to investigate, accuse and sentence those involved in this bribery. However, in many of the major cases of (suspected) corruption something else is going on. While individuals were either sentenced for or cleared of bribery claims, the overall impression remains that the issue at stake is more complex, involving dense relationships in which bribery and other forms of abuse occurred; it appears to be a systemic problem.

1.1.2 *The Reason for This Research*

In this research, three such complex case studies are presented: the cases concerning the international football governing body FIFA, the News of the World (NoW) case from the United Kingdom and the case of the municipality of Roermond in the Netherlands. During the initial investigations, public prosecution communicated that these were complex cases, with various forms of abuse occurring within the relationships of individuals. The FIFA case and the Dutch case are referred to as corruption scandals, both by law enforcement officials and the media, while the case from the United Kingdom was presented as the Phone-Hacking-Scandal, in which corruption was a means to facilitate the other abuse, phone hacking. Unintentionally but not surprisingly, the images of Sepp Blatter and Michel Platini (FIFA), Rupert Murdoch and Rebekah Brooks (NoW) and Jos van Rey and Piet van Pol (Roermond) come into our minds when thinking of these scandals. It is common to seek to place the blame on a few individuals who are found to be connected with the criminal and, in this case, corrupt conduct. Individual responsibility is something we can comprehend. The fact that many individuals might have been connected, and that these connections led to serious wrongdoings, is difficult to process.

While national public prosecutors hinted that the misconduct was part of a collective behaviour or reflected the culture of the context in which the abuse could emerge, affairs like these result in very few prosecutions, or the prosecutions fail during trial. Although not all three cases are presented as corruption cases, they do appear to present a different category of corruption: those in which the interaction of multiple actors within a social network results in corruption but in which the individual behaviour as such is not necessarily corrupt. This means that these individuals have organised themselves in networks, which function as a social system. Although officials are aware of and do consider the role networks played in the emergence of corruption, this network character cannot be taken into account when assessing the individual acts, nor can the network itself be assessed due to the legal way in which corruption is approached. An important argument which is used to exclude networks from the application of criminal law is that networks are not formal organisations like companies, nor are they criminal organisations established to commit crimes.

The first reason for this research is that a gap appears to exist in the available theories on corruption; very little research is available on corruption by a network, nor does the network theory thoroughly discuss the risks or pitfalls of networks. The second reason for this research is the observation that policies and investigations appear to be limited in dealing with corruption in network-like structures, while at the same time international and European organisations refer to 'trading in influence', political and high-profile corruption and the need to eradicate these forms of corruption. As will be described in paragraphs 3.3 and 3.4, the descriptions of both trading in influence and 'political corruption' are such that they refer to a web, circle or network in which corruption occurs.

1.2 Research Purpose

This research introduces the concept of 'network corruption' to address the issue of social networks becoming corrupted. The issue at stake is more complex, involving dense relationships in which bribery and other forms of abuse occur; it appears to be a systemic problem. Here corruption seems to be more than the sum of all individual acts; individual acts are mutually reinforcing, through which another form of corruption emerges. The Council of Europe (CoE) has called upon states to criminalise trading in influence and the European Commission has referred to the need to stand up to political corruption. Both of these appeals seek to address forms of corruption in which the trading in influence is done by means of connections. When most of the corruption cases involving networks are investigated, policy- makers and law enforcement authorities do not have adequate anti-corruption tools at their disposal. Although extensive research has been carried out into corruption, its causes, its appearances, its prevention and its punishment, corruption within or by a network has received little attention.

The starting point of this research is the fact that there is a public desire to gain a better understanding about networks generating social capital as well as forming unacceptable social structures, combined with the gap in available research on corruption by networks. This conceptual research is a prelude to improving anti-corruption policies. The research will lay a foundation for the assessment of social networks by introducing criteria for networks, which distinguish accepted ways of networking from network corruption and social capital from unacceptable social structures. This research will also offer an alternative and useful view to the concept of responsibility in corruption cases, which can be used by policy-makers and law enforcement officials in corruption prevention and repression. Here social networks are considered to be social systems, thereby recognising the different roles individuals adopt in social networks.

The EU has increasingly made its fight against corruption one of its major priorities and is thereby seeking for more effective policies to eradicate corruption. This is one of the reasons to address the EU in this research. This does not mean that the implications of this research are limited to the EU. On the contrary, they have consequences for the entire international scientific community. The FIFA case, as well as some references to non-EU legislation, has been used to explore network corruption in a wider sense. As the author of this research, I have been a member of the LRCC network, a network of research correspondents who report to the European Commission on corruption developments at the national level. Therefore, I have knowledge of and access to data on corruption within the EU, which is a second reason to address the EU in the practical outcomes of this research.

Klitgaard (1988: 95-96) was firm when stating that scholars have to do better when their goal is to be of practical use to policy-makers, by which he meant that, theoretically, policies are often built on restrictive and unrealistic conditions. He called for "(.....) rough-and-ready frameworks and checklists (....)" (Klitgaard, 1988: 95). Concrete practical knowledge on corruption is scarce, but by using case studies, it is the intention of this research to contribute to the international body of knowledge on corruption and in particular offer a useful set of ideas to make anti-corruption policies more effective. As such, this research can be considered as offering policy advice. The introduction of norms and responsibility for networks allows all individuals creating, participating and cooperating within social networks to preserve the social capital while not ignoring the risks of corruption.

1.3 Research Question

According to Knoke and Yang (2008: 8) a social network is a "structure composed of a set of actors, some of whose members are connected by a set of one or more relations." Mitchell (1969: 2) emphasised the impact or result social networks can bring about. In his definition of social networks he refers to "a specific set of linkages among a defined set of persons, with the additional property that the characteristics of these linkages as a whole may be used to interpret the social behaviour of the persons involved". This latter definition stipulates that the network is more than the sum of its connections, and that this has to be considered when assessing individual behaviour. It is therefore essential to consider the structure of the network and the responsibility in these networks in real-life cases: what consequences this has in terms of how the conduct should be assessed; what it means when corruption is a collective behaviour; and whether the behaviour of individuals can be assessed independently of the network. Furthermore, we need to understand which norms are laid down in the anti-corruption policies and models and compare them with the norms upheld in social networks, to explore whether it is possible to distinguish networks from network corruption. In particular, the various roles that individuals take on in such networks needs consideration. The FIFA case, the News of the World case and the Roermond case concerned serious misconduct by a given set of persons having some form of loose association, but sometimes with little individual behaviour being criminal. In this research the link between networks and corruption will be explored by means of the following central question:

In what way and to what extent is corruption linked to the functioning of social networks, and what does this entail for our knowledge of corruption and networks and the policies to eradicate corruption?

Sub-questions:

- What is corruption and what is the problem with this concept?
- What are social networks and how are they linked to corruption?
- What is the moral and legal status of a network?
- What features of networks and corruption make up network corruption?
- How does the concept of network corruption work in practice?
- What are the consequences of the introduction of network corruption in terms of law and policies for the EU?

This research is first of all written with an EU perspective in mind, because the EU is considering ways to eradicate corruption. However, international conventions, international literature and international cases are used, so the research implications reach beyond the EU region. Although the focus of this research is not an EU-US comparison in anti-corruption, some of the US' perspectives on fighting corruption are included because the US appears to be at the forefront in the prosecution of (international) corruption. The US was the first to have specific laws on corruption such as the 1977 Foreign Corrupt Practices Act. Although the US remains fierce on fighting foreign corruption, a recent verdict by the Supreme Court in the McDonnell case indicates that the US also encounters difficulties in distinguishing corruption from everyday politics. There is no consensus between the federal courts and federal prosecutors and the Supreme Court on when influence becomes corruption. In the case *McDonnell v. United States,* the court leaves room for 'pay-to-play politics', making it no longer a crime for someone to pay for 'access' to government decision-makers. Legal scholars such as Zephyr Teachout, a law professor at Fordham University in New York and Jessica Tillipman, an assistant dean at the George Washington University Law School, said that this decision will face significant challenges in bringing and winning public corruption cases (Feuer, 2017). Activity that may be distasteful, such as arranging meetings for wealthy sponsors, is now legal. "It's the legacy of Bob McDonnell, making life easier for corrupt public officials everywhere," said former federal prosecutor Randall Eliason (Zapotosky, 2017). This recent case is illustrative for the difficulties which coincide with corruption prosecution.

Both the EU and its member states try to curb corruption through anti-corruption legislation and anti-corruption agencies. The policy-makers and scholars share the view that this requires a joint approach, an approach in which central and decentralised institutions work together. As such, there is an awareness of the need for a systemic approach. Partly for that reason, the international anti-corruption NGO Transparency International (TI) has developed the National Integrity System (NIS) model (Transparency International, n.d. c). This model makes it possible to investigate the extent to which a country's system of institutions, policy instruments and laws and regulations is effective enough to stimulate integrity and prevent corruption; it is built on a system approach. The European Commission supported the pan-European NIS Assessment, and in 2014 it launched its first and only EU Anti-Corruption Report (ACR), which was based on the corruption reports of the network of local research correspondents on corruption (LRCC) (European Commission, 2011b).[1] The ACR provides a picture of the situation in each member state: the measures in place, the policies that work and areas that could be improved (European Commission, 2014c). The NIS and the ACR both describe the anti-corruption framework in place and the need for public and private institutions to work together to fight corruption.

In the NIS, the ACR and their corresponding country assessment reports, national and international corruption cases were named, yet the reports do not go as far as using these cases as case studies to understand how corruption could occur and translate this into policy recommendations.[2] Their approach is basically to assess whether independent institutions have their anti-corruption provisions in place (the formal anti-corruption system to prevent corruption), thereby not addressing the concept of corruption nor concrete cases of corruption or its systemic character. The issue of how a system can be fertile ground for these cases was never raised. Both TI and the European Commission play a role in law-setting and policy recommendation; but investigating case studies is not part of their day-to-day work. Their aim is to ensure that important anti-corruption safeguards such as the criminalisation of corruption offences, the rules on procurement and whistle-blower protection are available in the various EU member states. What I will

1 The LRCC (Local Research Correspondents on Corruption) is a network of research correspondents, one for each member state, appointed by the Commission as article 3 paragraph 1 sub of the Commission Decision (dd. 6.6.2011) Establishing an EU Anti-corruption reporting mechanism for periodic assessment ("EU Anti-Corruption Report").

2 For instance in the Country Chapter of the United Kingdom (European Commission, 2014d: 7) the Phone-Hacking Scandal is mentioned and the corresponding recommendations of the Leveson Commission which was set up to investigate the corruption allegations. Among other things, it was recommended that police officers were to receive clearer guidance on what is acceptable behaviour. Another example is that of the Country Chapter of Germany (European Commission, 2014e: 8). In brief, the corruption cases, prompted in part by investigations by the US Securities and Exchange Commission (SEC) and involving German multinationals such as Siemens, are mentioned foremost to illustrate that compliance programmes have become a central issue. The National Integrity Assessment of the Netherlands (Slingerland, Eijkelhof, Hulten Van, Popovych & Wempe, 2012a:25-30) presents Dutch corruption cases, but the NIS model does not allow a thorough analysis to be made to understand their occurrence and what this implies in terms of policy or institutional design.

explore as part of this research is to what extent case study research on corruption has its own value and can contribute to the work of policy-makers and NGOs.

1.4 Relevance and Importance of the Research

The Phone-Hacking Scandal, which is being examined as part of this research, led to a judicial public inquiry (the Leveson Inquiry) into the culture, practices and ethics of the British press and their (too close) connections with politicians. One of the reasons such an inquiry was considered necessary was in fact the general constraints faced by the police and the courts in the investigation, detection and prosecution of this crime, and the alleged crimes which took place in this case (The Right Honourable Lord Justice Leveson, 2012: 1481). In his report, Lord Leveson points out the constraints in which the criminal law operates and the practical limitations the police and prosecuting authorities are faced with, however much they wish to detect all those committing criminal offences (The Right Honourable Lord Justice Leveson, 2012: 1481). Similarly, the criminal court proceedings of the third case study which is part of this research (Roermond, the Netherlands) show a similar constraint felt by the Dutch prosecuting authorities.

Although this research is focused on corruption cases, the analysis presented is also useful in dealing with other complex issues in modern society. Recent scandals such as the Volkswagen Emission Scandal, where the automotive industry had close links with politicians and monitoring bodies but also the ongoing concerns about the power and gas regulation in Europe due to political interference at national level, underline the importance of understanding how networks function in our democracy and internal market. Both examples have made clear that connections, ties, networks and other informal relationships have a risk of undermining the checks and balances in our societies.

The current literature and research on corruption in network-like structures is not extensive, nor do literature and research on networks extensively discuss the pitfalls of networks or how such a collective can become corrupt. This research seeks to bridge both themes, thereby learning from the day-to-day reality of large corruption cases which are difficult to investigate, and comparing them to what is described in the existing bodies of literature on corruption and networks. Thus, understanding network corruption is relevant to prevent, detect and address corruption in our modern society. It will help create awareness and understanding of when social capital becomes corrupted.

1.5 Research Method

The research at hand is foremost an analysis of current ways to curb corruption by recourse to law and policies. In contrast to methodological individualism, this research does not assume that everything can be explained by means of rational individual decision-making without regarding the behaviour of others. If we were to only take into account the legal framework and individual conduct, the broader interaction contexts within which social actors are embedded will be overlooked (Knoke & Yang, 2008: 4). The social phenomenon of corruption can only be understood by taking into account the social structure it occurs within. In the conceptual analysis, I consider corruption to be a social system in which it is difficult to distinguish individual causal relations (French, 1984: 2-18). In doing so, I make use of methodological holism, which will be further explained in Chapter 2. The characteristics of social networks and the features of corruption are presented. The overriding question is how corruption emerges in network-like structures, and how we should understand it and recognise it in our policies. By using a network perspective, it is assumed that individuals participate in social systems connecting them to others, whose relations comprise important influences on one another's behaviour (Knoke & Yang). Social network analysis is a multidisciplinary research method, which investigates the process of social structures through the use of networks. It characterises network structures in terms of nodes (individual actors, people, or other elements within the network) and the ties or links (relationships or interactions) that connect them. For the research on networks and corruption, I will draw upon at least three disciplines: law, social sciences and (business) ethics. Literature research will allow the collection of relevant information on current anti-corruption instruments. However, the purpose of this research is to contribute to the effectiveness of these anti-corruption laws and policies. This effectiveness appears to be undermined by the fact that law enforcement authorities and policy-makers struggle with the collective nature of corruption. To fully investigate the latter, I will present three case studies which offer an analysis of the relation between networks and corruption. In order to present an objective description of the case studies, official documents were used, for instance, indictments, court verdicts, reports by investigative commissions and reports and articles from independent quality newspapers and broadcasting corporations. Various independent experts have read the case study descriptions to check the facts. Among others, investigative journalists, criminal investigators and scholars have fact checked the cases, some of whom wish to remain anonymous.

These illustrative cases in the introduction show the complexity of the corruption phenomenon, its legal interpretation and the far-reaching effects this can have on the prosecution of corruption in practice. I increasingly came to the realisation that the current legal concepts of corruption are failing and that in order to assess the link between connections, networks and corruption I needed to take on a multidisciplinary approach in this research. This research is the result of multi-disciplinary research in law, (business) ethics, public administration and organisational studies. Although I have an academic background in International and European Law which helps me to understand the legal approaches to corruption, I do not consider myself an expert in any of the other disciplines. I do, however, consider myself to be well equipped to undertake a multidisciplinary approach, which in my opinion is important to understand the link between networks and corruption. This allows for a useful perspective on prevention and repression of corruption.

In Chapter 8 a table of networks, their influence, their nature and their possible characterisation as corrupt will be presented. This overview can serve as an analytic and explanatory model that helps to understand what network corruption is, why network corruption cannot be reduced or simplified to individual (bribery) acts, how networks are related to the corruption and how network corruption varies, but also corresponds, across a broad range of countries or regions.

1.6 GUIDE TO THE SUBSEQUENT CHAPTERS

The methodology used in this research is justified in terms of method selection and its reliability and validity (Chapter 2). One of the methods used is that of case study analysis, which makes it possible to see whether the findings of the theoretical chapters on corruption and networks become visible in real-life situations. Before being able to fully understand the phenomenon of network corruption and the implications its recognition has for European and national anti-corruption policies, a literature review of existing corruption definitions and the way this is covered in international and European law and academic research is required, with a particular focus on corruption in the sphere of networks (Chapter 3). Thereafter, Chapter 4 will provide an overview of the existing literature on networks. Chapter 5 introduces the link between networks and corruption because certain issues concerning corruption in network-like settings require further exploration. Chapter 6 presents the three case studies. In this way a comparison can be made between the way in which this form of corruption is dealt with in law and policies and its emergence in real life. Once the scope of this research has been clearly defined, the link between networks and corruption is further assessed in Chapter 7, the analysis. The specific relation between social networks and corruption will be examined by means of the literature review and case studies. The specific characteristics of networks and corruption are presented and the link with the cases is made, in order to assess whether the theoretical findings also become apparent in real cases (Chapter 7). Chapter 8 presents an overview of networks and influence. Chapter 9 presents ideas on how to organise routes for developments based on the findings of this research. Conclusions are presented in the final section in Chapter 10.

2. Methodology

2.1 Introduction

The previous chapter provided an introduction to the topic of this research, its purpose and relevance. A brief description of the methodology used was given. This chapter will elaborate on the foundation of this research. Because this research is about the relation between networks and corruption, the body of knowledge of both topics will be analysed to gain a better understanding of the features of networks and the features of corruption and whether both bodies of knowledge entail any references to the other. By means of this conceptual analysis I explore what the link between corruption and networks is. Empirical case study research makes it possible to further develop a concept or theory on network corruption and allows this concept to be applied in real-life cases.

2.2 Conceptual Analysis

2.2.1 Criteria to Consider

The method of conceptual analysis is used to unravel existing concepts of corruption before introducing a new concept, specifically: network corruption. My aim is to assess whether it:

1. is justified to use the definition of 'network corruption' (a question of its legitimacy)
2. helps in understanding the issues which policy-makers, practitioners and public prosecutors have to deal with (a question of insight: does it offer a better insight into the phenomenon of corruption?)
3. contributes in a practical sense (pragmatic value/user value: does it have added value for the practice of policy-making and investigation?)

In this assessment I will have to take consideration of the need to be economical or thrifty when introducing new concepts. Additionally, I will assess whether network corruption is a phenomenon which has not otherwise been captured in a definition or concept. Also, it has to be argued that it is simply logical to define this phenomenon as network corruption. Lastly, there needs to be proof that this concept will effectively work in practice; that it clarifies debates and has value in the practice of individuals, networks and policy makers.

In order to be able to lay the foundation for this research and in order to assess the value of the network corruption definition, methodological holism is used. In doing so, I react against the usual way of looking at corruption (methodological individualism) which is dominant in policy-making and investigation. Corruption is a social phenomenon which cannot only be understood by assessing it at the level of the individual. Methodological holism allows the assessment of social-level rather than individual-level mechanisms (Zahle, 2016). Zahle (2016) explains methodological holism as an approach which views social phenomena as being present in their own right. Social scientific explanations need not always be confirmed by looking at what happens at the level of individuals. On the contrary, moral responsibility for social phenomena can be attributed to collectives and groups. Methodological individualism explains social phenomena by means of an individual's actions, beliefs, attitudes and so on. Methodological holism is a way of assessing what elements, actors and factors play a role in the emergence of a social phenomenon. Among others, Chapter 3 will present current theories on corruption and the importance of seeing it within its context which is crucial to understand how corruption comes into being. This in itself is a prerequisite for preventive and repressive policies to have effect. Nevertheless, current concepts still focus on individual acts in a context and causality, whereas this research explores corruption and the dynamics of a social network and as such looks at collective acting and non-causal relationships. This ambition does not imply disqualifying the current practice; in fact, I hope to contribute to the existing body of knowledge concerning corruption by coming up with alternative lines of thinking to solve the issues in anti-corruption activities which policy-makers, practitioners and law enforcement authorities struggle with.

2.2.2 Conceptual Analysis

This research involves a conceptual research into the role of social networks in the emergence and prevention of corruption. Instead of isolating corruption from its environment or context as if it is a thing on its own, an attempt is made to understand its appearance by looking at the underlying foundations and mechanisms in which it emerges. Contrary to methodological individualism such as that of Lewis (1948a; 1948b), this research does not consider corruption to be caused by a rational individual deciding to commit corruption in his interaction with another individual. Even when rational choice theories are used to describe how individuals seek to benefit or pursue their own interest, it presupposes some social structure to succeed (Kincaid, 2014: 147). Most social phenomena cannot be reduced to individual agents and actions and their causality to a phenomenon (the causal overriding argument). Meadows (2011: 4) describes how it is still much more attractive to blame something or someone, because this shifts responsibility away from ourselves and makes us look for quick fixes. The (sudden) emergence of these phenomena is another important argument in favour of a more systemic or integrated approach (Bhaskar, 2000; Meadows, 2011). To hold someone responsible for complex social phenomena such as corruption, obesity, poverty or terrorism is not only difficult in itself, but also does not help us to come up with real solutions if the system structures which produced them are not understood. Such social phenomena have an identity of their own and exist above and beyond the individuals it is composed of (the composition argument). I will explore whether network corruption is a complex collective conduct which cannot be traced back to individual acts and individual responsibility. The social phenomenon of corruption can only be grasped by regarding the structure in which it emerged. Through conceptual analysis, corruption is regarded as a social system in which it is difficult to distinguish individual causal relations. By assessing the network character of corruption, this research aims to find the underlying mechanisms which allow these networks to become corrupt. Scholars and practitioners agree that corruption cannot really be understood without reference to the political, economic, institutional and social system in which it emerges. The definition of network corruption concerns a new layer in the definition of corruption.

2.2.3 Literature review and case study analysis

After the literature review, I will present the available research and literature on corruption and networks. The second method used in this conceptual and explorative research is that of case study analysis. These case studies provide additional empirical data to assess how the findings of the literature research match the facts of real cases. There is a need to compare these cases by means of case study research and to distinguish their main characteristics. The combination of both methods helps to develop a definition of network corruption and a corresponding framework for analysis which can be applied in various contexts. I will explore the gap between the traditional definitions of corruption and the corruption cases in reality and whether 'network corruption' can help to fill this gap. The definition of network corruption is stipulative. This stipulative definition intends to attach a meaning to a term which does not already have an established use. This is considered to enrich our understanding of corruption and in particular for it to be useful in developing a theory on corruption in network-like settings. The aim is firstly for it to be a useful concept to fill the gaps in all mainstream anti-corruption theory and policies, and secondly for us as a society to change our way of thinking about networks, from considering these to be informal connections for which no policies or laws can be made to addressing networks in policies and laws and attributing responsibilities to them.

2.3 Case studies

2.3.1 *Case Studies as a Method to Develop a Concept*

The case studies are used to explore and analyse what current policies and investigations are confronted with. In all cases there is suspicion of corruption and there is a linkage to networks. It is clear that it is far from easy to understand what is really going on in these cases, because the embeddedness of the individual conduct is largely undisclosed. The case study analysis is therefore part of empirical research. The cases are summarised by using the available official information from public prosecution authorities, court proceedings and a parliamentary investigation. In addition to these primary sources of information, further information is presented by well-respected investigative journalists. These sources of information made it possible to present the processes of each case. For all three case studies a time span or period was set to use the information available for analysis. The developments leading up to these cases could possibly be earlier than my case study descriptions reflect. To the best of my knowledge I have incorporated the information available on these cases when my research was finalised. The case study descriptions are foremost based on official documents such as indictments, independent inquiries and court verdicts. The case descriptions are a summary of the facts as described in these documents, which varied from documents of a couple of pages up to the more than 2000 pages of the Leveson Report used for the second case. A secondary source of information used for the case study descriptions is that of newspaper articles on the three cases. This way additional information could be included which provided a better insight into the networks because of the 'off-the-record accounts' of witnesses and participants. The facts of each case study were checked by an independent expert with thorough knowledge of the case. Some of these experts expressed the wish to remain anonymous.

The first thing which will be assessed is whether the informal connections presented in the case study are in fact networks. Thereafter, I will consider whether these networks show the features of network corruption. In this research a distinction is made between the social network in which corruption occurs (corrupt network) and the networks which become corrupted themselves (network corruption). After all, it is not necessary to refer to the entire social network as network corruption in order to understand part of it as such. Within a network, (sub-) networks appear which will be referred to as 'corrupt'. This starts with the classical and obvious corruption, which encompasses a limited social structure. This can be bigger when it concerns a larger social structure, with the involvement of more individuals and more roles. The three cases of suspected corruption allow the focus to be on the question of what the nature of this corruption is and who or what can be considered to be the actor. This methodological holism allows the assessment of the social level, the mechanisms and actors beyond or in addition to the individuals. If networks can be linked to corruption, questions arise concerning its status and responsibilities.

This research is based on a multiple case study research design (Eisenhardt, 1989: 534). According to Yin (2003: 22), a case study design is to be considered when: the study seeks to answer "how" and "why" questions, the behaviour of actors involved in the study cannot be manipulated, the contextual conditions are believed to be relevant to the phenomenon under study or the boundaries between the phenomenon and context are not clear. I will present three case studies which were brought in connection with corruption and/or abuse of power in network-like settings. This case study analysis implies that the social phenomenon is demarcated and studied in depth. These cases cannot be considered without the bounded context of the formal institutional setting, and more importantly the informal social network setting. Yin (2003) differentiates between single, holistic case studies and multiple-case studies and categorises case studies as explanatory, exploratory, or descriptive. This multiple- case study consists of multiple holistic cases. They describe a phenomenon and the real-life context in which it occurred and therefore can best be referred to as descriptive. Besides the in-depth analysis offered by the case study method, it also ensures a certain degree of broadness. A disadvantage of the case study method is that only a limited number of cases can be analysed and therefore the findings and conclusions are not absolute. Notwithstanding this limitation, the case study does justice to the complexity of the subject of this research.

The case selection allows an analysis to be carried out on the way in which network corruption functions in concrete cases and to assess whether this definition is of added value in trying to understand when networks become corrupted. This consequently concerns a conceptual analysis and an explorative research. The research method of case studies is exploratory in nature and therefore the context and the experiences of actors are critical. The concept of network corruption will be introduced to assess whether this will work in practice. This concept is the start of a new theory and according to Eisenhardt (1989) this approach to case study research is popular among scholars when the phenomenon under examination is not adequately explained by pre-existing theories. (Freeman *et al.*, 2017: 3). By remaining close to the underlying ideas of the case study, the emergent theoretical explanation is inductively driven by observations. However, applying a new concept to real-life cases also depends on the richness of the underlying case descriptions. The purpose of this type of case study is less to confirm or refute the appropriateness of competing or complementing theories, but rather to explain a particular phenomenon to which the theory pertains and to determine whether its application helps to reveal its presence and features in real cases. I observed the struggle with networks and corruption in practice and noticed the implicit way of referring to networks. Therefore, case studies are used to explore whether the concept of network corruption offers an insight into the mechanisms which lead to network deterioration. The three cases are also useful in elaborating and challenging a pre-existing theory. By applying a general theory to a specific empirical context, I seek to explore the theory's weaknesses and problems in order to elaborate it. In this process, applying a concept to empirical cases is regarded as a possibility to reconcile the initial theory with contextual characteristics encountered in the empirical case (abductive reasoning) (Freeman *et al.*, 2017: 4). The concept of network corruption is applied to a national, European and global context.

2.3.2 *Selection of Cases*

This research investigates the contemporary phenomenon of network corruption within its real-life context, but it would be unreasonable to look at all corruption cases in which a network played a role. The three case studies in this research concern the network of the international organisation FIFA, a network in the United Kingdom and the network of the municipality Roermond in The Netherlands. Three cases were chosen; in my view this is the required minimum number to make a real comparison and understand the similarities and differences in the cases. At the same time, this is the maximum number to be analysed thoroughly and within the time limitation. The focus was on understanding the mechanisms in each case, which help in assessing how we should understand corruption which arises in the sphere of networks. The case studies offered an analysis of the corruption phenomenon, its context and the actors involved. This allowed for specific characteristics to be distilled and to practise methodological holism, making it possible to get to the essence of corruption, which would not be possible if methodological individualism had been used. Selecting these cases was not done at random. On the contrary, specific cases were selected. With the primary research question in mind (Yin, 2003: 24-25), the following logic was upheld:
- they were presented as large scandals, both in terms of the number of individuals involved and the size of the corruption involved;
- whereby the network was the centre of attention and brought in connection with corruption;
- they have (and/or had) a major impact on society;
- they emerged in developed democracies;
- besides corruption, other forms of misconduct were reported.

The cases selected are still under investigation by law enforcement authorities and at the time of writing of this research, there are no final analyses or conclusions made about the nature of the corruption. It was a conscious choice to present cases which have not been crystallised out entirely. If final verdicts are made, cases are likely to be assessed from a legal view, appearing to have a clear structure and an obvious manner in which each individual should have behaved. The absence of this kind of oversight is exactly one of the main characteristics of corruption. Based on this logic, three cases were identified for case studies.

The first case concerns the FIFA corruption and has had a global impact. For years allegations have been made about the corruption taking place within FIFA. In 2015, US federal prosecutors disclosed cases of bribery, fraud and money laundering by officials and associates connected with FIFA. Soon after this discovery, the embeddedness of FIFA in influential international circles was reported. In this case, the organisation can be seen as a network. The second case is from the United Kingdom. Years before the NoW Scandal became public, society had known about the close connections between the printed media (tabloids), politicians and the police force. Newspapers had reported highly confidential information, which could only have been obtained with the help of those working in law enforcement. The Phone-Hacking Scandal appeared to have been the final incident to convince the decision-makers to investigate the corruption and other forms of misbehaviour by national elite networks consisting of journalists, politicians and police officers. The third case is from the Netherlands and is centred around the network in the municipality of Roermond. Law enforcement officials investigated the local corruption between a senior council officer and an entrepreneur, but soon noticed that the close connections involved many more. This case study describes the local network.

Through the triangulation of data sources (press releases of the public prosecutor, court hearings, independent forensic investigation reports, parliamentary inquiry reports, newspapers and informal anonymous talks) this case study research views and explores the phenomenon of network corruption from multiple perspectives. Concrete practical knowledge of corruption is scarce, but by using case study methodology, I hope to contribute to the international body of knowledge by developing a theory on corruption which is not only academic but practical. Scholars, investigators and investigative journalists who closely followed these cases have been asked to fact-check the case descriptions. The generalising from case studies to theory is known as 'analytical generalisation', contrary to statistical generalisation. This theory helps to evaluate existing policies and more particularly can offer a useful set of ideas to make anti-corruption policies more effective.

3. Corruption: Definitions Across Disciplines and Addressing it in Policies

3.1 Introduction

The purpose of this chapter is to get an overall picture of the corruption phenomenon by looking at the way corruption is defined across various disciplines and by taking a closer look at how policy-makers try to address it in their policies. This chapter explores the available research and literature on corruption and presents the body of knowledge on corruption and whether there are any references to networks to be found in it. After presenting the major international treaties on corruption, this chapter continues with a focus on the EU's position in anti-corruption. The chapter therefore addresses the following questions:

- Why is corruption a concern?
- What is corruption?
- What is the EU's perspective on corruption?
- What is the problem with the corruption concept?

3.2 Why is Corruption a Concern?

3.2.1 *International Organisations Against Corruption*

Since 1999, the major international organisations have enacted anti-corruption conventions. Each international organisation tries to be effective against corruption.

The mission of the Organisation for Economic Cooperation and Development (OECD) is to promote policies that will improve the economic and social well-being of people around the world. By attempting to reduce bribery in international business it hopes to strengthen development, reduce poverty and bolster confidence in markets (OECD, 2014).[1] The OECD Anti-Bribery Convention establishes legally binding standards to criminalise bribery of foreign public officials in international business transactions. Its focus is foremost on the 'supply side' of the bribery transaction.

1 OECD Convention on Combating Bribery of Foreign Public Officials in International Business Transactions.

The Council of Europe (CoE) is the organisation which promotes human rights, solidarity and democracy on the European continent. Its Conventions against corruption seek to restore citizens' trust in the rule of law.[2] The CoE has developed various legal instruments dealing with matters such as the criminalisation of corruption in the public and private sectors, liability and compensation for damage caused by corruption, the conduct of public officials and the financing of political parties. These instruments aim to improve the capacity of states to fight corruption at the national as well as international level. The monitoring of compliance with these standards is entrusted to the Group of States against Corruption (GRECO) which monitors and evaluates the way in which states have implemented and enforced the anti-corruption instruments (Council of Europe, n.d. c).

Among other things, the United Nations (UN) strives for world peace and an end to poverty and considers corruption to be a root cause of war and poverty. The UN came up with the only universally applicable, legally binding anti-corruption instrument.[3] The Convention covers many different forms of corruption, such as bribery, trading in influence, abuse of functions and various acts of corruption in the private sector. It covers five main areas: preventive measures, criminalisation and law enforcement, international cooperation, asset recovery, and technical assistance and information exchange. The Conference of the States Parties (COSP) is the main policy-making body of the Convention, supporting states parties and signatories in their implementation of the Convention and giving policy guidance to the United Nations Office on Drugs and Crime (UNODC) to develop and implement anti-corruption activities. The actual implementation of the Convention into national law by states parties is done via peer review evaluations by the Implementation Review Mechanism (United Nations Office on Drugs and Crime, n.d.).

The EU is concerned that corruption seriously harms the economy and society as a whole. In the EU Anti-Corruption Report (ACR) (European Commission, 2014c: 2) corruption is said to hamper economic development, undermine democracy and damage social justice and the rule of law. The EU's perspective on corruption will be discussed in paragraph 3.4.

Although these international organisations have different missions (economic development, human rights protection, world peace etc.) they all try to fight corruption because they consider this to be a major risk to achieving their goals. The harm caused by corruption is hard to measure; it is economic, political and moral as well as material (Klitgaard, 1988: 6).

---

2 Council of Europe Criminal Law Convention on Corruption (ETS No.173.) and Civil Law Convention on Corruption (ETS No.174.).

3 United Nations Convention against Corruption.

3.2.2 Freedom and Fair Competition

Corruption continues to be one of the major issues of our time. If power and influence can be bought instead of earned in an honest way, this means that the rule of law, the principle of fair competition and good governance are directly undermined. The European democracies and market economies are built on the idea of rule of law. Corruption slows down economic development and destabilises government. The damaging effect corruption has on democracy and the market economy is straightforward and widely recognised. However, in the last decade the relationship between corruption, democracy and the market economy also received attention for other reasons. An economy based on the principle of freedom and competition is believed by some to be steering behaviour in the direction of corruption. According to Sandel and Johnston, the market economy is not only at risk due to corruption, the market economy itself is also increasing the risk for corruption. Although using different examples and arguments, both argued that the choice for the market model economy meant that we have created a society in which everything is for sale, including political influence (Johnston, 2005; Sandel, 2012: 13-14). Klüver (2013) indicates that it is important to gain a better understanding of why some interest groups win and others lose, in particular in the EU arena. The EU provides a particularly promising opportunity structure for lobbying due to its multiple access points and its general open attitude towards interest groups, which can be explained by the desire to ensure the legitimacy of the European Union. Klüver argues that if public policy is systematically biased in favour of some interests while others are constantly losing, this means the democratic legitimacy of policy outcomes is seriously undermined. Johnston refers to these societies as 'influence markets' (Johnston, 2005: 60-88). Since 2010 the new term 'lobbycracy' has been heard more often, referring to western democracies where networks of society's key figures are so interwoven that they influence the thinking of legislators or other elected public officials for or against a specific cause to such an extent that they are more powerful than voters casting their vote.[4] This results in a society divided into insiders and outsiders: those who are connected with key figures and thereby have influence and obtain advantages and those who function independently in society, thereby missing out on the chance to receive benefits or be observed in other ways.

4 Examples of references to lobbycracy: The Alliance for Lobbying Transparency and Ethics Regulation (ALTER-EU), Public debate on lessons from a #Lobbycracy 'Transformation for Transparency and Rules for Revolving Door'(dd. 2 April 2013). Available from: https://www.alter-eu.org/documents/2013/04/lessons-from-a-lobbycracy (Accessed 25/09/17); Transparency International EU posted a tweet on Twitter: "Lobbycracy has the potential to degrade and destroy democracy" @javorbenedek in the @Europarl_EN #lobbying" (dd. 3 September 2015); Corporate Europe Observatory (n.d.) Lobbycracy, Available from: https://corporateeurope.org/tags/lobbycracy (Accessed dd. 25/09/17).

3.2.3 Morality and Public Trust in Democracy and the Market Economy

Sandel (2012: 13-20) not only considers inequality itself to be a concern, but in addition to the legal corruption also points to the moral corruption which takes place when market thinking oppresses non-commercial values. If decision-making processes and competition in EU Member States are hampered because politicians, civil servants, businessmen, journalists or teachers abuse their discretionary powers to serve other interests than those they were assigned to protect and in return they get a favour, this means the informal circuits are stronger than the formal institutions. Warren (2004, 328) referred to this as "duplicitous violations of the democratic norm of inclusion". People lose confidence that public decisions are taken for reasons that are publicly available and justifiable. The real evil is done by an organisational context and not by individuals. As will be presented in the subsequent chapters, this organisational context is crucial to understanding and preventing corruption. This realisation is one aspect of the justification of the network corruption concept of this research. As early as 1949, Sutherland argued that white collar crime tears the social fabric more than street crime because it corrodes trust in authorities and institutions. Public trust in institutions, government and fair elections will deteriorate; there will be a downward spiral, leading to the failure of democracy and the market economy. These negative externalities generated by corruption are the major reasons for concern.

3.2.4 Health and Safety

Another reason for concern is the consequences of corruption on health and safety. A clear example of how corruption is related to safety is illustrated by citizens' response to the deadly fire that broke out in a nightclub in Bucharest in 2015. Immediately after the fire broke out, thousands of people gathered in anti-corruption demonstrations holding banners with 'Corruption kills', because they suspected that municipal authorities were bribed not to carry out the safety measures at the nightclub, which could have prevented the tragedy form happening (Maurice, 2015). Another example of corruption and its link to health and safety can be found in the many ways in which the pharmaceutical and food industry can influence governments and regulatory agencies, at the expense of other interested parties such as patients' organisations, which has led to the public debate about the risks of such relationships setting the political agenda and priorities of government and regulatory agencies, often referred to as 'regulatory capture' (Abraham, 2002: 1498; Herxheimer, 2003). This leads to favourable law-making in which the general interest of the people is no longer observed by the legislative and executive branches of government. Pharmaceutical firms with connections will see their profits rise, while honest competitors fall out and the consumers and patients pay more for the medicine, which will influence whether and what medicine they use. This will have an effect on their health. Johnson & Johnson, one of the world's largest pharmaceutical companies, was forced to pay a fine of $70 million after being accused and convicted of offering bribes to well-known doctors in Greece, Poland and Romania to persuade them to prescribe Johnson & Johnson products (Securities and Exchange Commission (SEC), 2011).

Another way to influence policy-makers and supervisory bodies to allow medicines on the market is to send them 'objective information' on the health benefits of the medicine from a researcher, who in fact was paid by the pharmaceutical company to carry out the research. *The Washington Post* reviewed the publications in *The New England Journal of Medicine* for a year and found that of those articles, 60 were funded by a pharmaceutical company, 50 were co-written by an employee of a pharmaceutical company and 37 had a lead author (often an academic) who had previously accepted outside compensation from the drug company who sponsored the research (Whoriskey, 2012). In one of its articles, that same journal had positively featured the arthritis drug Vioxx. Five years later, journal editors discovered that the researchers had omitted key incidences of heart problems, thereby falsifying the conclusion on the drug's safety. The drug was pulled from the market, but had already caused an extra 27,000 heart attacks and cardiac-related deaths (Whoriskey, 2012). Both these strategies, paying doctors to persuade them to prescribe your medicine or paying scientists to write a positive report on your medicine, may have serious consequences on the health and safety of patients and have a devastating effect on public trust in the medical profession. Abraham (2000) referenced the fact that the transparency rules to prevent expert scientific advisors from having industrial or commercial interests do not solve this as long as those scientists who are critical of industry products may notice that their consultancy is no longer asked for by the industry or that they might lose their large grants (Abraham, 2000: 1500). As will be discussed later in this book, such corruption is often referred to as 'regulatory capture' or 'collusion.

Other examples of corruption related to health and safety risks can be found in public contracting. If a company pays bribes or grants other favours to a civil servant who in turn 'selects' this company as the bid winner, this will mean that the public organisation pays far more than necessary for the actual work done. This money is tax payers' money which cannot be allocated to other projects or works. Additionally, an honest competitor loses the bid due to this unfair competition. The corrupt company pays extra money to win the bid, which in reality means that it has to save money on other items, for instance by using materials of inferior quality. Premature damage to, for instance, roads or buildings means extra repair costs and a risk of incidents occurring. There are regular reports on the collapse of buildings or infrastructures linked to corruption. In recent years, the collapse of bridges and buildings and explosions at plants in China were directly connected to corruption (Xuecun, 2015).

These aren't virtual examples. They illustrate the complexity of corruption and the damage which it can cause. Corruption is a serious concern and the EU is considering what its anti-corruption strategy should be. The amount of money annually lost in the EU due to corruption is believed to be €120 billion, which almost equals the EU's annual budget (European Commission, 2014b). 'Believed to be' because corruption is difficult to measure. It is not possible to simply add up the 'bribes' paid because the corrupt deals most likely stayed under the radar and the benefits did not always come in the form of money. If we consider the damage only in financial terms, other considerations have to be taken into account. Klitgaard (1988: 24-25) argued that if we consider the costs obtained by reducing corruption, the costs entailed by the very efforts to fight corruption also have to be taken into account. The hours spent on a corruption investigation will be balanced with the costs which could be earned if the same time could be spent on, for instance, a case on tax evasion. Analogue to this line of reasoning in financial terms, the corruption cases involving the foreign bribery practices of Siemens, Philips, Petrobras, SBM Offshore and Johnson & Johnson need to be considered. Here, one can also balance the fines and settlements with the costs of the corruption in financial terms. Notwithstanding the financial damages, these examples show that the damage caused by corruption can be expressed in terms of undermining democracy and the rule of law, harming public trust, and can even cost human lives.

3.3 WHAT IS CORRUPTION?

3.3.1 *Classifications of Corruption*

The previous paragraph explained why corruption is such a major concern. Corruption is a polymorphic concept, which means that different meanings or usage are assigned to it. Before going into the various definitions of corruption, it is useful to try to categorise existing corruption literature in the way it looks at corruption. The growing body of research can be classified as a dichotomy.

Relativist and Universalist view

The first dominant dichotomy in literature is that of corruption being seen as an accepted phenomenon in society (relativist view) versus corruption being a criminal offence (Universalist view). In some countries, sectors or communities, informal payments to secure access to services or to increase the quality or speed of services received is widely accepted behaviour and elsewhere it is common to appoint a friend or family member in an official position or to donate a large amount of money to a political party to ensure favourable decision-making. The relativistic approach found in the literature argues that such examples are accepted because they are either part of a cultural system or reflect the dominant social norms, or these corrupt acts circumvent inefficient and unjust policies (Klitgaard, 1988: 47). Leys (1965: 221-224) criticises the moralist concept of corruption and leaves the group or society concerned to determine whether it is corruption or not. However, the universalistic approach (Alatas, 1968) does not acknowledge contextual factors such as national or local culture to be a justification for such practices and considers corruption to be a universal phenomenon, nor does it recognise the positive function of corruption, because even if individuals profit from it, eventually it will distort the whole economy. One can hardly do anything without using corruption (Alatas, 1968: 30-32). Rothstein and Torsello (2013: 3) put forward two other arguments in favour of the universalistic approach. First, having to pay bribes for what should be free public services and the right to equal and respectful treatment does not differ much from what is considered to be a basic human right. Secondly, they point to empirical evidence which suggests that people in very different cultures seem to have a very similar notion of what should count as corruption (Rothstein & Torsello, 2013: 3). According to Klitgaard (1988: 3-4), the majority of countries and cultures condemn most forms of corruption.

Corrupt Individuals, Corrupt Organisations and Corrupt Systems

The second dichotomy in corruption literature is: corrupt individuals ('bad apples') versus corrupt organisations ('bad barrels') versus corrupt systems ('bad barrel makers'). The examples of corruption in paragraph 3.2 all had in common that somebody with power and influence knowingly used this influence to refrain from carrying out safety measures, to write a scientific report, to assign a public contract or to prescribe a specific medicine, in return for a favour given by a third party, who acted on behalf of themselves or others. Notwithstanding the possibility that extortion or other means of pressure were used to get these persons to do so, their way of acting was a conscious and rational choice of the individual; it is the individual who is corrupt. Trevino and Youngblood (1990) distinguished these two kinds of influences on unethical behaviour in organisations. The 'bad apple' perspective blames the immoral individual whose personal characteristics cause the unethical behaviour. Warburton (2013: 222) and Klitgaard (1997) see corruption foremost as a matter of personal choice or decision as to whether the individual will instigate or accede to an attempted corrupt transaction. Here, corruption is a rational choice of the individual when arguing that corruption; a crime of calculation or a matter of choice (Klitgaard, 1997).

Another approach is to consider corruption to be something at the level of the organisation. The 'bad barrels' perspective links unethical and immoral organisational culture to corrupt practices. Pinto *et al.* (2008: 688) distinguish these two distinct phenomena at the level of the organisation referring to the cases in which a significant proportion of an organisation's staff act in a corrupt manner, but primarily for their personal benefit (an organisation of corrupt individuals) and the cases in which a group collectively acts in a corrupt manner for the benefit of the organisation (a corrupt organisation). Here, corruption can be seen as a social process, within the context of the organisation, allowing the group to be organised in such a way that it commits corruption on behalf of the organisation (Pinto *et al.*, 2008; Warburton, 2013).

Besides seeing corruption as a matter of individual choice or seeing corruption as a social process or related to the organisational context, corruption is also regarded as being understood from a system or 'bad barrel maker' perspective. Andvig & Moene (1990) offer a model of bureaucratic corruption, focusing on the demand as well as the supply side. Their model is based on the link between profitability of economically motivated corruption and the frequency of corruption. They point at multiple equilibria, which emerge as a result of complementarities between the actions of different bureaucrats. Here the expected gains from corruption crucially depend on the number of other people who are expected to be corrupt. When corruption is rare, the economy is in a "low corruption-equilibrium", in which both demand and supply are limited. Although Andvig & Moene (1990) do refer to 'bribes' and 'bribe paying' when they describe how exploring bribe paying opportunities is more risky when bureaucrats hold high ethical standards, their model explains corruption by considering the (economic) system as the context which requires consideration. As soon as corruption levels increase, the request for bribes becomes easier as does the proposal of bribes. This way corruption leads the economy into a vicious circle, ending up in circumstances under which corruption is the standard, where honesty is too costly, with a general disregard of law and a higher level of crime, and where each individual is involved in making the most for him/herself, feeling no obligations for the country. The situation is often referred to as a "corruption-trap". (Andvig & Moene, 1990; Søreide, 2002: 9). Andvig & Moene's work sheds a light on the varying incidence of corruption across similar societies and activities. This theory on the dynamics of corruption also includes positive feedback loops, in which a small reduction of the general corruption level may result in a significant improvement of the situation.

Theories from economist and political scientist do explain how modern economic and political systems 'allow' mechanisms of undue influence of economic interests over legislative and regulatory authorities (Carpenter, 2013; Lessig, 2010; Johnston, 2005; Søreide, 2002). Lessig argues that institutional corruption is different from the kind of public corruption for which individuals and organisations are often found criminally liable. "Institutional corruption does not refer to the knowing violation of any law or ethical rule. This is not the problem (...) of bad souls acting badly. It instead describes an influence, financial or otherwise, within an economy of influence, that weakens the effectiveness of an institution, especially by weakening public trust in that institution. (An "economy of influence" rather than the simpler "system of influence" to emphasize the reciprocal character of such influence, often requiring little or no direct coordination.)" (Lessig, 2010). Johnston (2005) refers to such institutional corruption as 'influence markets'. This is further explained in paragraph 3.4.2. where similar and/or related phenomena collusive corruption, regulatory and state capture are presented.

This economic or political science perspective is in line with the existing theories on social system dynamics. Individuals and organisations are embedded in a larger societal system which influences their behaviour. Zimbardo (2008a: 259; 2008b: 18:52) points to the influence this systemic factor, in addition to the dispositional and situational factor, has on behaviour leading to diseases such as bullying and violence. By analogy, his reasoning can be used to reflect on corruption as a disease and the need to recognise it is a phenomenon embedded in the situation and system. Johnston (2005) also stressed the importance of understanding the system level of corruption. He understood corruption from the setting in which it evolved, both in terms of a country's level of economic development and its level of democracy. The system level of corruption is acknowledged by scholars, policy makers and NGOs. Klitgaard (1997) and Nielsen (2003) have tried to capture the elements of corrupt systems and introduced strategies to fix the systems that breed corruption. Transparency International has come up with its National Integrity System (NIS). Huberts and Six (2012) have developed the Local Integrity System (LIS) model in an attempt to capture corruption from a system level. As I will explain in paragraph 3.5.1, these approaches either refer to system failure or how to design a preventive system. This system approach is valuable because it builds on the idea that there is no single cause for corruption. On the contrary, these models look at the coherence of institutions, policies and individuals in an anti-corruption context and prescribe or describe what an anti-corruption system would ideally look like. The next step would be to understand corruption as a system. I will contribute to the existing theories on corruption by arguing that corruption is a (sub)system of the larger societal system by analysing the social relationships of actors (the network). Here the (formal) organisation is not the source of the corruption, but corruption is the result of a loosely organised network.

3.3.2 *Definitions Across Various Disciplines*

These dichotomies illustrate that there are great differences in the way scholars look at corruption. In line with the variations of this concept in corruption literature, the concept differs in the sense that some consider corruption to be related to an individual person (the person is corrupt) (Chugh, 2012; Klitgaard, 1997; Haines & Leonard, 2007), while others, even though they refer to corrupt individuals are in fact describing the corrupt (individual or collective) behaviour (Huberts *et al.*, 2006; Pinto *et al.*, 2008) and yet some others see corruption at the level of systems (whether organisations, branches or nation states) (Klitgaard, 1997; Huberts & Six, 2012). Klitgaard (1997) and Huberts (2012, 2009) show that although the concept of corruption varies greatly, the concepts they use are not mutually exclusive. Each discipline looks at a different actor and context of corruption. Additionally, what is violated in the case of corruption varies in the eyes of an economist, ethicist or lawyer. The following descriptions illustrate how various scholars try to capture the phenomenon in a definition which all states, their respective law-makers and their politicians can more or less agree upon. The definition debate is ongoing and definitions vary across disciplines. To get an idea of the wide variety across these disciplines a few references to corruption from other literature are presented. The following overview does not do justice to the extensive body of literature across the various disciplines. It is merely to provide a valuable reference point for understanding the complexity of the polymorphic corruption phenomenon.

Definitions From Behavioural and Social Sciences

Definitions from social sciences vary from seeing corruption as corrosion of the state of mind of the individual or a process of decision-making to public power-holders misusing their power for interests which are private. Examples of the first are given by Van Duyne or Divyanshi. Van Duyne (2001) used a behavioural definition: "Corruption is an improbity or decay in the decision-making process in which a decision-maker consents or demands to deviate from the criterion which should rule his or her decision-making, in exchange for a reward or for the promise or expectation of a reward, the promise or expectation of it." Divyanshi (2012: 2) defines corruption as "a process which perverts the original nature of an individual or group from a more pure state to a less pure state." This psychological definition sees corruption as a deviating mind of the individual or a group of individuals. Criminologists such as Van den Heuvel distinguish corruption from collusion, whereby the first is the abuse of power for oneself or a third party at the individual level, whereas the latter is the institutionalised version where public authorities abuse their power in the interest of one selves or third parties (1998: 7-8).

Examples of definitions centralised around the abuse of power can be found in Huberts and Lasthuizen (Huberts, 2014: 113), who present the three definitions used in Heidenheimer and Johnston's *Handbook on Political Corruption* (2002:7-9) as a 'tripartite division' of corruption definitions, all of which relate to public power-holders who misuse their power for private interest. First is Nye's (1967:417) definition, which is centralised around the public office: "behaviour which deviates from the formal duties of a public role because of private-regarding (close family, personal, private clique) pecuniary or status gains; or violates rules against the exercise of certain types of private-regarding influence." Huberts and Lasthuizen cite van Klaveren's definition, which they refer to as 'market-centred':

> [A] corrupt civil servant (or business administrator) regards his (public) office as a (separate) business, the income of which he will seek to maximise. The office then becomes a 'maximising unit'. The size of his income depends upon the market situation and his talents for finding the point maximal gain on the public's (or client's) demand curve (2014:113).

The last part of this division is the public-interest-centred definition from Friedrich cited by Huberts and Lasthuizen (2014:113): "The pattern of corruption can be said to exist whenever a power holder who is charged with doing certain things, i.e., who is responsible functionary or officeholder, is by monetary or other rewards not legally provided for, induces to take actions which favour whoever provides the rewards and thereby does damage to the public and its interests." Huberts (2014) defines corruption as:

> [...] the promising, giving, asking, or receiving of personal benefits or favours that (are meant to) influence the decisions of a (public) functionary; in other words, the intrusion of improper private interests into the decision-making process. Corruption, therefore, means that authority is misused because of the favours or benefits offered by external parties with an interest in past, present, or future decision-making (2014:4).

Definitions From Economics

Economists frequently refer to corruption as "acts in which the power of public office is used for personal gain in a manner that contravenes the rules of the game" (Hodgson & Jiang, 2007: 1043). This definition from economics considers the acts to be corrupt only if the acting is done by someone from the public sector who thereby violates the rules of our economic model. This line of reasoning does not acknowledge private corruption (business to business) nor does it consider companies to be corrupt when they pay public officials to influence decision-making. In this definition, only that particular public official can be blamed for corruption. Hodgson and Jiang argued that a possible reason for economists' focus on public sector corruption is the widespread influence of individualistic and libertarian ideology (2007: 1047-1048). According to them, the misuse of power by directors of large firms does not raise the same level of concern among leading individualistic and libertarian thinkers such as Friedman and Hayek. In this line of thinking, "most voluntary contracts between consenting adults are moral and legitimate, as long as they do not harm others."(2007: 1047). From a libertarian perspective, corruption in the private sphere foremost has benefits. By contrast, corruption in the public sector is the misuse of powers within state institutions. If corruption is defined as essentially a state phenomenon, this individualistic and libertarian perspective sees the reduction in the size of the state and privatisation to be the solution to the problem of corruption (Hodgson & Jiang, 2007: 1047; Pellegrini, 2011: 13-14).

In economic terms the outcome might be no different. If government is replaced by market, not only would the corrupt bribe be called the market price and still be inefficiently high (Klitgaard, 1988: 65-66), it would still be corruption even if it is between private parties. Pellegrini (2011: 17) describes corruption as:

> [...] the misuse of entrusted power for private gain; it is behaviour which deviates from the formal duties of a given role because of private-regarding (personal, close family, private clique) pecuniary or status gains; or violates rules against the exercise of certain types of private regarding influence. This includes such behaviour as bribery (use of a reward to pervert the judgment of a person in a position of trust); nepotism (bestowal of patronage by reason of ascriptive relationship rather than merit); and misappropriation (illegal appropriation of public resources for private-regarding uses).

This definition sees corruption in the way of acting and instead of referring to the public official the act is done by misuse of a role by someone entrusted with public or private power. It includes a distinction of various forms of corruption. It is an attempt to come up with a definition which is operational for the purposes of economic analysis (Pellegrini, 2011: 16).

Another economic perspective on corruption is to be found in the large body of literature on collusion. In fact, economists will often use the term collusion when they describe corruption, thereby referring to cases of bureaucratic rent seeking in which several parties are involved. While collusion is often associated with violations of competition law and its detrimental effect on private investment, thereby reducing economic growth, the economic body of knowledge goes further than that and explains the potential impact of collusion. Søreide (2014: 5) refers to corruption often being oversimplified as if it were a one phenomenon. In reality, there are different forms of corruption, and the world map of perceived corruption levels can look different depending on what form of corruption is being considered. In cases of collusive corruption, those involved collaborate to create the perception that all rules and procedures have been respected, which makes the crime much more difficult to control. Søreide thereby also refers to the examples of state institutions which are "captured" by private interests to bias the policy-making process in favour of particular firms, leaving the operation of government non-transparent (Søreide, 2002: 6-7). Paragraph 3.4.2 deals with the definitions of collusive corruption.

Definitions From Philosophy, Ethics and Political Sciences

Scholars in philosophy, ethics and political sciences consider corruption to be a moral phenomenon, opposed to a legal phenomenon. Acts can be corrupt, even though they are legal (Miller, 2011). Anechiarico and Jacobs (1996: 3) state that, "Corruption is the name we apply to some reciprocities by some people in some contexts." This is not to say that all immoral behaviour is corruption. Here one can think of gossiping about colleagues or cheating in a relationship. Although this is not illegal nor does it have any direct economic effects, it undermines moral values like respect and honesty. Anechiarico and Jacobs (1996) and Warren (2004) reference the popular use of the term corruption, and how nowadays it's not only a matter of lawful or unlawful, it's enough to regard the people's view on whether a conduct is considered to be moral and ethical or corrupt. This is seen in the persistent appeal to civil servants to prevent any "appearance of corruption" (Anechiarico and Jacobs, 1996: 3). Sandel uses a fundamental method of definition when he argues that it is no use to talk about corruption of certain aspects of life, if we as a society do not consider certain forms of for instance parenthood or citizenship to be better than others (2012: 20). With the moral definition of corruption in mind, we can say that it is corrupt if multinationals can hire expensive public affairs firms to develop their strategy to influence decision-makers while a small NGO without resources has to fall back on the traditional ways of interest representation. Although legally we could not consider this to be corruption, morally it would be corruption because money determines whether or not an organisation is being consulted in decision-making. This broader definition of corruption is also presented by Anechiarico in his 2016 speech on Political Corruption (Anechiarico, 2016). Anechiarico refers to corruption as "private gain for public office" and the practice of massive influencing by corporate and other special interests by means of financing electoral campaigns to be corrupt, albeit legal. He thereby uses the notion of inclusion as referred to by Rawls, Sandel and Warren (2004). Good governance and the absence of corruption can only be upheld if those interests most likely to be affected by the decision-making are included (Anechiarico, 2016).

Sandel argued that "the increasing commodification of our existence is a form of corruption which undermines both our relationships with each other and the relationship of the individual with society." Sandel's ethical approach to corruption implies that something becomes corrupt if it is only appreciated in terms of economic value and not in moral value. If friendship, love, political influence and organs are seen as commodities which can be bought or sold, the corruption becomes a fact (2012: 18-19). Seeing corruption in the commodification of our society is a fundamental method of definition and an absolute contradiction of the libertarian definition of corruption. The problem is that morality and the definition of corruption in moral terms are established by scholars, journalists and the wider public, while in reality law enforcement officials or organisations themselves cannot investigate immoral behaviour which is not illegal. This is not to say that this approach has no effect. Criminal, private and administrative laws and self-regulation do change over time because of changes in societal perceptions. Not long ago, smoking was allowed everywhere, including in companies, trains and airplanes. In less than two decades smoking not only became tightly regulated (only allowed in designated areas) but, more importantly, smoking has almost become an immoral practice which the public disapproves of. Another example of the moral definition of corruption is the high bonuses paid to board members of semi-public organisation in the Netherlands. All of a sudden people began referring to this practice as corrupt, while up until that time nobody had addressed these bonuses. The main argument was that it is immoral to receive high bonuses because it concerned public money which should first and foremost be allocated to the organisations' primary cause: education, health care or social housing. This public outcry eventually resulted in the regulation of these bonuses up to a maximum limit.

Welten (2012) has an alternative ethical view on corruption and compares the way in which the business sector looks at corporate social responsibility (CSR) with that of corruption. If companies implement CSR standards which are not intrinsically motivated, it would be similar to asking a corrupt tradesman if he is honest (Welten, 2012: 15). He uses the metaphor 'zombie-ethics' to capture the examples in which actors' interest is to appear or even be ethical by asking third parties what it is they need to have in place. Such external motivation corrupts the company, because in reality they have not internalised these ethics. For zombies society is nothing more than something from which you can extract money. If we consider companies and individuals not to be corrupt because they have all the self-regulation in place and have ticked all the boxes, it is no use talking about corrupt or non-corrupt (Welten, 2012: 16-17). These ethical perspectives on corruption show that it is not enough to abide by the rules to prevent corruption. Even if persons or organisations respect laws or observe their self-enacted integrity policies, it can be considered corrupt if important values are undermined. If bonuses granted to board members of semi-public organisations are lowered, or if corporations respect their anti-corruption standards, it can still be corruption if those involved do not personally value and appreciate this, but feel forced to accept it. Their intrinsic belief that this is the only moral way to act is missing.

No General Corruption Definition

The legal definitions make up a separate category because they are used by public prosecution authorities to decide whether or not it is opportune to prosecute individuals suspected of corruption. This category is presented in paragraph 3.4.2. The definitions already presented here show that there are various ways of looking at corruption and defining it. Most definitions come down to corruption at the level of the individual, whereas others focus on the context or system. The corruption definition most commonly used by the international community is that of Transparency International (TI) and the World Bank (WB), which define corruption as "the abuse of entrusted power for private gain" (OECD, 2008: 22). This behavioural definition is similar to those from social sciences referring to the misuse of power for private interest and captures four elements of corruption. One, corruption takes place in both the public and private sector. Two, it involves the abuse of power held in a state institution or a private organisation. Three, the bribe-taker, the bribe-giver or a third party benefits in terms of money or another advantage (Plougmann, n.d.). Four, the element of reciprocity ('*for*'), albeit implicit, is the link between the abuse and the private gain. This definition has a wide scope which makes it difficult to use in assessing whether something is corruption or another form of abuse, done by someone in an official capacity. For instance, an employee falsifying an expense report so that he receives more money than he has spent, also abuses his entrusted power and gains from this abuse but this is fraud and not corruption. The difference is that with fraud or other abuses the last two elements of corruption are missing. Corruption involves two or more parties and the reciprocity is the linking pin between them. It's about a favour and return favour, whereas in the example of fraud, the employee disadvantages the company and gains from this abuse but it is no return favour.

There is no agreement on the general definition of corruption. There appears to be even less agreement in literature on what specific types of behaviour are included in this phenomenon (Huberts, 2014: 114). Huberts *et al.* (Huberts, Pijl & Steen, 1999: 449-451) distinguish two types of corruption which express the public management point of view. The first is bribing which is described as "misuse of public power for private gain; asking, offering, accepting bribes." The second is nepotism, cronyism, patronage, which is described as "misuse of public authority to favour friends, family, party." Alatas (1968: 11-12) distinguishes three types of corruption: bribery, extortion and nepotism, because they have a common thread: "the subordination of public interests to private aims involving a violation of the norms of duty and welfare, accompanied by secrecy, betrayal, deception and a callous disregard for any consequence suffered by the public." Alatas' non-exhaustive set of criteria to classify corruption is still useful four decades onwards, because it can be used independently of the time or place where the corruption occurs. Additionally, the criteria allow an assessment of corruption which would otherwise be regarded as falling outside the legal definition. The following criteria are used: corruption involves more than one person (1); corruption on the whole involves secrecy, except when it is so deeply rooted that there is no need for this secrecy (2); corruption involves an element of mutual obligation and mutual benefit (3); those who practise corruption resort to some form of lawful justification (4); those involved are those who want definite decisions and those who are able to influence those decisions (5); corruption involves deception of, for instance, the public body or society at large (6); corruption is a betrayal of trust (7); corruption involves a contradictory dual function of both office/business interest and self-interest (8 and 9) (Alatas, 1968: 13-14).

Definitions are not static (Klitgaard, 1988: 23) and societies' understandings of what is to be counted as corrupt will evolve over time. At any time in a society it will remain common for every discipline to define corruption in its own way. By analogy, doctors, psychologists and environmentalists will all interpret the term 'health' in a different way, and what an economist, philosopher or lawyer deems 'sustainable' can vary a lot. Corruption definitions also vary greatly and this is problematic for two reasons. First of all, states and international organisations want to prevent and redress corruption and therefore knowing what is corruption, and what is not, is essential. If corruption definitions are based on conceptual misconceptions, this can drive policy-makers to apply specific measures that would have little potential to affect corruption if differently defined (Pellegrini, 2011: 14). Secondly, criminal corruption cases are initiated but often reach a deadlock, or corruption charges have to be dropped or lowered because in the process of translating corruption into legal terms, characteristics of corruption are left put, thereby limiting the scope of the definition. The current legal approach in most EU states is that corruption either takes the form of bribery, whereby bribes are paid to alter a certain decision-making, or alternatively corruption comes in the form of facilitation payments, paid to speed up decision-making. The last form of corruption is that of favouring somebody in decision-making whereby favour and return favour are not explicitly agreed upon. In these cases, suspicions of corruption might exist, but the legal definitions fall short. As will be discussed in paragraphs 3.4.1 and 3.4.2, putting corruption in legal writing means that trading in influence is not covered in criminal law, while there is a need for it in real-life.

3.3.3 ***Model Integrity/Anti-Corruption Systems***

The body of knowledge on corruption is increasingly growing. Corruption typologies help in thinking about new legal frameworks and policies which take the context of corruption, its embeddedness in certain systems, into account. This thinking of comprehensiveness and integration of anti-corruption institutions and policies is incorporated into the current corruption assessment tools. Policy-makers and scholars share the view that corruption can only be fought if the system around corruption is coherent in terms of prevention and investigation. The complexity of corruption calls for a wide range of institutions and instruments. In the last two decades, models have been developed which try to describe how such an anti-corruption system should look. Most of these come down to a collection of institutions, laws and policies. But how do the different elements of these integrity systems interact? For every system, in order to be able to realise a certain objective, it is necessary that all actors have this same objective in mind (Meadows, 2008: 14). It is therefore a requirement that all local, regional and central institutions are aware of the role that they play in relation to the tackling of corruption and the promotion of integrity. A system is dynamic and is subject to many different influences (Meadows, 2008: 76-85). A system that functions well will be resilient enough to manage changes of this kind and corrective measures can be taken.

The NIS and NISA Model

TI's NIS model (known as the Greek Temple and designed by Pope) (Slingerland *et al.*, 2012: 221) builds on the idea of societal foundations (political, social, cultural and economic) on which institutions rest (Legislative branch of government (1), Executive branch of government (2), Judiciary (3), Public sector (4), Law enforcement (5), Electoral management body (6), Ombudsman (7), Audit institution (8), Anti-corruption agencies (9), Political parties (10), Media (11), Civil society (12) and Business (13)). All institutions need to have their own rules and integrity policies in place, fulfil the role attributed to them and collectively take on the responsibility to safeguard integrity and take a stand against corruption. The term 'NIS' illustrates a major change in anti-corruption strategies. From 1999/2000 it was recognised that the answer to corruption did not lie in a single institution, let alone a single law, but in a number of agencies, laws, ethical codes and practices (Brown *et al.*, 2005). A couple of years later, the Australian National Integrity Assessment (NISA) brought new insights to the integrity model. By using the metaphor of a bird's nest, this model is built on the idea of a great multiplicity of individually small and weak elements that make up the system, and which are incapable of providing any significant support by themselves (Brown *et al*, 2005: 17). The NISA consists of a new methodological framework based on assessing an integrity system's 'consequences/impacts' (achievements) (1), 'capacity' (resources and competences) (2) and 'coherence' (3) (Brown *et al*, 2005, iii), whereby the latter seeks to evaluate whether the various elements coherently interact and enforce each other, and collectively support the overall aims of the anti-corruption and integrity policy (Brown *et al*, 2005: 78).

LIS Model and Models for Integrity Networks

Huberts *et al.* (2008) amended Pope's NIS model into a Local Integrity System (LIS) model. This model is used to assess the integrity system of a city. A LIS consists of nine elements to be assessed at the 'local' level: the actors involved (1), the regulatory context (2), the subject (whose integrity is at stake) (3), interpretation of the term integrity (4), the position and role of the local integrity bureau (5), the combination of compliance-based and value-based strategies (6), the presence of internal and external checks and balances (7), the political and public support for the system (8) and its effectiveness and efficiency (9) (Huberts *et al.*, 2008, 2012). Descriptive-empirical research (Huberts *et al.*, 2008; 2012; Brown *et al*, 2005 and Transparency International n.d.) proposed that there are various configurations of institutions, laws, policies and practices resulting in similar outcomes. As such, there is no 'Grand Model' to control corruption, but a need to assess corruption with a systems approach in a given context. Scholars such as Anechiarico (2010) and Hoekstra (2016) both point to the importance of integrity networks, whereby anti-corruption agencies have to be independent but also need to develop network connections with other key actors, whether internally, for instance, communications, compliance officers, audit, (top) management, HRM and legal (Hoekstra, 2016) or externally, for example, public administration, the media and the private sector (Anechiarico, 2010); (Hoekstra, 2016) As such, they engage with these key actors in developing both corruption control and public management networks (Anechiarico, 2010: 92). In this way the network approach is seen as providing an effective structure to work together on anti-corruption activities; the network is considered to be an answer to corruption, regarding the effective policy-making and implementation to be a complex system of its own (Anechiarico, 2010: 92).

3.3.4 *Corruption Embedded in a Social System*

The preceding paragraph described how newly introduced model integrity systems focus on the role systems play in the occurrence and prevention of corruption. This paragraph explores existing literature on corruption which is different from the immediate influencing (favour and return favour). De Graaf (2005: 56) and Höffling (2002: 78) present a typology of corruption, whereby corruption is either seen as deviating behaviour (situational corruption and intimate corruption) or whereby corruption is the norm (systemic and network corruption). According to Höffling (2002: 45), corruption networks are based on a sustainable relationship between the briber and the person being bribed in which both trust each other. These relationships exist in the context of a social system in which corruption is accepted and justified (Höffling, 2002: 45; Ashforth and Anand, 2003). De Graaf (2005: 58) references at the substitute mechanism. If a public office holder leaves office, the sub-systems will soon try to get the newly appointed office-holder 'on board'. Ashforth and Anand (2003) refer to this process of 'socialisation' as being one explanation for how organisational or system corruption can persist despite the turnover of its initial practitioners.

De Graaf (2005: 58-59) highlights the conclusions from the 2002 parliamentary inquiry into large-scale corruption in the Dutch building industry (Parlementaire Commissie Bouwnijverheid, 2003). Here one of the findings was that the corruption cases happened within the context of corruption networks, where there was not a one-on-one relationship with a clear favour and return favour (Parlementaire Commissie Bouwnijverheid, 2003, 270). De Graaf finds (2005: 59) that in the case studies, individuals involved refer to "unspoken agreements" in networks, where individuals can do things paid for by others who trust that at some point this will lead to favourable decision-making. Anechiarico and Jacobs (1996: 4) point at the great deal of uncertainty in labelling exchanges and reciprocities bribes and others lawful reciprocities or gifts. One argument they use is the fact that the payoffs are often complex and not 'money-filled paper envelopes' but instead come in the form of investment opportunities and campaign support and more often they do not involve the official personally but can be beneficial to one's colleague, friend, family member or acquaintance. Della Porta & Vannuci (1999; 2005) analyse in great detail the corrupt exchanges in political corruption in European countries, whereby they argue that friendships or relationships are instrumentally used by business politicians as a basis for the exchange of favours (1999: 90). In this way the basis for illegal transactions is created and the electoral support created which is required to further individual careers and maintain the party system.

Warren (2004) also criticises current conceptions of corruption for being too static. According to Warren, current corruption conceptions provide little insight into or guidance on the corruption of norm-creating processes at the heart of democratic politics (2004, 330). He proposes a democratic conception of corruption which extends to any person or group in a position enabling them to make use of collective powers or make collective decisions. In the eyes of an individual, "(...) a public matter is any in which a collectivity has the capacity to affect her life." (2004, 332). Warren's references to political corruption coincide with his view that corruption does not only include the state or government:

> "but also any collectivity with control over resources that people need or want. A corollary involves the broadening of the concept of collective power to include not only state power, but also (a) the "force" of collective judgment and argument (as in the ancient conception), and (b) control over economic resources sufficient to generate harms." (2004, 332).

Warren considers the norm violated by corruption to be that of democratic inclusion in collective decisions and actions of all affected. Here corruption is broader than immediate influencing; the corruption involves exclusion: it's about exerting control over resources to achieve gains at the expense of those excluded in collective decision-making and/or organisation of collective actions (2004, 333). Insights from organisational behaviour help in understanding the processes of collectives. Ashforth & Anand (2003: 3) present a model to examine collective corruption. Although they still build their model on the idea of corrupt acts, their research is a step in the direction of understanding corruption to be embedded in collective structures and processes. Ashforth & Anand argue that there are three reinforcing and reciprocally interdependent processes (institutionalisation, rationalisation and socialisation), which conspire to normalise and perpetuate corrupt practices so that the system beats the individual (2003, 37). This will be further discussed in subparagraph 4.8.4.

Some authors provide typologies of corruption, which reflect their recognition that corruption can only be understood in a certain context or social system. Johnston concludes that there are four different categories, which he calls 'syndromes' (Van Hulten, 2010: 22-23). In his search for syndromes of corruption, he asks "What are the underlying developmental processes, and problems, of which a society's corruption is symptomatic?" (2009: 38). Johnston clusters countries among four major corruption syndromes: Influence Markets, Elite Cartels, Oligarchs and Clans and Official Moguls. According to Johnston these distinctive corruption syndromes reflect deeper problems of democratic and economic participation and institutions (2005: 2). Influence Market corruption (Western Europe, Canada, Japan and the USA) is described as "efforts on the part of private interests to rent access and influence within well-institutionalised policy processes, often through political figures acting as middlemen."(2005: 3). Elite Cartel countries (Central Europe, Chile, Botswana, and South Korea) are said to be known for their "corruption which occurs among, and helps sustain, networks of political, economic, military, bureaucratic or ethnic and communal elites."(2005: 3). This corruption is economic, military, bureaucratic, or ethnic and communal elites, present in a system with increasing political competition and moderately strong institutions."(2005: 3). Oligarch and Clan corruption (Russia, Turkey, India, Philippines, Thailand, and Ghana) is present in systems with expanding economic and political opportunities and weak institutions. "It is dominated by figures who may be government officials or business entrepreneurs, but whose power is personal and attracts extensive followings."(2005: 3). The corruption which is symptomatic for countries with weak institutions, weak political competition and scarce economic opportunities is referred to as Official Moguls (China, Indonesia, many Sub-Saharan and Middle Eastern states like Jordan and Emirates): "government officials, or their protégés, who plunder an economy with impunity."(2005: 3). Johnston's typology is an attempt to capture corruption by seeing it as recurring and continuous improper influence mechanisms emerging in various systems.

All these scholars acknowledge the existence of improper influences and corruption embedded in the context of a system, subsystem and/or network and the complexity of addressing this in policies and responsibility attribution. These scholars' views of regarding corruption not from the individual act-perspective call for different approaches in anti-corruption policies and frameworks.

3.3.5 ***Corruption and Networks***

Two decades ago, Cartier Bresson (1997) argued that corruption networks aim at including pieces of the environment in their organisation. He indicated in this regard that networks are alliances between individuals from diverse sectors, aimed at reducing the parties' dependence on legal or formal boundaries, by creating instead a favourable environment (1997: 471-473). Thus, the network function is that of intermediary of exchanges (1997: 474). Cartier-Bresson (1997), Nielsen (2003) and Uribe (2014) make this reference more explicit by pointing to the importance of understanding the network nature of corruption. According to Nielsen, these stable corruption networks are pervasive corruption subsystems which function across geographical areas and political-economic systems (2003: 125) and are foremost built on trust. Nielsen identifies twelve key elements in the operation of corrupt systems.

According to the author (2003: 126-127), the first element is the existence of a reciprocal sub-system with parasitic and destructive win-win relations. The second element is the extortion conducted by government officials and political parties. The third element recognises the fact that corruption activities are often related to productive activities, thereby ensuring sustainability of corruption networks. The fourth element is how unethical behaviour conducted by reform agents can be used against them, and obstructs the application of an anti-corruption policy. The fifth element is the variety of relations that can exist among the members of a corruption network, based on their qualities to enable and maintain social relations. The sixth element refers to norms that are laid down in widely accepted laws, but which coincide with high costs. The seventh element is the existence of links among, for instance, political parties, law enforcement, the judiciary and the legislature. The eighth element is about the importance of analysing the connections among political parties and the checks and balances in a democratic system. The ninth element considers the large amounts of money needed in the financing of political campaigns and candidacies, and how this kind of funding requires political favours in the future. The tenth element is about those in charge of reform refusing corrupt offers and the threats they receive when they refuse. The eleventh element is about how the principal-agent problem can emerge in relations among public sector participants. The twelfth element refers to the risk of financial rescue programmes leaving the corrupt system undisturbed while forcing austerity measures on the population. In his description of corruption networks, Nielsen considers corruption network relationships among individuals across organisations to negatively influence corruption behaviour within organisations (2003: 142).

Uribe concludes that for anti-corruption policies to be effective, it is essential to understand how the networks of social trust can influence corrupt behaviour and corrupt outcomes (2014: 176). Cartier-Bresson (1997), Nielsen (2003) and Uribe (2014) all stress the importance of understanding the social structure of this network and the need to translate this understanding into policy design. They foremost describe how social networks influence individual corrupt behaviour. Without explicit reference to the network character of the corruption, Johnston's description of the Influence Markets and Elite Cartels are in fact examples of forms of network corruption which are linked to the given societal systems (2005). Heywood (1997) argues that from the 1990s onwards 'political corruption' generated wide public concern. Heywood does not provide a general definition of 'political corruption' because the rules of fair politics and political order vary from one country to the other, but in his article he refers, among others, to 'business politicians' and 'career politicians', thereby also referring to Della Porta's distinction between (Italian) traditional forms of clientelism, involving localised relationships between patrons and clients, and clientelistic networks, which are linked to broad institutional contexts (Heywood, 1997: 427; Della Porta, 1997). Heywood describes how developments such as the decline in membership of political parties and trade unions and the transfer of decision-making authority, both upwards through transnational organisations like the EU and downwards through decentralisation, have blurred the division between the public and private spheres (1997: 429; 2015: 2). The opportunity structures for influence peddling have become greater due to third-party sector involvement and 'new public management' (1997: 429). Heywood points to the fact that the most striking corruption scandals have precisely involved the inter action between the public and private sectors. Any over-emphasis upon the public sector thus risks missing many actual instances of corruption (2015: 2). He calls for refining our understanding of corruption to allow consideration of sub- national and supra- national variation, as well as the particular actors in question (2015: 4).

This paragraph presented the various ways corruption is defined and looked at. Each discipline has its own way of defining corruption and scholars from the same discipline can use different corruption definitions. This research seeks to assess the link between networks and corruption with an EU perspective in mind. In addition to the scientific approach of networks and corruption, this chapter will also detail the current EU policy perspective on corruption. The next paragraph deals with EU references to corruption in law and policy.

3.4 WHAT IS THE EU PERSPECTIVE ON CORRUPTION?

3.4.1 *International Anti-Corruption Law*

This research looks at the EU perspective on anti-corruption, but before this topic became a priority for the EU, other international organisations had already set up their anti-corruption laws. The international community started to actively make rules against corruption at the end of the 70s. Already in 1977 the International Chamber of Commerce (ICC) issued its Rules of Conduct to Combat Extortion and Bribery (International Chamber of Commerce. (n.d.). The ICC was at the forefront in trying to eradicate corruption and the ICC Commission on Corporate Responsibility and Anti-corruption is actively involved in making and promoting anti-corruption rules, concerning among other things anti-corruption in public procurement and in model commercial contracts. In that same year, the US Foreign Corrupt Practices Act (FCPA) was enacted.[5] Although this is a piece of national anti-corruption law, it has far-reaching territorial effect and applies to any person who has a certain degree of connection to the United States and engages in foreign corrupt practices.[6] In 1989, a Seminar on Corruption in Government was organised by the UN's Department of Technical Co-Operation and Development (DTCD) and the Dutch government. The seminar was held in The Hague and was organised in anticipation of the eight UN Congress on the Prevention of Crime and the Treatment of Offenders (Posadas, 2000: 370) This is probably the first initiative where the necessity for international cooperation to control corruption was concretised. The UN has since developed and encouraged several activities related to corruption matters.

At the same time, also other international organisations developed their anti-corruption measures. In 1994 the OECD recommended that its member states criminalise foreign bribery (Posadas, 2000: 373) In 1996 the *UN Declaration Against Corruption and*

5 The Foreign Corrupt Practices Act of 1977 (15 U.S.C. §§ 78dd-1, et seq.).
6 Note: Among others, the Johnson & Johnson bribery case and the Siemens bribery case were investigated and settled based on the FCPA.

Bribery in International Commercial Transactions was adopted by the General Assembly. Though not legally binding, the resolution expressed the interest and concern of the international community in the development of anti-corruption measures. This Declaration presented a model definition of the basic passive and active elements of bribery[7], following to some extent the OECD. The *OECD Convention on Combating Bribery of Foreign Public Officials in International Business Transactions*[8] entered into force in 1999 and soon afterwards the CoE[9] and the UN[10] followed with their own anti-corruption conventions. Carr (2007) examined the current legal frameworks adopted by the eight regional and international conventions and concludes that their scope differs significantly.[11] Except for the South African Protocol, all other Conventions refrain from providing a general definition of corruption but focus on specific types of corrupt behaviour (Carr, 2007: 131). Carr argued that it would be reasonable to expect that with so many anti-corruption treaties a form of mutual cooperation between the international organisations would take place, resulting in a largely harmonised and comparatively uniform legislative approach to fighting corruption (Carr, 2007: 129). Unfortunately the conventions and protocols vary in terms of both substantive and procedural provisions, and comprehensiveness. Lack of conformity between the conventions means that states are likely to tackle the issue of corruption in different ways, which might result in (legal) uncertainty. It also means that states have to go through various evaluation mechanisms, which is time-consuming because all the provisions on the various forms of corruption differ from one piece of law to the other, but all need to be translated and implemented in national law.

Instead of coming up with entirely new policies, the EU by voice of the European Commission announced it will make use of the existing international instruments and their mechanisms to monitor and evaluate effective implementation. Therefore the following subparagraph will deal with the major legal definitions of corruption in these international instruments.

---

7 Annex 3 a and b UN Declaration Against Corruption and Bribery in International Commercial Transactions

8 OECD (1999) OECD Convention on Combating Bribery of Foreign Public Officials in International Business Transactions.

9 Council of Europe (1999) Criminal Law Convention on Corruption (ETS No.173.) and Council of Europe (1999) Civil Law Convention on Corruption (ETS No.174.).

10 United Nations (2004). United Nations Convention against Corruption.

11 i) Organisation of American States Inter-American Convention Against Corruption 1996, ii) Organisation for Economic Cooperation and Development Convention on Combating Bribery of Foreign Public Officials in International Business Transactions 1997, iii) Convention drawn up on the basis of Article K.3 (2) (c) of the Treaty on European Union on the Fight Against Corruption involving Officials of the European Union Communities or Officials of Member States of the European Union 1999, iv) Council of Europe Criminal Law Convention on Corruption 1999, v) Southern African Development Protocol Against Corruption 2001, vi) African Union Convention of Preventing and Combating Corruption 2003, vii) United Nations Convention Against Corruption 2003, viii) Council of Europe Additional Protocol to the Criminal law Convention on Corruption 2003.

3.4.2 Definitions in Law

As seen from the definitions in paragraph 3.3.2, corruption is a complex economic, moral, social, and political phenomenon. It has proved remarkably difficult to define in general terms. To this day there is no universal legal definition of corruption because this complexity makes it difficult to capture the corruption phenomenon in a legal definition. Firstly, corruption can take on all sorts of agreements, payments, favours, kickbacks and other transactions in power and influence. Secondly, the actors involved in the corruption are different in nature, varying from natural persons such as citizens, public officials, civil servants or even football players to legal persons such as companies and governmental organisations. Thirdly, the damaging effect of corruption is diverse; corruption can undermine moral values and result in unfair competition, lower investment levels, loss of public money and decrease in public trust, which ultimately undermines the rule of law and democracy. Fourthly, there is the cultural component which makes it impossible to reach agreement among states on what the scope of corruption is. Fifthly, the concept of corruption inspires emotions which make it difficult to define corruption without a strong moral component (Pellegrini, 2011: 14-15). This has led to the compromise that international organisations concentrate on the definition of certain forms of corruption (Council of Europe, 2009: paragraph 2).

The TI/WB definition 'the abuse of entrusted power for private gain' (OECD, 2008: 22) is referred to by international organisations (including the EU), national law-makers and civil society as an umbrella definition for policy and advocacy purposes. It is by no means a criminal definition. It is useful because of its wide scope, including all sorts of corruption. The alternative approach is to refer to corruption as bribery, but as stated before this definition is not suited to dealing with the variety of corruption offences. This paragraph will compare the two officially recognised corruption offences bribery and trading in influence as they are defined in the CoE Convention and the UN Convention.

Before we look at these legal definitions, it is wise to distinguish the various references to corruption in other wordings. The references below are some examples of references to corruption commonly used. Some of them overlap to some extent.

References to Corruption in Common Language

1. Abuse of discretion

The three forms of corruption which can be clustered under this heading are favouritism, nepotism and clientelism. This is a form of corruption in which an individual abuses his/her discretionary power thereby serving the interests of someone linked to him or her through membership in a group (United Nations Office on Drugs and Crime, 2004).

2. Old boys' networks
An informal system through which men are thought to use their positions of influence to help others who went to the same school or university they did, or who share a similar social background (Oxford Dictionaries).
3. Collusion, crony capitalism, state capture and regulatory capture
Cambridge Dictionary defines collusion as an "agreement between people to act together secretly or illegally in order to deceive or cheat someone" (Cambridge Dictionary). The Anti-Corruption Glossary of Transparency (n.d. b) International defines collusion as: "A secret agreement between parties, in the public and/or private sector, to conspire to commit actions aimed to deceive or commit fraud with the objective of illicit financial gain. The parties involved often are referred to as 'cartels'." Van den Heuvel defines collusion as "secret relations foremost to hinder the investigations of crimes." (1998: 6). Another reference to corruption is crony capitalism, which Oxford Dictionary defines as "an economic system characterised by close, mutually advantageous relationships between business leaders and government officials." This phenomenon appears to be related to the phenomenon of state capture, which the Vice Presidency of the World Bank referred to as "the efforts of a small number of firms (or such groups as the military, ethnic groups and kleptocratic politicians) to shape the rules of the game to their advantage through illicit, non-transparent provision of private gains to public officials." (World Bank, n.d.). Another definition of state capture is "the domination of policy making by private, often corporate, power" (Encyclopedia Brittanica, 2018). Regulatory capture is defined as "The tendency of regulators to identify with the interest of the industry they are supposed to regulate." (Oxford Reference, n.d.). This is the case when public authorities in charge of regulating a certain industry in the public interest, start to identify the public interest with the interests of producers in the industry, hereby not considering the interests of its customers or the general public any longer. Posner (2013) simply defines is as "the subversion of regulatory agencies by the firms they regulate."
4. Conflicts of interest
This form of corruption can be distinguished to refer to the conflict between the professional responsibilities of a corrupt individual and his or her private interests (Transparency International, n.d. b). Individuals in the public and private sector are often confronted with circumstances in which their personal interests conflict with their professional responsibility to act in the best interests of their organisation or the general interest. The Anti-Corruption Glossary of Transparency International defines it as "the situation where an individual or the entity for which they work, whether a government, business, media outlet or civil society organisation, is confronted with choosing between the duties

and demands of their position and their own private interests." (Transparency International, n.d. b).

5. Bribery

This form of corruption involves a "payment given personally to a government official in exchange for his use of official powers." (Huberts, 2014: 114). Both the official abusing his power and the person offering the favour (bribe) are considered to be committing bribery.

6. Influence peddling/trading in influence

This form of corruption involves an individual who sells his influence over a decision-making process to a second person who acts on behalf of a third party.

7. Nepotism, patronage, cronyism and favouritism

Phenomena linked to clientelism, which is a social relationship linked to informal rules (Wolfgang, 2013: 37), which include forms of corruption that involve the use or abuse of one's professional influence to favour individuals or groups because they are family, relatives, friends or party members, or for other reasons that result in a sense of connectedness.

These descriptions all have characteristics in common, such as the element of connections and blending professional with personal interests. These descriptions are used in policy documents and not in law. The international conventions do require states to adopt legislative and other measures as may be necessary to establish the criminalisation of basic forms of corruption such as 'bribery' (such as bribery of foreign public officials in international business transactions (OECD, 1999)) and trading in influence (United Nations Office on Drugs and Crime (n.d.); Council of Europe (n.d.)). The Conventions entail numerous provisions on the criminalisation of bribery, each dealing with active bribery (bribe offering) or passive bribery (bribe taking) by a specific official (whether for instance, civil servant, judge or politician, whether domestic or foreign). However, corruption is more than bribery alone.

Trading in Influence

Trading in influence is a separate form of corruption defined in the Conventions of the UN and the CoE.[12] These two conventions are applicable in nearly all EU Member States. To get an idea of the scope of corruption, for both conventions a provision on bribery is compared with one regarding trading in influence, of both Conventions, in order to see what these specific corrupt behaviours entail.

12 The OECD Convention is not analysed further because its scope is limited to foreign bribery, while this study seeks to capture corruption which is the result of social networks, particularly within various European states.

Bribery of domestic public officials	Trading in influence
Art. 2 and art. 3 Council of Europe's Criminal Law Convention on Corruption:	*Art. 12 Council of Europe's Criminal Law Convention on Corruption:*
When committed intentionally, the promising, offering or giving by any person, directly or indirectly, of any undue advantage to any of its public officials, for himself or herself or for anyone else, for him or her to act or refrain from acting in the exercise of his or her functions. When committed intentionally, the request or receipt by any of its public officials, directly or indirectly, of any undue advantage, for himself or herself or for anyone else, or the acceptance of an offer or a promise of such an advantage, to act or refrain from acting in the exercise of his or her functions.	When committed intentionally, the promising, giving or offering, directly or indirectly, of any undue advantage to anyone who asserts or confirms that he or she is able to exert an improper influence over the decision-making of any person referred to in Articles (…….) in consideration thereof, whether the undue advantage is for himself or herself or for anyone else, as well as the request, receipt or the acceptance of the offer or the promise of such an advantage, in consideration of that influence, whether or not the influence is exerted or whether or not the supposed influence leads to the intended result.
Art. 15 United Nation's Convention against Corruption:	*Art. 18 United Nation's Convention against Corruption:*
(a) The promise, offering or giving, to a public official, directly or indirectly, of an undue advantage, for the official himself or herself or another person or entity, in order that the official act or refrain from acting in the exercise of his or her official duties;	(a) The promise, offering or giving to a public official or any other person, directly or indirectly, of an undue advantage in order that the public official or the person abuse his or her real or supposed influence with a view to obtaining from an administration or public authority of the State Party an undue advantage for the original instigator of the act or for any other person;
(b) The solicitation or acceptance by a public official, directly or indirectly, of an undue advantage, for the official himself or herself or another person or entity, in order that the official act or refrain from acting in the exercise of his or her official duties.	(b) The solicitation or acceptance by a public official or any other person, directly or indirectly, of an undue advantage for himself or herself or for another person in order that the public official or the person abuse his or her real or supposed influence with a view to obtaining from an administration or public authority of the State Party an undue advantage.

Bribery, as described in these articles, is the straightforward classical form of corruption: person A, who is in power, accepts a (future) favour from person B and as a return favour A does something while in his official duties which is beneficial to B. Both A and B can do this for themselves or at the interest of person C. Trading in influence is a more complex form of corruption. Here person A accepts a (future) favour from B and in return there is a chance that B or C benefits from favourable decision-making. Whereby person A can be anyone who is able to exert an improper influence on the decision-maker, meaning that this does not need to be the public official himself. Also the use of the wording 'improper' influence indicates that it is already enough to prove that undue pressure is used to influence decision-making.

Both the provision on bribery and that of trading in influence define the corruption to be individual acts, either active (the promising, giving or offering) or passive (request, receipt or acceptance of the offer or the promise). However, according to the Explanatory Report of the CoE, trading in influence was included "to reach the close circle of the official or the political party to which he belongs and to tackle the corrupt behaviour of those persons who are in the neighbourhood of power and try to obtain advantages from their situation, contributing to the atmosphere of corruption." (Council of Europe, 2009). This explanation is an attempt to look beyond the unethical individual corrupt act of the bribe taker and bribe giver and to consider a wider circle of individuals involved in corruption. It is not only about the persons who have power and influence, but also about the persons who are near those who have power and influence.

The Problem of Distinguishing Trading in Influence From Lobbying

The Group of States against Corruption (GRECO)[13] (Council of Europe, n.d. b) would like member states to criminalise this behaviour in their national criminal law, allowing those who try to use improper influence in decision-making to be convicted (Macauley, n.d.). The Explanatory Report goes on to say that 'improper' influence must contain a corrupt intent by the influence peddler; acknowledged forms of lobbying do not fall under this notion. The CoE did not intend the offence to include traditional lobbying, but it lacks in offering a clear distinction of 'proper' and 'improper' influence. The topic of lobbying is on the agenda again, with the European Commission calling for stricter rules on lobbying groups, amid controversies that former top officials have used the so-called 'revolving door', thereby taking on positions with big business (Eriksson, 2016). Lobbying is generally considered to concern ways to influence decision-makers (a legislator). The regulation of lobbying is on the EU agenda. In 2018 the European Parliament, European Commission and European Council started talks about setting up joint rules that will bring more transparency and openness to the activities of interest representatives in the decision-making process at the EU level. Seven EU member states (France, Ireland, Lithuania, Austria, Poland, Slovenia and the UK) enacted legislation on the issue of lobbying (European Parliament, 2018).

The United Nations Office on Drugs and Crime (2006) distinguishes active from passive bribery. Trading in influence is explained further in the *Legislative Guide to UNCAC* (United Nations Office on Drugs and Crime, 2006). The element of 'undue advantage' may be something tangible or intangible.[14] *The Guide* explains that:

---

13 In 1999 the Council of Europe established the Group of States against Corruption (GRECO) to monitor States' compliance with the organisation's anti-corruption standards.

14 United Nations Office on Drugs and Crime. (2006). *Legislative Guide for the Implementation of the United Nations Convention against Corruption.* Paragraph 283.

> "The undue advantage does not have to be given immediately or directly to a public official of the State. It may be promised, offered or given directly or indirectly. A gift, concession or other advantage may be given to some other person, such as a relative or political organisation. The undue advantage or bribe must be linked to the official's influence over an administration or public authority of the State."[15]

It is necessary to prove that "some link must be established between the offer or advantage and inducing the official to abuse his or her influence in order to obtain from an administration or public authority of the State party an undue advantage for the instigator of the act or for any other person."[16] The undue advantage "may be for the official or some other person or entity."[17] Both provisions of trading in influence seek to capture and criminalise a form of corruption in which various persons or entities are involved and whereby some link must be proven between A, B and C's behaviour in influencing decision-making.

Although trading in influence is an ambitious and not fully developed concept within GRECO, the UN and member states, its introduction is a step in the direction of network thinking. An important element in GRECO's explanation which hints at the collective behaviour of corruption is that the close circle has contributed to the atmosphere of corruption. Reference to a 'close circle' indicates that the CoE/GRECO is convinced that the social structure itself is the actor to consider corrupt. Thereby the definition of corruption is extended beyond the briber and bribe taker and includes others that helped create a corrupt environment. This is a subtle reference to a joint or collective form of corruption; a form of corruption, that is more than the sum of individual acting, or corruption which is the result of individual acts which are in themselves acceptable.

The desire to capture corruption in a universal definition is not a semantic issue; how corruption is defined actually ends up determining what will be allowed and what will not. Also it means that it is a step in the direction of measuring corruption and the effectiveness of anti-corruption policies. What these articles from the UN and CoE Conventions show is that both Conventions do not define corruption but instead define separate forms of corruption. Bribery and trading in influence are seen as different forms of corruption. The legal definitions in the CoE and UN Conventions are formulated in such a way that they can be used as criminal offence provisions; here corruption is brought back to an individual act, whereby trading in influence is different from bribery, because its seeks to include an element or organisation. This entails that there is a sense of awareness or recognition of the many parties and social structure involved in corruption. However, criminalising separate forms of corruption is not a guarantee that corruption

15 Ibid. Paragraph 284.
16 Ibid. Paragraph 285.
17 Ibid. Paragraph 288.

will be fought more effectively. There will continue to be major differences in what is considered corrupt conduct across different societies and over time in the same society (Anechiarico & Jacobs, 1996: 3-4). Johnston (2005) and Warren (2004) are among those scholars who criticise the modern legalistic understanding of the individual conception of corruption. Considering the incorporation in criminal law of forms of corruption which go beyond this bilateral reciprocal relationship is a step in acknowledging and recognising the corruption caused by joint actions, but in itself the legal approach is not enough, as will be demonstrated in paragraph 3.5.1.

This paragraph provided a comparison of the corruption offences of bribery and trading in influence, as laid down in the two major international conventions which the European Commission uses in its evaluations (European Commission, 2014c: 2). In Chapter 8 I will present a table which distinguishes, among other things, lobbying from trading in influence and network corruption. The following subparagraphs will specifically deal with the EU's position on anti-corruption.

3.4.3 *The Position of the EU*

EU Competence in Anti-Corruption

The preceding paragraphs explained why corruption is a concern and what the difficulties are in defining corruption. Now it is time to look at the role of the EU in anti-corruption and its possibilities to take action against corruption in network-like structures. Initially, EU integration was aimed at securing peace on the continent through economic and political cooperation. This integration was intensified and most policy fields now fall within the exclusive or shared competence of the EU. The EU's competence to act in the field of anti-corruption policies is twofold. This entails first of all the EU's obligation to ensure high levels of security. This entails the prevention and combating of crime by means of cooperation between police and judicial authorities and where necessary by adjusting criminal laws.[18] The Treaty on the Functioning of the European Union (TFEU) lists corruption among those crimes for which directives may be established, providing minimum rules on definition of criminal offences and sanctions because corruption often has implications across, and beyond, internal EU borders.[19] The focus here is particularly on preventing social harm. Secondly, the EU has the obligation to protect the internal market by promoting fair competition and tackling market distortion.[20] The EU can take action to protect financial interests: businesses which obtain orders after having paid bribes commit a crime and violate the principle of fair competition. On the basis of this competence, the EU enacted the *Framework Decision 2003/568/*

18 Art. 3 (2) TEU and Art. 67 (3) TFEU.
19 Art. 83 (1) TFEU.
20 Art. 3 (3) TEU.

JHA on combating corruption in the private sector, aimed at criminalising both active and passive bribery, establishing more detailed rules on the liability of legal persons and deterrent sanctions. This Decision together with the *1997 Convention on fighting corruption involving officials of the EU or officials of Member States* forms the specific anti-corruption acquis. European legislation in other areas, such as anti-money laundering and public procurement, include important anti-corruption provisions. The 2011 implementation report on the 2003 Framework Decision on combating corruption in the private sector showed that several states still had not fully transposed all elements of active and passive bribery in their criminal provision and neither was the liability of legal persons regulated as prescribed.[21] Without the adequate implementation and enforcement of these international and European anti-corruption standards by states, their effect in curbing corruption will remain negligible. It is important to understand the reason why enforcement is problematic.

EU Strategy 'Fighting Corruption in the EU'

It is clear why corruption is such a concern to the EU. In 2010 EU member states adopted the 2010 Stockholm Programme entitled "An open and secure Europe serving and protecting citizens" (European Council, 2010). With the adoption of the Stockholm Programme, the Commission was given the political mandate to measure the existing efforts in the fight against corruption and to develop, in close cooperation with the Council of Europe Group of States against Corruption (GRECO), a comprehensive EU anti-corruption policy (European Commission (n.d. b). In 2011 the European Commission announced its comprehensive strategy 'Fighting Corruption in the EU' to reduce the problem of corruption (European Commission, 2011a). It will largely make use of the existing international instruments and their monitoring and evaluation mechanisms to oversee implementation. The Commission expressed itself to be particularly worried about the fact that some member states have not ratified these important international anti-corruption conventions and where anti-corruption institutions and legislation are in place its enforcement has often turned out to be insufficient in practice (European Commission, 2011a: 4). The Commission expressed its concern about the lack of firm political commitment by national governments to combat corruption in all its forms (European Commission, 2011a: 4).

Political Corruption

Although the Commission states that it wants to reduce all forms of corruption (public corruption, private corruption, corrupt activities committed by organised criminal groups and petty corruption), it emphasises the importance of particularly fighting 'po-

---

21 COM(2011) 309 final. The Report found that only nine member states (i.e. Belgium, Bulgaria, Czech Republic, France, Ireland, Cyprus, Portugal, Finland and UK) have correctly transposed all elements of the offence as laid down in Article 2 of the Framework Decision.

litical corruption' and therefore attributes a special paragraph to it in its communication. The Commission reiterated that:

> "As political scandals have repeatedly shown, complex connections are sometimes developed between political actors, private undertakings, media, trade associations and foundations. These connections are driven by mutual benefits in influencing key political and economic decisions, putting democratic institutions and procedures at risk and rendering the detection of corrupt practices more difficult." (European Commission, 2011a, 14).

In its description the Commission refers to those scandals which made the press and thereby became known to the public at large and which revealed networks of individuals with a certain authority who unlawfully traded power and influence in return for a preferential treatment or favour for themselves or another individual belonging to the network. The Commission introduced a new mechanism for periodic assessment of Member States' efforts against corruption: the EU Anti-Corruption Report (European Commission, 2011b). This should allow for a clear picture of the effectiveness of anti-corruption efforts in the EU, "helping to step up anti-corruption efforts, facilitate the exchange of best practices, identify EU trends and stimulate peer learning and further compliance with EU and international commitments." (European Commission, 2011b).

3.4.4 ***EU ANTICORRP, Anti-Corruption Report, and the European Semester***

The ANTICORRP Research Project

From 2012 to 2017 the large-scale ANTICORRP research project took place, funded by the European Commission's Seventh Framework Programme (n.d. b). Its official name was *Anticorruption Policies Revisited: Global Trends and European Responses to the Challenge of Corruption*. Researchers from various disciplines and various countries conducted research into various topics, such as comparative perspectives on the history of corruption, media and corruption and individual values and motivations to engage against corruption. Many research reports deal with specific forms of corruption in individual member states. Although the link between networks and corruption was not a specific topic in this research project, one of the ANTICORRP policy pillar leaders Alina Mungiu-Pippidi, presented some of the findings during the 2016 OECD Integrity Forum and stated: "Government favouritism is still seen as "rule of the game" by many citizens in Europe and other parts of the world. The need for more evidence-based policies is thus clear. New measurements and insights are a first step for these reforms." (ANTICORRP, n.d. a). This quote underlines that public trust in fair politics and decision-making is low in many EU States. This matches the descriptions of lobbycracy, trading in influence and favouritism as described in the previous paragraphs 3.2 and 3.3.

EU Anti-Corruption Report (ACR)
Besides this academic research project, the European Commission also made use of the policy assessments provided by the network of Local Research Correspondents on Corruption (LRCC), and based on these findings, the first and only EU Anti-Corruption Report (ACR) was published in 2014 (European Commission, 2014c). Among other things, the report compares how states implemented and enforced the OECD, CoE and UN anti-corruption conventions. The Commission chose not to come up with yet another piece of law to prevent additional administrative burdens and duplication of efforts by member states and recognised that some issues are solely national government's competence, but that it is in "the Union's common interest to ensure that all Member States have efficient anti-corruption policies and that the EU supports the Member States in pursuing this work." (European Commission, 2014c: 2). In its 41-page ACR the European Commission assesses what the overall status is of EU member states' preventive policies (such as financing of political parties and campaigns, asset disclosure, conflicts of interest, whether codes of conduct are in place) (European Commission, 2014c: 8-13). Thereafter it describes whether member states have their criminal law against corruption in place and whether there is enough capacity in law enforcement, prosecution and the judiciary (European Commission, 2014c: 13-16). It also highlights specific corruption risks, for instance, local and regional level, healthcare and urban development and public procurement (European Commission, 2014c, 16-19: 21-36). The Commission considers transparency and freedom of information policies, protection of whistle-blowers and transparency of lobbying as important background issues (European Commission, 2014c: 19-20). The overall ACR is supplemented by national reports highlighting country-specific information.

The approach the Commission chose in its ACR is similar to that of the NIS model, albeit it is not referring to a system approach nor does it look in detail at all central institutions in the member states. It describes a wide spectrum of anti-corruption laws and policies, both preventive and repressive. Additionally, it assesses whether state institutions are equipped and willing to prevent and address corruption. As such, it takes on a rather piecemeal and fragmented approach that lacks coherence. Also, the focus is mainly on traditional corruption such as bribery. With the original descriptions of trading in influence and political corruption in mind, the main concern with corruption is not so much on the individual corrupt behaviour, but the existence of these complex connections between powerful individuals acting on behalf of public institutions, businesses, media and civil society and being guided by the principle of reciprocity of returning a favour with a favour, thereby hampering the fair decision-making process. The Commission is aware of the complexity of corruption when it states: "corruption is a complex phenomenon with economic, social, political and cultural dimensions, which cannot be easily eliminated. An effective policy response cannot be reduced to a standard set of measures; there is no 'one size fits all' solution." (European Commission, 2014c: 3). However, it appears as if the Commission is falling back on traditional, existing ways of reporting about corruption without touching the core of the phenomenon. With the EU's statement in mind, that it wishes to support its member states in making their anti-corruption policies more effective, it is time to explore what can be done about complex corruption cases in which trading in influence takes place in networks. Three years after the first and only Anti-Corruption Report was published, the European Commission announced that this Report would no longer be used because the European Semester on economic policy coordination provided the information needed to determine how corruption can best be fought in the EU and its Member States.

The European Semester

The European Semester was introduced in 2010 and enables the EU member countries to coordinate their economic policies throughout the year and address the economic challenges facing the EU (European Commission, n.d. a). The European Semester's approach is to streamline processes aimed at ensuring sound public finances (avoiding excessive government debt), preventing excessive macroeconomic imbalances in the EU and supporting structural reforms to create more jobs and growth-boosting investment (European Commission, n.d. a; European Commission Directorate-General for Migration and Home Affairs, 2017). In the overarching Communication in the 2017 Spring European Semester Package, the Commission noted that, to improve the efficiency of investments, further efforts are needed to improve the performance of justice systems and to prevent and fight corruption. Challenges identified are: the fragmented corruption prevention frameworks and inadequate control mechanisms; gaps in the anti-corruption legal framework or enforcement of existing anti-corruption rules; insufficient initiatives on whistleblowing and letterbox companies; insufficient prosecution of high-level corruption; informal payments in healthcare and lack of competition and transparency in public procurement operations (European Commission Directorate-General for Migration and Home Affairs, 2017; European Commission, 2017: 14-15).

The Remaining Challenges of the EU in Fighting Corruption

According to the European Commission, challenges remain. Firstly, corruption prevention frameworks are regarded as fragmented. Secondly, there are inadequate control mechanisms. Thirdly, the anti-corruption legal framework has gaps and so does the enforcement of existing anti-corruption rules. Fourthly, there are insufficient initiatives on whistleblowing and letterbox companies. Fifthly, high-level corruption cases are insufficiently prosecuted. Sixthly, there are still too many examples of informal payments in healthcare. Seventhly, competition and transparency in public procurement operations are lacking (European Commission 2017: 14-15). To address these issues, on 22 May 2017 the Commission adopted targeted, country-specific recommendations for a number of member states to improve the fight against corruption and inefficient practices in public procurement, strengthen the regime for preventing conflicts of interest, improve accountability and transparency in public administration, strengthen provisions concerning the statute of limitations for corruption offences, combat informal payments in healthcare, reinforce the anti-corruption framework and better enforce existing legislation. Additionally, Experience Sharing Workshops will be organised in which experts, NGOs and policy makers present their good examples of anti-corruption to learn with and from each other (European Commission, n.d. c).

The European Commission has prioritised anti-corruption measures in recent legislative initiatives. It has proposed to revise the *Fourth Anti-Money Laundering Directive* to further improve transparency of beneficial ownership. The *Directive on the Protection of the EU Financial Interests* will replace an important part of the EU anti-corruption acquis, facilitate the recovery of misused EU funds and improve investigation and prosecution across the EU. Other Commission proposals include a regulation on the mutual recognition of freezing orders in which the Commission will further explore the possibility of introducing non-conviction-based confiscation. Integrity and transparency in public procurement are likely to be improved with the national implementation of the 2014 Public Procurement Directive (European Commission Directorate-General for Migration and Home Affairs, 2017). The Commission decided to favour the mainstreaming of anti-corruption in the European Semester rather than adopting a second Anti-Corruption Report (European Commission Directorate-General for Migration and Home Affairs, 2017). It considers this to be more efficient and also to yield more results because it is more operational. The EU has the power and legitimacy to make rules and policies to fight corruption.

3.5 The Problem with the Concept of Corruption

3.5.1 *Broader Than the Individual Act, Broader Than Immediate and Obvious Influencing*

Scholars' References to the Structure of the Social Network and Corruption

The previous paragraphs presented the available theory on corruption and the EU's position on corruption. The majority of the corruption definitions and concepts consider corruption to be caused by individuals who act individually. These individuals can be natural persons or legal entities such as corporations. This acting can take on all sorts of forms. There are a few scholars who refer to systemic corruption. By this they refer to the ongoing corruption by many individuals. That countries are suffering from 'systemic corruption' is another way of saying that the majority of individuals commit bribery and are involved in corruption. Sometimes references to 'systemic corruption' point at the economic or political systems which have developed over time and which have become characterised by close, mutually advantageous relationships between e.g. business leaders and government officials or between regulatory authorities and interest of specific industries or other private parties. As was described in paragraph 3.3.1 and paragraph 3.4.2, such mechanisms of influencing are referred to as 'institutional corruption', 'collusive corruption', 'crony capitalism', 'regulatory or state capture'.

There are only a few scholars who do not refer to 'act' or 'acting' and who regard corruption as including another layer to the individual acting in a corrupt manner. For instance, Anechiarico and Jacobs (1996: 3) who state that "*corruption is the name we apply to some reciprocities by some people in some contexts.*" Cartier-Bresson (1997), Nielsen (2003) and Uribe (2014) argue the importance of understanding the structure of social networks and its effect on corrupt behaviour. They consider social networks to be the context in which individuals can become corrupt. Such a social system approach is also underlined and explained by scholars such as Ashforth and Anand (2003), who assess the normalisation of corruption in organisations. They criticise the body of knowledge on corruption for its general emphasis on the individual as evildoer, because it misses the point that systems and individuals are mutually reinforcing (2003: 1).

Models on Formal Anti-Corruption Systems

The NIS and Anti-Corruption Systems are attempts to look at the system and its role in preventing corruption. It regards the coherence of institutions, policies and practices to assess whether their interplay poses a corruption risk. Although the literature and research on NIS and integrity networks provides a promising outlook on effective corruption eradication, they remain rather static and focus on the formal system consisting of institutions and their staff. The UN and CoE (GRECO)'s call to criminalise trading in influence is an attempt to capture a form of corruption which is different from individual corruption committed by individuals and corporations, but policy makers are hesitant to incorporate the concept into law because its definition is too close to legitimate forms of influencing.

3.5.2 ***The Link Between Networks and Corruption***

This chapter illustrates that various disciplines are concerned with the corruption phenomenon. It also shows that corruption is a layered concept, which emerges in various contexts and that each context requires adaption of the concept of corruption. In this research, I will add an important layer to the corruption concept: that of the network.

This is necessary because hitherto the forms of corruption which occur in real-life are not adequately conceptualised. Policy-makers and law enforcement authorities at the EU and national level struggle to deal with the more complex cases of corruption related to networks. This conceptualisation is foremost meant as a valuable contribution to the renewed interest of the European Commission in tackling corruption. However, the findings of this research can be used across the globe.

The previous analysis is a step in the direction of seeing corruption as the outcome of a collective conduct, whereby the individual's acts do not necessarily have to be corrupt. This form of corruption is more sophisticated and collective by nature than bribery. Here corruption is the result of multiple interactions between connected individuals (a network). It is a prerequisite to acknowledge that corruption itself has a network character, in which the immediate and obvious influencing is either not present or difficult to distinguish (the 'quid pro quo'). What is missing in the current literature and research is a clear description of how collective acting and influencing by informal groups of individuals can deteriorate into corruption. What features can be distinguished which can be used to evaluate these collective ways of influencing? In the cases referred to in the introduction, individuals and formal organisations played a role and the body of knowledge related to both is quite extensive. As was illustrated, this network character of corruption receives much less attention from scholars. This underlines the importance of further exploration of the available body of knowledge on corruption and networks, to develop alternative approaches to corruption which can help international organisations in their search for effective anti-corruption policies. This requires exploring the available literature on collective acting and networks.

3.6 Sub-Conclusions

This chapter described why corruption is a major societal concern and explains what makes corruption such a complex phenomenon. Corruption undermines the rule of law, our democracy and public trust. Corruption hampers economic development and can pose a threat to our security and health. There is a growing body of corruption literature and research available which consists of various corruption theories. The relativist view considers corruption to be an acceptable phenomenon while the Universalist view sees corruption as a criminal offence at all times. The other dominant theory is that which distinguishes corrupt individuals, corrupt organisations and corrupt systems. There are great differences in the way scholars define corruption. Some definitions relate the corruption to the mind of the individual (intention), while other definitions see corruption in the economic consequences of a certain conduct. Although there is no universal definition, the World Bank and TI's definition "the abuse of entrusted power for private gain" is most often referred to in policies and literature. The fact that every discipline will continue to define corruption in its own way is problematic for two reasons. It is essential for states and international organisations, such as the EU, to know what corruption is and what it is not in order to initiate policies. Additionally, many corruption cases are initiated but they result in very few convictions because of the need to translate corruption into legal terms. If corruption definitions are based on conceptual misconceptions, we might not be able to recognise and address it.

International law distinguishes bribery from trading in influence to indicate the social structure in which the more sophisticated forms of undue influencing take place. In common language corruption linked to networks is for instance referred to as 'nepotism' or 'old boys' networks'. The difference between appropriate and inappropriate ways of influencing is sometimes difficult to distinguish. This is also the reason why there is hesitation among states to criminalise trading in influence, as it bears many characteristics which are similar to the characteristics of lobbying. Since 2011, the EU has been particular active in organising anti-corruption activities. The LRCC, ANTICORRP and European Semester are different examples of EU initiatives in which it facilitated research by independent experts and scholars into the corruption phenomenon. These initiatives are meant to help the EU in determining what its (future) anti-corruption policies should consist of. The European Commission uses the term 'political corruption' in its existing policies to address the form of corruption in which complex connections between representatives from various institutions undermine democracy and fair decision-making. This in itself is considered to be a risk, but the European Commission also sees this as an extra context in which corruption is difficult to detect. Scholars such as Heywood (1997; 2015) point at the major developments which blurred the lines between the private and public sector. Too big a focus on seeing corruption as something related to the public sector minimises the chance of recognising the trading in influence which takes place.

Corruption is translated into a legal wording for pragmatic purposes but if we explore the link between social networks and corruption, the essence of corruption is missing. While there are attempts to define corruption in such a way that the environment which contributes to corruption is also considered, the current integrity system models depart from a rather classic interpretation of corruption. The NIS and the ACR, as well as the European Semester offer a description of the necessary ingredients of an anti-corruption framework and try to make the integrity or anti-corruption safeguards coherent. In doing so, these approaches fail because they have not thought through the concept of corruption. In assessing how society's institutions and the legal framework prevent corruption, the interrelatedness between institutions is overlooked and the role played by networks is not recognised.

The body of knowledge on corruption leads to the conclusion that corruption is a polymorphic concept. Recent literature on corruption does present the system and network approach of corruption, mostly by looking at how individual corrupt acts are in fact caused by the collective behaviour of groups and organisations (corruption is the norm and many are committing corruption). This, however, is still a focus in which corruption is understood as an act in a context, while this research seeks to explore corruption linked to networks, even if there is no individual corruption such as bribery. Having assessed the most used corruption definitions and typologies, I've come to define corruption as: "allowing improper interests to influence decision-making at the expense of the general interest." This definition does not differentiate between active and passive influencing, public and private sector involvement, individual and collective actors or the reciprocal relationship. The core of the corruption concept is that those with a form of decision-making power which directly affects the general interest take into account interests which should not be part of their consideration. This definition lies at the core of most definitions described above; this is what makes corruption to be a concern. Contrary to most bribery definitions or TI's definition, the 'private gain' or the reciprocal element of exchange ('favour and return favour' or 'in return for') is not explicit but implicit. Each individual who allows improper interests to influence decision-making has a reason for doing so but this reason is not as concrete as most scholars tend to think.

Both scholars and law enforcement officials see corruption caused by networks and recognise this, but little is done in terms of theory development. This is why it is important to do research into corruption in the sphere of networks. A next step would be to assess the body of knowledge on networks to explore whether network theory provides reference points to networks and corruption. This will be done in Chapter 4.

4. Social Networks: From Social Capital to Corruption and the Attribution of Responsibility

4.1 Introduction

This chapter gives an overview of the available literature and research regarding networks, their features and their status. The available body of knowledge on networks and the social capital they can bring about is voluminous. I will explore whether there is network literature available on the risks networks bring about and whether the body of knowledge on networks links networks to corruption. If there are risks or pitfalls in networking to be found, the question is who should be aware of this. Therefore the second part of this chapter explores whether networks form a collective which can be subject to moral and legal judgments.

The questions that need to be answered are:

- What is a social network?
- What value do social networks have?
- Can a network be regarded as a moral actor to which responsibility can be attributed?
- What risks do social networks pose?

4.2 Social Networks

4.2.1 Definition

Brass *et al.* (1998) apply a broad definition of social network. They see a social network as "a set of actors and the set of ties representing some relationship or lack of relationship between the actors." Owens and Young (2008: 23) incorporate some features of a social network into their definition, stating that a social network is "an arrangement of people crossed at regular intervals by other people, all of whom are cultivating mutually beneficial, give-and- take, win-win relationships." A social network is composed of actors and relations. Actors can be individual natural persons or a collective. Relations can best be described as the specific kind of connection or tie between these actors. Almost by definition, social networks imply mutual obligations (Putnam, 2000: 20). They are not mere contacts. An individual's network entails everyone from family members, friends and acquaintances to business contacts. Organisations such as student associations, business clubs, political parties or chambers of commerce are formalised networks with a formal structure and a formal hierarchy of their own. The official membership of such a formal organisation is only one facet of social connectedness, which also includes the membership of informal collectives such as these social networks. A social network distinguishes itself from official organisations because it is not formally founded but instead has an informal horizontal structure in which these beneficial relationships emerge. Putnam (2000: 58) distinguishes formal 'card carrying' membership from actual (informal) involvement in community activities, whereby the latter has more effect in terms of value. This will be further discussed in paragraph 4.3.1. Networking requires individuals to stay in touch with their contacts formally or informally to know what they are up to and to stay informed about their needs (Putnam, 2000: 25). Actions of individuals and groups can be facilitated by their memberships in social networks, foremost because of their direct and indirect links to others in these networks. Social networks are not abstract concepts, they are existing concepts. However, they are not equally as real as chairs, cars or trees. They do have effects which are real and noticeable. Networks can act in a positive and in a negative way, but before I asses their conduct, their main characteristics will first be presented.

4.2.2 ***Characteristics***

Although there are many variations among networks, there are some features which are common to all social networks. According to Nielsen (2003: 125), the network nature of corruption implies the need to regard the network relationships among actors. These networks form sub-systems within the larger political economic system. Social networks are social systems, consisting of actors. Social networks have some distinguishing features.

1. The main characteristic of a social network is the absence of a formal structure and the presence of *an informal structure*. Networks are flat and horizontal, whereas formal organisations are governed by means of a certain hierarchy. Putnam (2000: 150) and Wuthnow (2002) both pointed to the fact that small groups add an important element to the way in which modern life is organised. It is a change from formal organisations in the direction of interpersonal unorganised or loosely organised connections.

2. A second characteristic is that a network does not have a formal leader or director but so-called *centres of influence* can be distinguished. This centre of influence is the actor which has been part of a network for a long time or who has a high-profile position (Owens & Young, 2008: 24). Although the actor may not be able to offer someone immediate advantages, he or she may be able to connect someone with others who can, while this connection might be useful in the future. The foundation for networking is based on the old expression "it's not what you know, but who you know." (Owens &

Young, 2008: 23). Granovetter did research into the strength of interpersonal ties and as an example showed that although person A has a close connection with B and A also is closely connected to C, even though B and C have no relationship, common ties to A will at some point bring about a certain interaction (1973: 1362). There is a likelihood that friendly feelings emerge once they met because of their expected similarity to A. A in this example can be seen as a centre of influence in such a network.

3. A third characteristic is that social networks are *dynamic, responsive and adaptive.* Formal organisations are rather static and bureaucratic. Social networks are systems which consist of nodes (individual actors, people, or things within the network) and the ties, links or connections (relationships) between them. These nodes can be tangibles such as individual persons, regulations, institutions, permits or money, and intangibles, for instance, success, pride or feelings of loyalty and fear. The interconnections are the relationships which hold these elements together. These are the flows and reactions that govern processes within the network. Such signals allow network members to respond to what is happening in other parts of the network, for example, communication, money flows or criteria for candidates to political parties or tendering procedures. Flows of information are the most important and common form of interconnections and become signals that trigger decision or action points in a system (Meadows, 2011: 14). If a consistent behavioural pattern over a long period of time can be seen, this means that the feedback loop mechanisms are working. Feedback loops can be either balancing or reinforcing. Granovetter explained the importance of interpersonal flows in social networks and how one rumour, innovation, piece of information etc. can have a large impact through the way in which (strong and weak) ties in such social systems work and adapt accordingly (1973: 1364-1366). Although Ashforth and Anand (2003) did not specifically refer to networks in their research, they did underline the importance of understanding (organised) groups to be social systems with reinforcing feedback loops, and the need to assess these forces further in the case of non-formal/hierarchical forms of organisation (2003: 41). They emphasise the point that systems and individuals are mutually reinforcing.

4. The fourth characteristic of the social network is that it has a *purpose.* The next paragraph will describe the difference between goal-directed networks and emergent networks. Purposes are deduced from behaviour as seen in human systems and not from stated goals (Meadows, 2011: 15). This implies that the purpose of a system has to be discovered by looking at the way the system works instead of noting what the official purpose is on paper. In the past, belonging to a group had one major purpose: survival. This evolutionary purpose has changed gradually and now survival is related to one's professional career and the welfare that coincides. Social networks provide informal structures of social interaction. They also create an opportunity that may facilitate access to a variety of resources (finances, information and political support) which ensures one has adequate means to exist and be successful in a competitive society. The purposes

which I distinguish in this research are: the purpose of helping one another and doing the other a favour, the purpose of influencing decision-making and the purpose of ensuring preferential treatment and exchange. These purposes help in distinguishing between the various forms of influencing and undue influencing which will be described in the table on networks and influence in Chapter 8.

The Centres of Influence play an important role in determining the purpose and can be seen as the establisher of the network. Networks form close communities which have as their main goal to serve the interests of oneself and other network members. However, there is never one single purpose or goal at stake. When several individuals cooperate, the purposes can shift. This conduct leads to an implicit agreement (a social contract) which binds members together and in a way isolates the network from the larger context of society. In paragraph 4.3.1 the purposes of social networks are further explained in terms of social capital. Equally, the existing norm within the social network is reflected in the attitudes and behaviours of the network members (Donaldson & Dunfee, 1999b: 102). Norm development will be discussed in the coming paragraphs.

5. Brass *et al.* (2004: 796) and Putnam (2000) both refer to the 'actor similarity' in networks. Similar people tend to interact with each other, or 'likes attract likes'. Similarity is thought to ease communication, increase the predictability of behaviour, and foster trust and reciprocity. This is a prerequisite for the fifth characteristic of networks, being that individuals *identify themselves with* the network to which they are a member. Turner *et al.* (1987) introduced this idea of 'self-categorisation'. When people 'self-categorise', they are motivated by social group goals rather than individual goals, make the group's characteristics their own personal characteristics, and thus incorporate social group identities into their personal identities (Davis, 2014). In social psychology, social identity theory is based on the idea that membership in social groups is an important determinant of individual behaviour (Davis, 2014). Social networks coordinate an individual's behaviour and ethical decision-making in a certain direction. Social identity theory explains how a person has a social group identity in terms of 'identifying with' the collective (Davis, 2014). As soon as a person identifies with others, their individual identity is re-framed in terms of others' identities. This implies that individuals contribute to the identity of the social group, which in turn influences their own identity. Ashforth and Anand (2003) refer to a similar process being that of socialisation. This process involves imparting to newcomers the values, beliefs, norms and conduct, that they will need to fulfil their roles and functions effectively within the group context. As individuals seek to make sense of reality, they compare their own perceptions with those of others (Brass *et al.*, 797). Ashforth and Anand use the metaphor of a 'social cocoon' or 'microcosm' where newcomers of a group are encouraged to affiliate and bond with older members, fostering desires to identify with, emulate and please them (2006: 26). As such, they not only identify with the other group members and the collective they form together, but also identify with their own role in the collective (2006: 27-28). The psychological and socio-

logical mechanism of wanting to belong to a group and being less critical towards the conduct of in-group members has had implications in other disciplines. There is a legal concept named 'wilful blindness', which refers to a situation in which a person intentionally fails to be informed about matters that would make one criminally liable (Heffernan, 2011). So there is a possibility to know something and a responsibility to be informed, but it is avoided. Wilful blindness originates from the fact that human beings have a tendency to build relationships that reaffirm their values, make them feel comfortable and blind them to alternatives. Heffernan (2011) illustrates how this form of negligence within networks has led to environmental disasters and the financial crisis. This mechanism is likely to play a role in social networks examined by this research.

6. The sixth characteristic of a network is that it is not simply the sum of its members. Current major societal successes but also concerns like corruption are embedded in social systems. If a phenomenon is caused by a collective, but cannot be reduced to individual acts and members, it can meet the criteria of an independent actor. If the type of network which is part of this research meets these criteria, it can be seen as a *separate entity* which has its own social impact. In paragraph 4.6 a distinction is made between two types of human collectivities: aggregates and conglomerates. This characteristic is linked to the use of methodological holism in this research.

4.2.3 ***Goal-Directed Networks and Emergent Networks***

Network literature varies from social networks to organisational networks. The literature on whole networks or inter-organisational networks is steadily growing, providing important insights into the way networks function and how social networks and organisational networks are embedded in the whole network. Whole networks are defined as three or more autonomous organisations collectively working together to achieve not only their individual organisational goals, but also a common network goal. These whole networks are complex systems and can either be goal-directed or emergent. Emergent networks develop organically and over time. Their relationships are maintained informally through the norms of reciprocity and trust. As defined by Provan *et al.*, whole networks refer to "a group of three or more organisations connected in ways that facilitate achievement of a common goal" (2007, 482). They point out that whole networks "are often formally established and governed, and goal-directed, rather than occurring serendipitously" and that "relationships among network members are primarily non-hierarchical and participants often have substantial operating autonomy." Goal-directed networks are maintained in a more formal way, such as by means of contracts and rules (Provan *et al.*, 2007: 503). The multilateral relations define a whole network and are essential for achieving a collective outcome. Such networks are critical for resolving many of the problems and issues that office holders are confronted with ('wicked problems'). There is less consideration in literature on how emergent networks are typically formed, strengthened and ultimately sustained. Such factors as friendship, trust, or the need to acquire legitimacy or power are the basis of successful relationships and cannot simply be discounted (Provan & Lemare, 2012: 638-639).

The goal or purpose of the network can best be characterised by looking at the conduct of the network members. Network theory and research notes that those who interact become more similar (Brass *et al.*, 2004: 797). As such, the common attitude of connected individuals is not only proof of the existence of a network; it is also evidence of the network's purpose. Goal-directed networks have been established with a goal in mind, while the emergent networks strive for a certain goal but this process is the outcome of an organically grown network. If we observe the network's conduct and distinguish its purpose, while also taking into account the degree to which such a goal-directed or emergent network is formal or informal and open or closed, we are able to distinguish whether its conduct is in fact: social capital, lobbying, trading in influence or network corruption. This will be presented by means of a table on networks and influence in chapter 8.

4.3 Social Capital

The Value of Social Networks

Networks are a type of social capital that encompasses the connections that people have with family, friends and acquaintances and which brings with it potential advantages granted by members of the network because they have power and influence. The relationships are based on the principle that people have a mutual concern for each other's welfare and well-being. Baumeister and Leary (1995) refer to "the need to belong" which is a human desire for interpersonal attachments which is a fundamental human motivation.

4.3.1 ***The Reward of Networks***

What differentiates social capital from other forms of capital is that this capital is not located in the actors but in the relations they have with others (Adler & Kwon, 2009: 94). Social capital, as defined by Putnam, "refers to networks and the norms of reciprocity and trust that arise from them" (2000: 19). Fukuyama states that "social capital is an instantiated informal norm that promotes co-operation between two or more individuals." (2001:7). The OECD defines social capital as "networks together with shared norms, values and understandings that facilitate co-operation within or among groups" (OECD, 2007: 103). The norms that constitute social capital can range from a norm of reciprocity between two friends to the larger and more complex examples such as religion, tradition or historical experience. Most scholars consider the source of social capital to be located in the structure of the network (Putnam, 2000; Adler & Kwon, 2009). With Fukuyama's definition in mind, networks arise as a result of social capital but do not constitute social capital itself. Others consider social capital creation to be the result of building a network with others through which both individual and collective actors can gain access to valuable contacts and information (Putnam, 2000; Adler & Kwon, 2009: 93; Granovetter, 1973). Social networks are not formed for economic reasons and people do not join a network for economic purposes. The reward of the social interactions is intrinsic. There is considerable consensus among scholars that the social interaction itself is the reward (Dasgupta & Serageldin, 2000: 3-5). This is not to say that people do not get economic advantages through the social networks, but this is not the initial motive for forming a network.

Brass *et al.* (2004: 799) refer to social capital often being referenced as "getting ahead to be a matter of who you know, not what you know", thereby emphasising the importance of 'social capital' as compared to 'human capital' in the form of education and intelligence. Social capital is the contextual complement to human capital. Burt (2000) refers to the social capital metaphor when concluding that the people who do better are somehow better connected. Certain people or certain groups are connected to certain others, trusting certain others, obligated to support certain others, dependent on exchange with certain others. According to Burt, holding a certain position in the structure of these exchanges can be an asset in its own right (2000: 347).

4.3.2 *Networks' Influence at the Macro Level*

The social network is seen as an important social organisation or structure in our society. Scholars such as Granovetter (1973) have pointed to the failure to recognise the importance of these networks of personal relations in the economic system, while Fukuyama (2001) states that civil society serves to balance the power of the state and to protect individuals from the state's power. If such social capital is absent, the states are likely to step in to organise individuals who are incapable of organising themselves. In this way, excessive individualism does not result in freedom, but rather in centralised tyranny and local government failure which can be the seed for corruption (2001: 11-12). In 1973 Granovetter noticed that many studies fall short in providing insight into how small group interactions influence large-scale or macro patterns (Granovetter, 1973: 1360). This social structure does more than fulfil an economic function; this 'embeddedness' generates trust, creates expectations and enforces norms (Dasgupta & Serageldin, 2000: 15). Warren connects social capital to today's democracies by stressing that democracies work when their people have capacities to associate for collective purposes (2004, 332). Human beings' ability to organise themselves in networks is essential to ensure interest representation in a well-balanced society, economy and political environment. With

Granovetter's observation in mind, the question remains what other macro patterns and phenomena social networking can bring about. But before getting into that aspect of social networking, a categorisation needs to be made of the various social networks which exist.

To assess the link between networks and forms of influence, the three most important network purposes are distinguished. Based on the findings in this paragraph, networks make up social capital for three major purposes:

1. *the purpose of helping one another;*
2. *the purpose of influencing decision-making;*
3. *the purpose of treating one another in a preferential way.*

These purposes will be taken into consideration when combining them with various types of networks, to assess how certain networks and specific purposes result in due and undue forms of influencing. This will be discussed in Chapter 8.

4.3.3 ***Network Variations and Social Capital***

If a network is considered to be a form of social capital or social capital to result in networks, the question is what varieties of such networks can be distinguished. Putnam (2000: 23) makes a distinction between bonding (close-knit homogenous groups (similar in a socio-demographic sense), inward looking, high degree of personal contact and reinforcing exclusive identities) and bridging (loosely knit dissimilar group, outward looking and developing broader identities). The bonding networks cultivate trust, cooperation and collective strength among individuals often with a shared history, experience and common purpose. The bridging networks allow different groups or networks to share and exchange information, ideas and innovation and build consensus among the groups representing diverse interests. A third type of social capital is that of linking social capital. This form of social capital has similarities with bridging but these relationships are with people across different hierarchical levels and power. According to Szreter and Woolcock (2004) networks of trusting relationships between people who are interacting across explicit, formal or institutionalised power or authority in society can be labelled as 'linking social capital'. Granovetter has distinguished one particular aspect of connections, namely their strength (1973). According to Granovetter, the strength of an interpersonal tie is a combination of amount of time, emotional intensity, intimacy (mutual confiding) and the reciprocal services which are exchanged (1973; 1361). Within networks, ties between network members can be strong, weak or absent. Granovetter has argued why some sets of ties or communities are able to organise themselves easily and effectively for common goals. He did not elaborate in this regard on the nature of these common goals and whether they are morally acceptable or not. Granovetter particularly looked at small-scale level linkages with one another and with larger non-organised networks (1973: 1376). These extended weak ties are seen as indispensable to increase an individual's opportunities and their integration into communities (1973: 1378). Small networks which only consist of strong ties can have internal cohesion but lead to overall fragmentation. Brass *et al.* (2014: 799-800) argue that the friendship link to individuals in senior prominent positions in an organisation boost the individual's performance reputation and promotion.

Burt (2000: 353) assessed the network structure of social capital. He referred to the weaker connections between groups as 'holes in the social structure'. Such structural holes create a competitive advantage for an individual whose relationships bridge these holes. The structural hole between two groups means that the people are focused on their own activities such that they do not attend to the activities of people in the other group. People on either side of a structural hole circulate in different flows of information. Structural holes are thus an opportunity to broker the flow of information between people, and control the projects that bring together people from opposite sides of the hole. Individuals functioning as brokers of a bridge reach more individuals indirectly, which gives them an advantage. The brokers' more diverse contacts mean that they are more likely to be candidates to involve in new opportunities. Having a network that yields such benefits makes them more attractive to other people as a contact in their own networks. Additionally, there is a control advantage by being in a position to bring together otherwise disconnected contacts, which gives these individuals disproportionate say in whose interests are served when the contacts come together. Stam (2010) examines how participation in industry events relates to entrepreneurs' brokerage positions in informal industry networks and how these positions, in turn, impact new venture performance. Stam shows that the network positions of entrepreneurs are also structured by the characteristics of the social contexts in which they build network relations. Irrespective of entrepreneurs' individual preferences for close, more homogenous relationships, industry events appear to constrain individual dispositions by limiting the pool of contacts whom entrepreneurs can meet and form ties with. Event bridging and prior experience on brokerage coincides with an observed positive interactive effect, which suggests that entrepreneurs who take advantage of brokerage opportunities at industry events increase their access to structural holes (Stam, 2010). Thus, individuals with contact networks rich in structural holes are the individuals who know about, have a hand in, and exercise control over, more rewarding opportunities. The behaviours by which they develop the opportunities are many and varied, but the opportunity itself is at all times defined by a hole in the social structure (Burt, 2000: 355). Similar to Granovetter, Burt emphasises the success that networks can have if they bridge or broker by means of weaker ties, compared to the advantages that go to individuals in a homogenous cohesive group which is rather closed. Most advantages go to people who build bridges across cohesive groups.

Strategy guided by brokerage involves locating a position at structural holes. The centre of influence fulfils such a position.

Although both Putnam and Wuthnow have focussed mostly on social capital in the United States, their findings are believed to be exemplary for western societies. Wuthnow (2002) criticises those scholars who believe that self-interestedness has led to a decline in civic involvement, resulting in a decline in social capital since World War II. Wuthnow pointed to the new ways people connect and the fact that if there is a decline in social capital, this mainly concerns the traditional forms of civic participation (for example trade unions) by the socially and economically marginalised. The OECD supports the view that social capital is not eroding but transforming. Individuals might not organise themselves in local networks as much as they used to do, they join groups which made up of people with similar views on societal issues (OECD, 2007: 104-105). In this way there is a variety of active social networks in real life and in the virtual world. Another example of this transformation can be seen in the social capital of the privileged and economically advanced, which has not eroded. On the contrary, they have found new ways of connecting in networks, based on what Wuthnow describes as 'cultural capital', whereby he refers to leadership skills, familiarity with rules within organisations and the confidence and skills to make small talk or to speak before larger groups (Wuthnow, 2002: 80). Such networks have great power and influence. According to scholars such as Wuthnow, there is also a downside to this form of social capital. This will be explained in paragraph 4.8.

4.4 COMMUNITARIANISM AND NETWORKS

The previous paragraphs describe the characteristics of networks and the links between networks and social capital from the perspective of sociology and organisational studies. Philosophical thinking offers complementary perspectives in understanding the valuable social capital of networks and the norms which develop consciously or over time.

4.4.1 ***Network Communities***

To be able to understand the norm development within these informal social networks, social networks have to be seen as communities. Communitarianism considers a person's social identity and personality to be largely moulded by community relationships, with a smaller degree of development being placed on individualism. Communities are understood, in the wider, philosophical sense, as a collection of interactions among a community of people in a given place, or among a community who share an interest or who share a history (Avineri & De-Shalit, 1992). Communitarian thinkers criticise the liberal notions of philosophers such as Rawls, who abstracts just and unjust from particular social contexts and presents justice as something universalistic (Bell, 2016). Contrary to classic liberalism, which will be described in the paragraph on the contractarian approach (paragraph 4.5), Etzioni (2015) points out that communities can be defined as: first, a web of affect-laden relationships among a group of individuals, relationships that often criss-cross and reinforce one another (as opposed to one-on-one or chain-like individual relationships) and second, a measure of commitment to a set of shared values, norms, and meanings, and a shared history and identity (a particular culture). Communitarian thinkers argue that contemporary liberalism fails to account for the complex set of social relations that all individuals in the modern world are a part of. Social networks have become communities that are dictated by communitarian thinking in which the community restores solidarity and goodwill in society, resulting in a strong moral awareness (Sandel, 2009). Loyalty, tradition and long-held relationships help bind these networks together. Communitarian philosophers stress the importance of human interdependence and the strength of a collective and criticise the liberal ideas of human independence.

They consider social organisations to be a vital countervailing power and answer to formal and hierarchal state institutions. Communitarianism points to the social, political and economic damage caused by the more liberal institutions and practices, having contributed to, or at least not able to deal with, modern phenomena such as alienation from the political process, unbridled greed, loneliness and urban crime (Bell, 2016). On the one hand, this line of thinking considers liberalism to be fuelling the self-interest and self-serving attitude of individuals, bringing out the worst in individuals. As such, it is only a small step for communitarian philosophers to link corruption to liberalism. Etzioni argued that when political systems are corrupt to the core, only extensive involvement in public affairs by citizens can remedy the situation (Bell, 2016). From a communitarian perspective, society foremost needs more citizens who are willing to scrutinize political decision-making: "Once citizens are informed, they must make it their civic duty to organise others locally, regionally, and nationally to act on their understanding of what it takes to clean up public life in America." (Etzioni, 1993: 244). On the other hand, it can also be argued that the communitarian perspective on communities also makes communities sensitive to corruption.

4.4.2 ***Compliance in Networks***

Bell (2016) distinguishes three types of communities: (1) communities based on geographical location, (2) communities of memory and groups of strangers who share a morally significant history and (3) psychological communities and communities of face-to-face personal interaction governed by sentiments of trust, co-operation, and altruism. Despite the differences between those communities, they all can bring about positive things, in the sense that constituent members have the good of the community in mind and act on behalf of the community's collective interest.

In a way, the communitarian approach of seeing communities as restoring a fair democracy because of their civic involvement can also be detrimental if the ties of friendship and acquaintance grow to encompass business and politics as well. These social networks form close communities in which the norms of loyalty and reciprocity 'steer' these networks; these norms are rooted in these communities with their own logic. Pearson (1995: 47) argued that communities are necessarily, and by definition, coercive as well as moral, threatening their members with the stick of sanctions if they stray, offering them the carrot of certainty and stability if they don't. Putnam (2000: 23) described such networks as 'bonding' (paragraph 4.3). Bonding in social capital is referred to as social networks between homogenous individuals or groups. This can be a valuable form of organisation for oppressed or disadvantaged members of a society to be heard by decision-makers and to support their collective needs. These networks can form strong collectives built upon common interests, shared social norms and the will to help or favour network members, particularly when the outside world (state, society, political parties and other institutions) does not provide the protection or care needed. This coincides with the risk of communities becoming closed, inward-looking and self-serving. From a theoretical perspective, communities can be the watchdogs and countervailing power in a system of formal, non-democratic decision-making, but as the examples of the case studies in Chapter 6 will illustrate, such communities with either a geographic location, shared history or personal networks based on trust, solidarity and cooperation, can deteriorate.

4.5 CONTRACTARIAN THEORY AND NETWORKS

Communitarian perspectives foremost underline the corruption (risks) which liberalism has created and argue that communal life can help to bring back a fair social order in society. Alter and Hage (1993) argue that the organisation of relationships is primarily based on the social contracts maintained. Some contract thinkers, such as Donaldson and Dunfee, respond to communitarianism by arguing that in fact it is a contract agreed upon by communities on the basis of which their behaviour is determined. When assessing the presence of norms in networks, the question about their validity comes into play. Communitarianism and Contractarian theory assess the norms for networks in different ways.

4.5.1 Norms in Microsocial Contracts

Contract thinkers Donaldson and Dunfee have proposed a neutral definition of community: "a community is a self-defined, self-circumscribed group of people who interact in the context of shared tasks, values or goals and who are capable of establishing norms of ethical behaviour for themselves." (1999b, 39). Such communities may be formally constituted, or they may evolve out of informal interactions. Membership in a community can be based on a contractual commitment or may involve participating in a group and being acknowledged by others as a member (Donaldson & Dunfee, 1999: 41).

Following the reasoning that social networks form communities whose conduct can be assessed, the question which follows is what norms we can apply to assess their conduct. Individuals are free to associate and form or join communities and to act jointly to establish moral rules applicable to the members of the community, a freedom that macro contractors would endorse, described as "moral free space" (Donaldson and Dunfee (1999a: 38-39). Donaldson and Dunfee (1999a: 38-39; 1999b: 139-173) argue that there is a moral-free space in which communities can develop their own community norms. The moral rules freely adopted by a community reflect its particular goals, environments, resources and experiences (1999a: 38). Contrary to communitarian thinking, such microsocial contracts should not only be regarded as an agreement developed over time by a community; rather they should be structured along the lines of the social-contract model. The term 'microsocial contract' represents an agreement or shared understanding about the moral norms defined by communities. Donaldson and Dunfee offer a few conditions under which they consider microsocial contracts to be valid, thereby building on the overarching supremacy of the macrosocial contract. That is, within the norms of the macrosocial contract, there is freedom for a community to develop its own norms. The macrosocial agreement simply sets limits on that freedom. Donaldson and Dunfee offered a few conditions that determine the legitimacy of the microsocial contract. As such, their Integrative Social Contract Theory (ISCT) does not specify requirements for the development of moral norms in a microsocial contract other than the norms having to be authentic, based on informed consent and the individual's right to exit (Donaldson & Dunfee, 1994: 262-263). They distinguish the norm emergence into change as a result of formal processes of debate and decision-making and norms formed in a distinctly informal way evolving out of interactions among members of a community (1999a: 38-39).

A network grows over time and its norms slowly develop in the direction of increasing the well-being of its members. Society is confident about the usefulness of a network (creating social capital). However, at the same time, a network needs to fit into this wider society and apply the applicable hypernorms to itself. This calls for the prevention of closed networks across societal institutions which in fact become the decisive actor in the decision-making process. Donaldson and Dunfee (1994, 1999a, 1999b), as Social Contract thinkers, have tried to resolve this conundrum by applying the contract approach to ethics. As introduced above, in their ISCT they distinguish two distinct kinds of contracts. First, there is the macrosocial contract, which has a normative nature (what 'ought to be'). This is a hypothetical societal contract in line with Rawls' contract thinking, and defines the normative ground rules (hypernorms) for the microsocial-level contract (Fort, 2000: 384). Second, there is a microsocial contract which is more concrete and occurs among members of a specific community and reflects the values of that community that have developed over time, thereby governing the community's behaviour (the what 'is'). For instance, firms, industries, chains, universities, municipalities and social networks can all be regarded as communities with their own microsocial contracts (Donaldson & Dunfee, 1994; Wempe, 2010, 2009). Such norms are 'simply there' and not the result of conscious agreements. These microsocial contracts have a largely communitarian character.

4.5.2 *Overriding Societal Hypernorms*

According to Donaldson and Dunfee, there are three distinct categories of hypernorms. First, there are the procedural hypernorms (1999a: 51) that specify the right of exit and the right of voice which are the prerequisites for microsocial contractual consent. Secondly, there are the structural hypernorms, such as the right to property and the right to fair treatment under the law (hypernorms that oblige one to respect justice and economic welfare) (Donaldson & Dunfee, 1999a: 52). Thirdly, there are the substantive hypernorms, which come down to the fundamental conceptions of the right and good (Donaldson & Dunfee, 1999a: 52). The first two categories are implicit or specified in the macrosocial contract, but the substantive hypernorms are to be found outside in the real world. Donaldson and Dunfee have developed a list of types of evidence which confirm widespread recognition of an ethical principle in economic activity, thereby constituting a hypernorm (1999a: 60). By analogy, these criteria can be used in the broader societal domain. This evidence in support of a principle being a hypernorm includes (1999a: 60-61):[1]

- A widespread consensus that it is a universal principle
- The principle being a component of well-known global industry standards
- Supported by prominent nongovernmental organisation such as TI
- Supported by regional governmental organisations such as the EU or the OECD
- Consistent reference as a global ethical standard by the international media
- Reflected in precepts of the major religions
- Supported by global business organisations such as the International Chamber of Commerce
- Reflected in precepts of major philosophies
- Supported by relevant international community of professionals, for instance accountants
- Supported by the laws of many different countries

1 The examples in the principles have been adapted by the author to reflect the up-to-date situation and their relevancy to the corruption topic.

If two or more of these types of evidence apply, the principle is presumed to be a hypernorm. An exception to this reasoning applies when, for instance, in a decision context the hypernorm application would result in the violation of a widely recognised human right. Donaldson (1989) presents a list of hypernorms, among which the following are at stake when social networks become corrupt: the right to ownership of property, the right to fair trial, the right to non-discriminatory treatment and the right to political participation.

4.5.3 *Microsocial Contract and Norm Development Being a Social Process*

The problem for policymakers and public prosecutors is that while the social network plays the major role in this form of corruption, and needs to be made visible, the legislation at their disposal only recognises individual corrupt behaviour. The case studies in this research describe how the norms of the microsocial contract conflict with the abstract hypernorms or societal norms of the macrosocial contract and result in abuse of power. The social contract approach is contextual (Donaldson & Dunfee, 1999b: 93). Its assumption is that many norms derive out of very specific contexts, in which the majority acknowledges the norms to be right and as such followed by the majority in future cases (Donaldson & Dunfee, 1999b: 93). Hypernorms represent norms by which all others are to be judged (Donaldson & Dunfee, 1999b: 44). Donaldson and Dunfee thereby regard microsocial contract norms which are incompatible with hypernorms, to be illegitimate. Their reasoning concerns cases in which legitimate microsocial contracts in various communities conflict with one another. Their way of thinking concerns which communal norm has priority.

4.6 The Moral Status of a Network

4.6.1 *Moral Responsibility Attribution in Complex Cases*

Moral responsibility is generally associated with individuals: individuals can bring about good or bad, and can be held responsible for the effects of their actions. However, without knowing and willing action by an individual, there is no moral responsibility: only where a person causes an unacceptable situation as a result of their knowing and willing action (*mens rea* and *actus reus*), can they be held morally responsible for the result. This moral responsibility is the reason why such a person is perceived as guilty and blamed for his action ('the evildoer'). In the 1980s and 1990s the debate was on the responsibility of collectives, more particularly that of corporations. This debate dealt with the question as to whether it was possible to assign moral responsibility to a collective in such a way that this responsibility was distinct from the responsibility of the individual members of the collective. Donaldson (1982), French (1984), Werhane (1985) and May (1987) debate this issue and argue that corporations should be seen as collective agents with their own moral responsibility. This meant that from then on corporations were considered to be moral agents, distinct from the individuals of whom they are composed. This responsibility was gradually accepted by businesses themselves in the late 1990s and by now the term Corporate Social Responsibility (CSR) is generally accepted.[2]

While the acknowledgement of moral responsibility of firms is now generally accepted, society faces many complex issues in which the question of where to locate responsibility appears problematic. For example, the prevailing notions of responsibility no longer work regarding issues such as the financial crisis (the responsibility of the financial sector), obesity (responsibility across sectors), the refugee crisis (responsibility across countries) and the corruption cases which will be presented in the three case studies in Chapter 6 (responsibility within social networks) (Wempe & Slingerland, 2016). In these examples, it is not possible to talk about the responsibility of specific or concrete individuals, and attempting to assign responsibilities to organised collectives, such as companies or countries, also fails. Still, it is important to localise responsibility, not only to talk in terms of liability, but more importantly to try to prevent future tragedies and crises and to address them as soon as they are about to occur. What theories exist on collective conduct and can a network be understood as a collective actor?

4.6.2 *Philosophical Theories on Collective Responsibility*

Social networks form social capital and this social capital is more than the sum of its parts. This in itself is not an issue as long as the networks operate according to the hypernorms or societal norms. This changes once the network operates in such a way that the collective results in corruption. Now the question of who is responsible for the corruption becomes a pressing one. Can the responsibility be attributed to the collective? This paragraph deals with the philosophical theories on collective responsibility.

4.6.2.1 The Controversies Surrounding Collective Responsibility

The notion of collective responsibility, referred to by some philosophers as 'group morality', associates causal responsibility and blameworthiness with groups and locates the source of moral responsibility in the collective actions taken by these groups understood as collectives (Smiley, 2017). The concept of collective responsibility is applied in various contexts. It reflects a variety of collectives, their potential to act and the responsibility that

2 The concept and definition of CSR has evolved over time. Carroll (1991: 289) states that for CSR to be accepted by the conscientious business person it should be framed in such a way that it encompasses four social responsibilities: economic, legal, ethical and philanthropic. This four-part definition of CSR should always be fulfilled at the same time. Caroll's concept of CSR has been influential in understanding and making concrete the type and nature of the obligations corporations have.

one may attribute to that collective. Among philosophers there are those who embrace the concept of collective responsibility, those who acknowledge the existence of collective responsibility in a limited number of cases and those who deny the notion of collective responsibility. Critics of collective responsibility such as Weber (1914) and Lewis (1948a: 17-33; 1948b: 3-18) deny the existence of group intentions and collective actions. According to them, groups do not have a mind of their own, nor can they make their own choices, thereby failing the requirement of intention (knowing and willing), necessary to attribute responsibility for the unacceptable outcome. Those philosophers who accept some form of collective responsibility are foremost concerned about the fairness of attributing collective responsibility to individuals who themselves did not directly cause harm or who did not bring about harm on purpose. Corlett (2001) therefore distinguishes the collective behaviour from collective action. The former is the action or behaviour that is the result of a collective, though not the result of its intentions. The latter is caused by the beliefs and desires (intentions) of the collective itself, independent of whether the beliefs and desires can be explained in individualistic terms (Corlett, 2001: 575). May (1987) argues that actions can be legitimately ascribed to groups in those cases where individuals are related to one another and act together in such ways that would not be possible if they acted alone. May (1987) and French (1984) both assert that only particular kinds of groups are capable of acting and intending collectively and that only particular kinds of groups are capable of being collectively responsible for harm. What kinds of groups are these?

The most common approach taken to distinguish situations in which collective responsibility is eligible, and when it is not, is to look at the level of organisation of the group or collective. Criteria which are used are, first of all, whether a moral agent can be identified (a board or representative body). Secondly, whether the decisions are made by the group consciously (with a purpose) and on a rational basis, thereby proving the existence of group intentions. French (1984: 13-14) argues that if a collective meets three important features (the availability of organisational mechanisms through which rational concerted action can be taken, enforced standards of conduct for individuals and the clearly defined roles by which individuals can exercise certain powers) the collective responsibility is appropriate. Attributing collective responsibility to such well-organised groups or collectives is widely accepted and such responsibility is assigned to states and corporations (Wempe, 2010; Wempe & Slingerland, 2016).

4.6.2.2 Aggregates and Conglomerates

Coincidental and Statistical Aggregates

Some (business) ethics distinguish collectives which form an aggregate, which is an unstructured collection of individuals, from collectives which are a conglomerate, which is a structured collection of individuals (French, 1984; Kaptein & Wempe, 2002). A key characteristic of aggregates is that there is no structure or any form of cohesion. Aggregates can be divided into coincidental aggregates and statistical aggregates (Kaptein & Wempe, 2002). A *coincidental* aggregate refers to a largely coincidental group of people, such as the individuals who live in the same neighbourhood or individuals who go to the same concert. In the latter example, the people share an interest in the same band or artist. Another example of such an aggregate is a spontaneous demonstration following a speech by a politician. We refer to these collectives as aggregate when there is no prior consultation between the individuals or any form of decision-making procedure. A *statistical* aggregate can be seen as a collective on the basis of a specific characteristic. One may think of characteristics such as gender, age, being unemployed or having a certain profession. If individuals form an aggregate, then there is no question of collective moral responsibility since we are not inclined to hold an aggregate, as a collective of individuals, responsible for its 'acting' or for 'failing to act', because there is no conscious act desired by the aggregate. An aggregate can be comprehensively described by putting the characteristics of the separate individuals together. The moral responsibility of an aggregate can therefore only be described in a distributive sense: each member is responsible according to his/her share. The moral responsibility of an aggregate is nothing more than the sum of the individual responsibilities. The fact that an aggregate cannot be held responsible for the collective effect of all the individual actions does not imply that it is not possible to hold separate actors accountable for their actions or inaction. The point is that the collective as such, and also the members for their membership of the aggregate only, cannot be held responsible for the effects that the aggregate brings about.

Conglomerates (Joint Actions and Actions of Organised Collectives)

A key characteristic of conglomerates is that there is a level of organisation. The joining or leaving of individuals has no consequences for the identity of the conglomerate (French, 1984, 13). A conglomerate is more than the sum of the individuals. What can be attributed to the conglomerate cannot necessarily be ascribed to its members. The moral responsibility of a conglomerate cannot be distributed among its members because the characteristics of a conglomerate cannot be reduced to the sum of individual characteristics. If all the members of a conglomerate left and were replaced by new members, the responsibility of the conglomerate would remain unaltered. Again, it is possible to divide conglomerates into two categories: joint actions and actions of an organised collective. Examples of *joint actions* are students who work on a group assignment, or several individuals involved in an armed robbery. In the latter example, the shared purpose is the robbery. The fact that this group of individuals brought weapons is evidence that they made this decision together beforehand. A joint action is a form of cooperation where individual actions are directed towards a common goal. In a joint action, the contributions of everyone involved are required to achieve the goal (Wempe & Slingerland, 2016). This form of cooperation is often incidental in nature and relies on some form of communication. There is an element of freedom: those involved could have decided not to take part. Additionally, there is an element of control: each individual can determine what he or she does; and an element of intervention: each individual can intervene while joint actions take place. Often, there is no intention or expectation that the cooperation will continue in the future.

Examples of *actions of an organised collective* are a strike called by a union or the dumping of waste by a corporation. A collective has the ability to act if several members of the collective make decisions for the whole and are able to carry them out. This collective differs from the joint actions in the sense that there is no dependency on contributions of each individual. Conglomerates can be judged in moral terms. The line of thinking of French (1984) is that a crucial element in speaking of an organised collective is that there is intentional action by that collective. That is, the intentions and actions of the collective can be distinguished from the intentions and actions of the individuals of which it is composed. The questions here are whether the collective is able to act and, if so, whether this acting is intentional.

Collectives' Acting Through Secondary Action

A collective can act through its members through 'secondary action' (Copp, 1979: 177-186). An agent's action is secondary if it is correctly attributable to this agent on the basis of either an action by some other agent, or actions by some other agents. Secondary action can apply to a natural person, who is represented by another person, but it can also apply to a collective that is represented by others. In the latter case, it is the collective that is acting secondarily. If, for example, the director of a corporation enters into a contract (in his capacity as director) on behalf of the corporation, the corporation is bound to it. Although the director is the one who actually signs the contract, the ensuing rights and obligations are incumbent upon the corporation. The natural person thus carries out the physical act of signing but the collective acts in a secondary, indirect sense. Natural persons can act in both primary and secondary senses, a corporation only in the latter. French (1984) argued that it is possible to attribute intentional acting to an organised collective such as a company. Consequently, it is possible to hold the company accountable for any damage it causes.

Most authors on collective responsibility perceive a conglomerate as a moral agent in its own right and an appropriate site for collective responsibility. Their argument to justify collective responsibility is the presence of a formal or hierarchical organisational structure. The organisation has a mission or goal. The organisation's structure directs the actions of the members of the conglomerate in such a way that the organisational goal is achieved. That justifies seeing the actions of the individual members as the actions of the conglomerate itself. The collective corruption which Ashforth and Anand (2003) identify is an example of an organisation being such a conglomerate to which collective responsibility can be attributed but which will be brought back to individual responsibilities. Ashforth and Anand consider corruption to be individual corrupt acts, which can be explained by three reinforcing and reciprocally interdependent processes (institutionalisation, rationalisation and socialisation), embedded in collective structures. These processes normalise and perpetuate corrupt practices so that the system beats the individual (2003: 37). This was discussed in paragraph 3.3.4.

However, this argument does not seem to hold for collectives such as the social networks presented in this and the following chapter(s), because they are less organised in the sense that it is not possible to perceive the actions of an individual network member as an act on behalf of the collective because these actions cannot be rephrased as a secondary action on behalf of the collective of the network. Among the scholars in favour of collective responsibility, there are those who argue that there is such collective responsibility but that ultimately it needs to be translated into individual responsibilities. Here collective responsibility is distributable or reducible to individual responsibilities and there are those who see ascription of responsibility to a collective as indivisible (Cooper, 1968: 39). The attribution of collective responsibility varies depending on whether the corruption subject in this research is in fact corruption in a network or corruption by a network. The latter will be dealt with in the paragraph 4.9 below.

4.7 Social Networks and Collective Responsibility

Social Networks Being Social Systems

Paragraph 4.2.2 described the characteristics of social networks. Social networks are systems consisting of elements, interconnections and a purpose. They are dynamic, responsive and adaptive due to the functioning of balancing and reinforcing feedback loops. Even when members leave, or political and economic circumstances change, the social network will soon bounce back and organise itself in an effective way. When a social network wants to achieve a desired goal, these reinforcing and balancing loops trigger actions which help to achieve this goal. For instance, if the social network aims at expanding its business activities, all individual persons will be acting to achieve this goal, for instance, sharing information on regional or sectoral opportunities or by connecting to individuals who have influence in the desired region or sector. Reinforcing feedback loops occur when a change in the social network ultimately comes back to cause a further change in the social network. If for instance a social network which is built on membership in a political party is confronted with the resignation of one of its politicians, others, out of solidarity, can decide to lay down their position as well. In this way, a reinforcing feedback mechanism is triggered. At the same time this can trigger a balancing mechanism, whereby the initial resignation stimulates other individuals to become active for this political party, because they perceive the resignation as proof that the political party is solid and professional etc. This response and adaptation is evidence that the network functions as a system, which indicates the presence of an independent moral actor. This raises the question whether this network fulfils the criteria of a conglomerate.

At first sight, none of the concepts in the previous paragraph appear helpful when it comes to analysing the responsibility of a network-like collective. Although there is an evolution noticeable in how we perceive responsibility, difficulties remain in applying current ethical concepts in relation to complex issues, because the model of individual responsibility is used as the model for all forms of collective responsibility. As such, we need to have an actor that is intentionally (knowingly and willingly) acting, damage which is felt by a third party and a link between the act and the damage. It is because of this relationship between the act and the negative outcome that we feel able to hold the individual or the organised collective responsible. However, it is difficult to apply this concept when attempting to attribute responsibility to social networks. Is there something like an autonomous (network) organisation?

Loosely Organised Collectives and Responsibility

Wempe (2010) concludes that with French's reasoning, only well-organised collectives, such as firms, can be identified as a site for responsibility. Apparently aggregates are only responsible insofar as an issue is reducible to the responsibility of the individual members. Wempe questions whether this is justifiable and therefore explores whether it is possible to hold what he refers to as 'loosely organised collectives' responsible, and if so, whether it is only possible to translate this into responsibilities of the individual members, or whether it is possible to hold the collective responsible as an entity in its own right (Wempe, 2010). Wempe (2010) applies the criteria formulated by McGary (1986) and May (1987) in order to determine whether a loosely organised collective of individuals can be perceived as a conglomerate. If members of a collection of individuals *share a particular interest or background*, this can be an argument to qualify these individuals as conglomerate. This can be seen in individuals expressing a strong interest in each other's interests. According to May (1987) and McGary (1986), the fact that these individuals share a common interest or participate in certain practices, or tolerate them, is a strong argument for perceiving a collection of individuals as a group. Here it is no longer a matter of a random collection of individuals, but a conglomerate with its own responsibility. Theory and research have noted that; just as similar actors are prone to interact, those who interact become more similar (Brass *et al.*, 2004: 797). The second argument which justifies perceiving people as belonging to a conglomerate is the presence of a *shared attitude*. In network theories this is referred to as 'attitude similarity'. Wempe (2010) disagrees with May (1987) and McGary (1986) on one point, as he does consider *self-consciousness* to be an essential criterion of the group for it to be a conglomerate.

Wempe (2016) uses the example of children who need to look after their father who has just been released from hospital to argue for this criterion of self-consciousness. He hereby distinguishes the individual obligation to provide care and the responsibility of the children and other carers as a collective to become organised in such a way that the father is well looked after (Wempe, 2010). He distinguishes three other features of this loosely organised collective. The first is that there is a *result* that can only be realised through this collective's cooperation. Secondly, there is an *awareness* that the loosely organised collective has to be turned into an appropriate organisation to reach this result. Thirdly, individuals take on *different role responsibilities* in getting the collective organised. Wempe argues that the feature of self-consciousness foremost has to be understood as active responsibility, which implies that the cooperation has to be organised in such way that abuse is prevented. This is an important remark, since loosely organised collectives can be successful in meeting their purpose, but it is problematic if the end result is a form of abuse.

In this respect, Hirschman's *Exit, Voice, and Loyalty* (1970) can be used to assess whether there is not only an awareness that a social network has to be turned into an appropriate organisation, but also whether network members can, in real and practical terms, exit (withdraw from the network) or voice (attempt to repair or improve the network through communication of the complaint or proposal for change). Where there is loyalty to the networks as a loosely organised collective exit may be reduced, especially where options to exit are not so appealing. If network members should reasonably be aware of their collective output and have the option to exit, voice and/or express loyalty, this is another argument to underline collective responsibility of social networks. This self-consciousness requires self-reflection to one's role in the larger context of a network.

4.8 The Risks of a Social Network

4.8.1 ***Tension Between Structure and Agency***

Most empirical studies on networks focus on networks with legal activities or illegal activities Baker and Faulkner (1993). The body of knowledge on networks with legal activities which deteriorate is rather scarce, even though networks and the associated norm of reciprocity are by no means always positive. Social capital is one of the concepts associated with corruption. Brass *et al.* (1998) argue that neither the individual bad apples perspective nor the organisational bad barrels perspective fully explains unethical behaviour in organisations. They argue that unethical behaviour is foremost a social phenomenon, which needs to be understood by looking at its embeddedness in the structure of social relationships. Brass *et al.* (2004: 800) stress the importance of applying a multilevel perspective on unethical behaviour, whereby the interpersonal networks within the larger contexts of organisations need to be included. They argue that interpersonal networks have an important effect on a variety of individual outcomes such as getting a job and gaining influence, but more work is needed on network antecedents to understand interaction patterns within organisations. This line of thinking considers organisations to have internal networks, which are to be understood from the inter-organisational networks they organisation is embedded in. This layer is the structure to which the organisations as an agency are part.

Emirbayer and Goodwin (1994) criticise the dominant thinking in network theory that understanding and acknowledging the structure is important to understand the behaviour in networks. This signifies tension between structure and agency or, alternatively, whether behaviour can be explained by reference to the context of the network or by reference to the rational behaviour of the individual because of his free will. They use an alternative approach in their attempt to explain social change over time, including the transformation of social networks themselves. They suggest that most conceptualisations of social structure are strong, yet analyses of networks have inadequately thought out the role that ideals, beliefs and values play and how the actors strive to realise them; as a result, it has neglected culture, actor and its social action (Emirbayer & Goodwin, 1994: 1446-1447). The network and its transformations, they argue, are under the influence of structural, cultural and discursive factors. The next paragraph will deal with the link between unethical behaviour and networks.

4.8.2 ***Specific Versus Generalised Reciprocity***

The reward of being a network member is that the network or its members return something of value. Granovetter, Putnam, Fukuyama and Wuthnow and other scholars refer to the network's dominant norm being that of reciprocity. Sometimes the reciprocity is specific, with an individual doing something and a particular person doing something in return (Putnam, 2000: 20). Putnam (2000: 20-21) describes how the generalised form of reciprocity in a network is even more valuable: "I'll do this for you without expecting anything specific back from you, in the confident expectation that someone else will do something for me down the road." This form of generalised reciprocity is of value in our society because not every single exchange needs to be balanced. This external focus is complemented by investments in the internal relations, thereby strengthening the social network's collective identity and its effective governance (Adler & Kwon, 2009: 93). This norm is derived from the network's purpose and is an intangible element which steers behaviour of the individual in the direction of the network's purpose. However, the advantages that social networks bring about are one side of the coin.

Warren (2004: 339-340) considers exclusive or specific reciprocity (the demand that any favour be reciprocated) to tend towards exclusive ways of associating. In this way, particularised (bonding) reciprocity is seen as being bad for democracy, because it builds on and reinforces group separations. Fukuyama also points to the 'negative externalities' if groups achieve internal cohesion at the expense of outsiders: the larger society in which they are embedded (2001: 8). According to Warren, generalised (bridging) reciprocity meets the democratic notion of inclusion because it enhances all to be included. The question is whether the generalised form of reciprocity linked to the bridging or broker networks is a guarantee that opportunities will be available to all. Szreter and Woolcock (2004) argue that all forms of social capital (bonding, bridging and linking) can be put to unhappy purposes such as suppression or corruption.

4.8.3 ***Inclusive and Exclusive Networks***

The Downside of Social Capital

Not all forms of social capital have a positive impact. Fukuyama (2001: 8) cautions that internal cohesion in networks is achieved at the expense of outsiders. In-group solidarity reduces the ability of group members to work together or cooperate with outsiders, thereby often imposing negative externalities on the latter. Fukuyama refers to the corruption this might cause, in particular when one becomes a public official (2001: 9). In such a case, in-group bonding can cause the cultivation of nepotism (in the interests of family or a group), thus depriving members outside the group from equal opportunity in accessing goods and services. The OECD also points to the risk of relationships which are too inward-looking and fail to take account of what's going on in the wider world (OECD, 2007: 104). In their article on the normalisation of corruption in organisations, Ashforth and Anand (2003) describe corrupt groups to be more homogeneous than a typical group (2003: 33). A corrupt group needs to pay greater attention to attracting, selecting, socialising and retaining individuals who have lower and more homogeneous levels of ethical reasoning to ensure continuity.

The Risk of Exclusion

Granovetter (1973: 1378), Wuthnow (2002) and Warren (2004) describe a similar downside to social capital when they argue how the underprivileged and economically disadvantaged lose their connections while the well-educated and privileged continue to bond and keep their social capital strong. They consider this form of association to operate on the basis of implicit norms, whereby the cultural capital associated with higher education is valued and used to favour some and exclude others. Ashforth and Anand (2003) point to similar social processes within the context of groups and organisations. Because they threaten the group's subculture, particular attention is paid to individuals who cannot be 'turned' (2003: 33). Newcomers may be pressured to encourage compliance with the group's norm of corruption. If unsuccessful, the punishment usually escalates and becomes exclusionary; a newcomer is rejected and induced to quit. Exclusionary punishment not only pushes the newcomer from the group, it reaffirms the norms and beliefs of the group by clearly drawing the line between acceptable (corrupt) and unacceptable (non-corrupt) behaviour (2003: 33). In this way, corruption is internalised by its members as permissible and even desirable behaviour, and passed on to successive generations of members (2003: 3). Tops and Tromp (2016) see another risk linked to networks and the underprivileged and economically and socially disadvantaged. Here, the disadvantaged are a 'victim' of today's elites in society, thereby falling back on the liberal notion of self-reliance and in return organise themselves in criminal networks actively trying to undermine local government. These criminal networks are beyond the scope of this research, but are an example of how the (elite) network structure in itself causes criminality by means of networks which again poses a serious threat to society. Kolthoff and Khonraad (2016) refer to social and family networks as a main resource in organised crime which is causing undermining of government. The topic of organised crime is further discussed in paragraph 9.3.

When regarding the risk of exclusion which networks bring about, Putnam distinguishes 'bonding' from 'bridging' social networks (2000: 23-25). Bonding is referred to as social networks between homogenous groups (exclusive). Bridging is referred to as social networks between heterogeneous groups (inclusive). Bridging allows different groups to share and exchange information and builds consensus among the groups representing diverse interests. Bridging contributes to an inclusive institutional structure that is more democratic in nature. In contrast, Putnam considers corruption to result from bonding networks; they are a negative manifestation of social capital (Putnam, 2000: 22). The question is whether this black and white distinction between bonding and bridging networks can be upheld. Burt (2000) refers to a similar type of networks, which he defines as 'broker networks', being large, sparse and non-hierarchical networks rich in opportunities to broker connections across structural holes. Although brokerage across structural holes is the source of added value, closure can be necessary to realise the value found in these holes. As such, the bonding or closed networks gain from the opportunities obtained by bridging or broker connections. This calls for at least three types of networks: a bonding network, a bridging/broker network and a bonding network with some bridging/broker connections.

By analogy, Wuthnow states that social capital may function in an exclusionary way when " it consists of limited networks that provide valuable information to some people but not to others (old boys' networks, for example) or when associations set up expectations about membership that cannot be easily met by everyone." (Wuthnow, 2002: 79-80). These networks can be considered homogenous in the sense that they consist of one or a few centres of influence with a closed group of individuals who are alike and share a certain background (study association, political party, historical roots). Also, they have successfully bridged with others because they work at or represent a wide spectrum of influential institutions or organisations in a given society. In this way, the social network bears features of bonding and bridging networks (Putnam) and strong and weak ties (Granovetter). Such social networks exist across democratic and societal institutions and are present in the heart of the decision- making processes.

The notion of inclusion does not imply that there is no longer room to freely associate, because whether there is a right or freedom to associate, there is also a right to exclude. Warren proposes three criteria to test whether associational exclusion becomes corruption. First, all individuals should be able to find the social attachments and memberships that provide opportunities for voice, representation, collective action and socialisation as part of democracy. Secondly, exclusion should not be combined with resources in such a way that the expenses or 'bill' is paid by others who lack recourse. Thirdly, there should be a certain overlap in membership so that civil society does not consist in mutually exclusive associations resulting in segregation (Warren, 2004: 339).

The beliefs of actors and the structure of the social network both play a role in the deterioration of the network. The homogeneity of close networks can lead to the insiders versus outsiders' mechanism and norm development. The bridging or brokering of the network can lead to the closure of the network once the additional advantages are obtained. Both the normalisation of reciprocity and the normalisation of corruption in networks need to be considered before dealing with corruption by a network.

Based on the theory on networks in this chapter, goal-directed networks are different from organically grown, emergent networks. Informal networks can also be distinguished from formal or organised networks. This latter type of network is similar to other organisations such as companies in terms of formalisation. Their deterioration can more easily be attributed to the organisation. I therefore also distinguish the informal networks and their level of openness to explore in Chapter 8 the extent to which this affects the risk of deterioration and what this means in terms of responsibility. To assess the link between networks and forms of influence, these four types of networks are used:

1. *A goal-directed network based upon a form of organisation* (legal and/or formal entities such as firms, associations, and (semi) public organisations
2. *A goal-directed network based upon an informal open structure* (open network)
3. *A goal-directed network based upon an informal closed structure* (closed network)
4. *An emergent network based upon an informal closed structure* (closed network)

The closure of an informal network can have an effect on the norm development within the network while influencing it at the same time. This will be dealt with in the following (sub) paragraphs.

4.8.4 *Normalisation of Corruption in Networks*

Social comparison theory explains how norm formation takes place. According to Festinger (1954), persons form their attitudes through social comparisons; they weigh and integrate the attitudes of others. In networks or other groups, attitudes are formed by interpersonal interaction and agreements. Often, individuals go back a long way and the norm formation in their closed networks was influenced by the social comparison among one another. If the networks emerge in the form of closed communities, this implies that the influence by outside attitudes is lacking, resulting in reciprocity being interpreted in a narrow sense; only applicable to the network members. This notion of inclusion and exclusion gets more attention from scholars. Warren (2004) points to the fact that in any democracy second-order norms of process can evolve that can quite properly bring new meanings of corruption in their wake. Although he looked at norm development within organised collectives such as institutions, like Ashforth and Anand (2003), he also explains how focussing on individual behaviour might detract attention from norm evolvement with corrupt consequences (Warren, 2004: 331). Warren and Ashforth and Anand therefore call for paying more attention to the norm development of collectivities instead of focusing on the behaviour of governmental organisations. Ashforth and Anand's concept of normalisation of corruption points at the norms within the collective violating the societal norms (2003: 2). In developed democracies, more and more influence and public purposes are attributed to nongovernmental organisations and profit-seeking businesses. Warren warns that such collectivities can become corrupt in a political sense "since political corruption is possible whenever a collective has within its power – because of its control over resources – to produce harms for which they seek to avoid accountability in order to benefit its members." (Warren, 2004: 332).

Baker and Faulkner (1993: 843) distinguish illegal networks from legal networks in their work on the network structure of three price-fixing conspiracies. Illegal networks differ from legal networks in important ways. Participants in illegal and criminal networks must conduct their activities in secret: they must conceal the conspiracy from outside 'guardians of trust' such as customers, non-participants inside their own organisations, and other internal company watchdogs. Various practices and organisational devices are used to protect the secrecy of such a network. Members may conceal its existence and their involvement in it by limiting face-to-face communication and leaders may be unknown to ordinary members. These goal-directed networks are established with the criminal objective as its purpose. Lauchs *et al.* (2011) have assessed the long lasting corruption network in the Queensland Police Force, a state police agency in Australia and looked at the socialisation processes in this criminal network. They describe how networks can have a dark side, where the network achievements come at the expense of other individuals, groups or societies. The bonding together of individuals to pursue particular or common interests is a key element of the network disadvantage, leading to exclusivity rather than inclusivity (2011: 4-5). Such exclusivity renders networks to be private in essence rather than public entities. In this way, they are not exposed to any form of monitoring or subject to external accountability checks. Because of this, networks can be quite secret and difficult to examine or regulate in their operation and endeavours (2011: 5). Lauchs *et al.* (2011) point out that this dark nature of networks and their lack of transparency, coupled with values and norms that support covert actions and goals, can provide a basis for corruption. Granovetter (1992: 45) argues that "networks can create their own norms at odds with the outside world to the point where they become a 'law unto themselves'." Lauchs *et al.* (2011: 8) refer to well established theories in criminology regarding dark networks and crime syndicates in which criminal operations such as drug trafficking rely on kinship and friendship networks to protect themselves from penetration by law enforcement agencies. In this case the illegal network operated within the legal police organisation. Systemic bribery led the network to become a corrupt network.

In their work *The Normalisation of Corruption*, Ashforth and Anand (2003) describe how corruption emerges within the context of organisation. Here, collective corruption is considered to be a slippery slope where initial unusual corrupt practices become institutionalised over time. The normalisation of corruption occurs and becomes an ongoing collective undertaking due to the process of institutionalisation, rationalisation and socialisation. Corruption becomes a property of the collective and thereby an integral part of the daily conduct to such an extent that individual members may be unable to see the inappropriateness of their behaviour (2003: 4). Ashforth and Anand distinguish three phases in this institutionalisation: the initial corrupt decision or act, the embedding of corruption in structures and processes, and the routinising of corruption (systemic momentum). The collective also steers the process of rationalisation. Corrupt individuals often acknowledge their conduct but deny the criminal intent (2003: 15). Most individuals still uphold values such as fairness, honesty and integrity, even as they engage in corruption, that is, until the momentum of a corrupted system provides its own seeming legitimacy. This distances individuals and groups from the moral stance implied by their actions and perhaps even forges a moral turn around, in which the bad becomes good. This mechanism becomes even stronger when institutionalised in the collective (2003: 15-16). The third process is that of socialisation which takes place in the collective. Newcomers are pre-socialised into corruption through, for example previous experience in corrupt organisations and industries, and through recruitment via personal or social networks (2003: 25). They explain the social influence by referring to the theory of differential association, which entails that criminal values, motives, beliefs and behaviours are learned through interactions within "intimate personal groups." (2003: 25). These three processes reinforce each other in such a way that corruption becomes the new normal. Heffernan (2011) and Palazzo *et al.* (2012) refer to the existence of 'wilful blindness' and 'ethical blindness' to point to the mechanisms which start to work from a complex interplay between individual sense making activities and context factors, which limits people ability to decide rationally and to be able to evaluate their decisions from a moral point of view. This collective corruption still builds on the idea of individual acts but liberates the idea of the individual evildoer and instead looks at the group dynamics steering a certain conduct. Their approach is a step in the direction of understanding how social capital can become corruption.

Cartier-Bresson (1997: 267) considers the generalisation of abuse in large-scale corruption among elites to be the result of informal social exchanges. Here, social capital becomes corruption. In practice, the distinction between bonding and bridging networks is not always easy to make because most networks bear features of both. Putnam argued that they are foremost dimensions through which different forms of social capital can be compared (2000: 23). The closed nature of the social network is an important characteristic to distinguish network corruption from other phenomena, as will be presented in the table of Chapter 8. I will argue that both bonding and bridging networks can become closed networks. Bridging with other actors and ensuring a certain degree of dissimilarity is not a guarantee that the division in insiders and outsiders is prevented. The collective corruption or generalised abuse which Ashforth and Anand and Cartier-Bresson, describe and which is linked to the bonding types of networks/groups, considers the corrupt way of acting to be adopted by all of its members. Corruption becomes the norm and everybody will eventually act corrupt. What is corruption is not the norm, but the generalised norm of reciprocity is such that all individuals favour the network (and its members) with corruption as a collective outcome.

4.9 Corruption by a Network

The previous paragraphs described how the structure of a network and norm development can be fertile ground for committing collective corruption. Although this is a risk to consider by social network members and policy makers, the legal provisions and policies available allow the prosecution and conviction of this form of corruption. This intentionally committing of corruption together with network members is of a different order than networks in which the norm of reciprocity slowly develops into corruption. Here they start to develop the characteristics of autonomous processes and organisations. This complex phenomenon is presented in the three case studies in Chapter 6 and can best be described as corruption *by* the network which exists alongside the corruption *in* the network. This is the main reason for using the holistic approach: network corruption exists above and beyond the individuals involved. As such, this research has followed up on the findings and recommendations of Ashforth and Anand (2003), who called for further research to examine what kinds of organisations and practices are most susceptible to normalised corruption (2003:40). If networks form the context in which corrupt practices such as bribery become the norm, I will refer to them as 'corruption networks'. Although this phenomenon also concerns the link between network and corruption, this research deals with another phenomenon in which networks themselves deteriorate and thereby result in corruption because generalised reciprocity becomes the norm and the networks close. This corruption by the network even exists without any individual acts of corruption taking place. The question therefore is: Who or what is responsible for such forms of corruption? New forms of organisations such as networks lack the checks and balances that are in place in the older, more hierarchical organisations; therefore the question is: To whom should this responsibility for their norm development be attributed? Paragraph 9.3 will explore how collectivity and attribution of responsibility are being approached in law.

Although contractarian thinking offers important insights into how to distinguish macro from micro social contracts, it does not offer a solution to the situations in which microsocial contracts have conflicted with hypernorms because they saw this as a violation of the moral free space. I will argue that network corruption occurs when communal endogenous norms conflict with these exogenous substantive hypernorms. Given that this microsocial contract is a social process, it is difficult to identify the precise turning point when social capital becomes corruption. This collective corruption is different from the collective corruption Ashforth and Anand present. In their examples, corrupt acting becomes the norm (corruption in a network), while in the examples I present, something else is going on: corruption by the network because of the normalisation of reciprocity. The norm development in social networks is not a conscious agreement in the form of a microsocial contract. People make group-serving or 'sociocentric' attributions to boost the performance of groups to which they belong, and this can turn into network corruption.

In terms of the type of network, I distinguish between a goal-directed network based upon a form of organisation, an emergent network based upon an informal open structure (open network) and a network based upon an informal closed structure (closed network). The closure of the network is a gradual process. There are a few signs which indicate the *closure of the network*:

- There is no general equality for individuals to be able to find the social attachments and memberships that provide opportunities for voice, representation, collective action and socialisation part of democracy
- Resources are used in such a way that the network members gain from them, while the 'costs' are paid by non-network members
- It is customary to inform about, select, hire or appoint network members to official positions without offering third-party candidates a real opportunity to gain the position.

These four types of networks can serve three different purposes: the purpose to help one another, to influence decision-making and to provide preferential treatment through the network. Helping one another lies at the heart of social capital. Networks can also be used to influence decision-making, whereby the decision-maker can be a network member or third party. However, the purpose to help one another or to influence decision-making can gradually deteriorate into the purpose of preferential treatment. There are a few signs which indicate the network's purpose *has become preferential treatment*:

- It is standing practice to incorporate network members' interests in decision-making while assigned to serve the general interest;
- The norm becomes to favour the network's members through favourable legislation or policies

4.10 Sub-Conclusions

The network literature is voluminous. Although the definitions of 'social networks' vary somewhat, most definitions include references to 'relationships between actors' or 'connections between individuals'. Social networks have an important function in our society. People join formal and informal networks and through this structure they develop a mutual concern for each other's welfare and well-being and collectively they can achieve goals which could not be realised independently. Foremost, networks provide a structure through which individuals can help one another but networks can also have a goal of making themselves heard in the political process of a democracy. This goal achievement can be the result of goal-directed networks or the result of networks which have grown more organically, so-called emergent networks. From a communitarian perspective, networks form valuable communities with a great influence on the way an individual thinks and acts in these networks and vice versa. The contractarian approach builds on the concept that networks can explicitly agree on their own norms through microsocial contracts as long as they match the macrosocial hypernorms. In reality this concerns a social process which can meet or come in conflict with the hypernorms and/or societal norms. The social processes of networks are influenced by their unique characteristics which influence its dynamics and adaptation. Most networks are informal forms of cooperation and are generally composed of like-minded people with a similar purpose who identify with the network because of the beliefs upheld by its members, the shared history of its members etc.

The key element in networks is reciprocity. The group-serving attributions which network members collectively bring about, can lead to the normalisation of reciprocity (generalised reciprocity) which, together with the closed and exclusive nature of the network, leads to exclusion of non-network members or outsiders. Networks form the important social capital needed in society. In network theory a distinction is made among 'bonding networks', which are close-knit homogenous groups, inward looking, with a high degree of personal contact and reinforcing exclusive identities and 'bridging networks' which are more loosely-knit heterogeneous groups, outward looking and developing broader identities, and 'linking networks', which are a form of social capital consisting of relationships with people across different hierarchical levels and power. The bonding networks cultivate trust, cooperation and collective strength among individuals often with a shared history, experience and common purpose. The bridging and linking networks allow different groups or networks to share and exchange information, ideas and innovation and build consensus among the groups representing diverse interests. Network theory also indicates that those network members who function as a broker and connect (through weak ties) the closed bonding networks with other networks across the structural holes, are the most successful. These 'bridging connections' give these brokers (centres of influence) an advantage. The broker has more diverse contacts and as such is more likely to be a candidate for involvement in new opportunities. Additionally, this position brings together otherwise disconnected contacts, which give this individual a disproportionate say in whose interests are served when the contacts come together. Closure can be necessary to realise the value found in these holes. As such, the bonding or closed networks gain from the opportunities obtained by bridging or broker connections but equally make the risk of the network's deterioration greater because of their exclusion of non-networks members, and this is what links networks to corruption.

The available network literature has linked networks to the aspect of inclusion and exclusion, but it has not thought through the question of when networks deteriorate and what this means in terms of responsibility. The literature does point to the dark side of networks when discussing corruption networks: networks in which the norm has become to act corrupt. These networks are criminal networks, goal-directed to make a living by organising criminal activities. Norm development in emerging networks is more of a social process which has been less exposed in literature. This gap in network theory is therefore followed by the fundamental question of who is to be held responsible for those emerging networks which become exclusive or, alternatively, who is responsible for preventing networks from becoming corrupted. (Business) ethics provide arguments which allow responsibility to be attributed to those networks which are not formalised per se. Networks can develop and at a certain moment they qualify as autonomous organisations which can bear responsibility for their conduct. Among others, loosely organised collectives, such as the informal emergent networks, can become an autonomous moral actor with a responsibility of its own, if this network of individuals share a particular interest or background, are shown to have a 'shared attitude' (attitude similarity) and manifest their 'self-consciousness' by showing that they as a collective become organised in such a way that a purpose is reached. The result is something that can only be realised through this collective's cooperation. Additionally, there is an awareness that the network has to be turned into an appropriate organisation to get to this result. Also, individuals take on different role responsibilities in getting the network organised.

This chapter makes clear that individual behaviour is much more steered by the social processes of the networks. We all participate in formal and informal networks because we understand that we can benefit from our networks. In particular, informal networks are less real than the organisations where we are employed at or with which we do business. There is already a great awareness on the context of formal organisations and how they determine and influence individual behaviour. The findings from the network literature underline the importance of acknowledging the roles networks play in decision-making and the perspective of individuals. This above all is the social capital of our society. Scholars point to the value of this form of social capital but to a lesser degree have thought through networks' dark side and deterioration and the corresponding questions regarding responsibility for networks.

Now that we know how networks come into being, what their unique features are and how responsibility can be attributed to them, this knowledge can be combined with the findings of Chapter 3 concerning corruption and how it is linked to networks.

5. The Link Between Networks and Corruption

5.1 Introduction

In Chapters 3 and 4, I provided an overview of the main literature and research on corruption and networks. Chapter 3 concluded that our current thinking about corruption is limited. Our current concepts of corruption do not give us enough hold on dealing effectively with corruption in network-like structures. Chapter 4 led us to conclude that theories on networks and their linkage to corruption are scarce. Notwithstanding that, some theories support the idea of collective acting and collective responsibility, which by analogy can be used when networks themselves form the corruption (corruption by a network). In this chapter both analyses will be integrated in one assessment frame which helps with distinguishing when the influencing in networks becomes network corruption and when social capital becomes corrupted. In the following paragraphs the features of corruption linked to networks are presented, followed by the features of networks which can bear responsibility (autonomous network organisations). Combining these two sets of features will result in the set of features of informal social networks which can bear responsibility for their deterioration: network corruption. In this way an assessment can be made on whether the characteristics and mechanisms found in the literature also appear in practice. The three case studies of Chapter 6 allow for the assessment of the link between networks and corruption in Chapter 7.

5.2 Features of Corruption and Networks from Both Bodies of Knowledge

5.2.1 *Features of Corruption*

In Chapter 3 corruption was characterised, with specific importance given to the notion of networks in literature and research. I define corruption as *allowing improper interests to influence decision-making at the expense of the general interest.* With this corruption definition in mind, the corruption literature was analysed on the aspect of corruption and its link to networks. Across the many corruption definitions, three features can be extracted which together form the elements of corruption which is linked to networks.

The first feature of corruption which is related to networks is that of (1) *collective misuse of professional roles for network interests.* This feature is reflected in references to corruption by wordings such as “close circle”, “connections driven by mutual benefits”, “any collectivity with control over resources” and “role conflicts”. Corruption linked to networks is not limited to individual or occasional behaviour. On the contrary, the connections allow sustainable benefits to arise out of these. The connections include those with power who can use their professional role for non-professional purposes, specifically: aiming to ensure the network benefits. This does not mean that networks do not gain from the misuse of professional roles. However, linked to the second feature of ‘generalised reciprocity’, the structure of the network will ensure all its members can fall back on or gain from the network at some time. The aspect of network interests is intertwined with the next feature. The term ‘professional role’ entails that network members apply their professional capacity in such a way that the network can benefit from it. Professional can be interpreted as the actual profession or job someone has, but can also be, for instance, the informal but powerful role of former businessmen or politicians. It concerns those who are experienced and qualified and have influence.

The second feature is that of (2) *generalised reciprocity*. In some of the corruption literature, corruption is presented as ‘bribery’, whereby a person abuses his power and in return receives a favour. Here, corruption is a matter of clear ‘quid pro quo’ (something is given to receive something else). Other references in corruption literature describe corruption as broader than the immediate and obvious influencing. As such, there is no specific reciprocity or ‘quid pro quo’, but abuse of power takes place in return for a previous, present or future favour from the network. Such references include: “unspoken agreements”, “undue advantage not given immediately or directly (…) but linked to officials’ influence over administration of public authority of the State”, “complex payoffs which more often do not involve the official personally but can be beneficial to one’s colleague, friend, family member or acquaintance” and “some reciprocities by some people in some contexts”. These references do implicate that abuse of power or role can become the norm; as such, something is done or given, with the confidence that someone else will return it at some time. The private or personal gain is implicit. My definition of corruption also sees reciprocity as something implicit, generalised as such. The next feature looks at the outcome of the corruption.

The third feature of corruption related to networks, is that of (3) *harming the rights of outsiders*. Paragraph 3.2 deals with the question of why corruption is a concern. Varying from safety and security arguments to more democratic arguments relating to fairness and equal treatment, corruption seeks to favour some at the detriment of others. These others may be specific parties such as the fair competitor who did not ‘win’ the tender or they may be the public or society in general. The literature refers to it as “corruption violating the norm of democratic inclusion” and “violation of the norms of duty and welfare (...) disregard for any consequence suffered by the public” and “the power (...) is used for personal gain in a manner that contravenes the rules of the game.” Corruption is not a victimless crime; this implies that networks can only be linked to corruption if this feature is fulfilled.

In addition to the three features extracted from the corruption literature and research, five features of the network literature were found which link networks to achieving a result (good or bad) and bearing some form of responsibility for this result (autonomous network organisation).

5.2.2 Features of Informal Social Networks Which Can Bear Responsibility (Autonomous Network Organisations)

To understand how corruption can be caused by social networks, it is useful to consider the network to be a loosely organised collective (conglomerate). Social networks are composed of a few key figures that bond together because they are very much alike. They determine the purpose of the network and play a key role in shaping the identity of the network. After the initial phase, other important persons are attracted. These individuals are identified by the centres of influence or older members. These persons become members of the social network not by any formal agreement, but through socialisation processes and by contributing to the network out of solidarity. Their commonality is that they all have influence and hold key positions in various formal organisations (municipality, police, media, business or politics). Membership is open to those who have power and influence and who want to use it for the common purpose of the network.

In Chapter 4 social networks and their downsides and risks were characterised, with a particular focus on the references to corruption in the network literature and research. On this basis, five features of autonomous network organisations are extracted. These features are not features of networks as were presented in paragraph 4.2.2, but are features of those social networks which can bear responsibility for the conduct, whether corrupt or not. I refer to them as 'autonomous' to separate them from the informal social networks which form an aggregate or conglomerate of individuals but which do not meet the criteria of a separate moral actor. As such, 'autonomous' means an identity or presence of the network in addition to its individuals. Non-autonomous network organisations cannot bear a collective responsibility.

One feature is that of (1) *informal structure*. The network literature distinguishes "formal from informal networks". Formal networks are official organisations, often with a membership and governance which is hierarchical. The network literature does refer to the risks, such as the norm development, which coincides with informal social networks. Such informal networks are described as "horizontal and without formal structure". The literature on networks and collective responsibility refers to the feature of (2) *shared interest* by wording such as "the purpose to survive" and "shared tasks, values or goals" and "common interests of individuals". This feature is linked to the feature of (3) *common attitude*, by which is meant that all network members take on a similar way of thinking and feeling towards their network. References in literature and research are "attitude similarity", "individuals share a common interest and participation in certain activities or at least not opposed to them" and "the process of rationalisation in the collective" or individual members "may be unable to see the inappropriateness of their behaviours" and "the networks are steered by sentiments of trust, co-operation, and altruism". The feature of (4) *self-consciousness* is essential for a network to be an autonomous organisation. If there are examples of the network members' awareness, that in order to serve their shared interests they must take on a common attitude with complementary "role responsibilities", it is a sign that network members are aware of the presence of their network. The individuals organise themselves in such a way that the network achieves a concrete result. References in network literature are that individuals "identify themselves with the network" or the reference to "self-categorisation". The last feature from network literature is that of the network's (5) *closed character*. This feature is referred to as "bonding and inward looking", "the cultivation of nepotism" or "social capital functioning in an exclusionary way." This aspect of networks is the most important reference in network literature which links networks to corruption. The following chapters will display the empirical part of this research. Thenceforth the concept of network corruption will be applied to the real-life cases.

5.3 Combining Features of Corruption Linked to Networks and Informal Social Networks with Responsibility (Autonomous Network Organisations)

With the basic body of knowledge on corruption and autonomous network organisations in mind, it is time to connect both, and present the integrated set of features which can be used to evaluate the functioning and status of a network. The legitimacy of putting the question of network corruption on the table is the observation that collective actions can bring about harm. The harm in this case is the corruption. Therefore, the first characteristics are derived from the network literature, followed by the characteristics of corruption from the corruption literature.

Together the eight features form a basic outline of those networks which can bear responsibility for their deterioration (corruption). One by one I will compare them and search for overlapping features, or alternatively, features which need to be complemented by a second meaning to be able to distinguish the original meaning given to the feature.

I will start with the autonomous network feature of *informal structure* and link it to the feature of corruption being the *collective misuse of professional roles for network interests* to clarify the singularity and wrongfulness of this cooperation as opposed to the common way of *cooperation*. Network literature has indicated that such an informal way of working together is human nature and a form of interaction which exists because no one in society is entirely isolated from others. As such, its connotation is neutral. Only when this informal collective cooperation results in the misuse of professional roles for network interests does the character of the cooperation change to the negative. The misuse is a collective misuse which can take on all sorts of forms, with the common denominator that it is linked to the professional roles of the individuals used for their network.

Thereafter I combine the autonomous network organisation's feature of *shared interest* with the corruption feature of *generalised reciprocity* (previous, present or future favour from the network) to distinguish the normal network's interest or purpose *to help one another* from the absolute norm which has influenced the network's shared interest over time. The network literature considers associations of individuals helping one another to be important in the sense that individuals have a better chance to survive and be successful if they help each other in their daily lives. The network literature does refer to the risks of the norm of reciprocity, which can be specific or generalised and thereby automatic. Corruption literature attempts to define the 'quid pro quo' or 'favour and return favour', and more and more the dominant thinking of scholars is that this is difficult to prove, because favours can be returned by others and/or at some time in the future, often referred to as the 'deferred expectation'. In this way, 'helping one another' can in fact be aimed, albeit implicitly, at the idea of having to contribute to the network, in order to be automatically rewarded when there is a specific need.

I continue with the autonomous network organisation's feature of *common attitude* and with the knowledge gained on self-categorisation, I link this to the *self-consciousness of the collective* to distinguish the networks whose identity coordinates the behaviour and role of its members from the networks in which individuals cooperate but foremost remain individuals with their separate and unique identities (*self-consciousness of the individuals*). From the observance of network behaviour the awareness in terms of identity is revealed. In order for a network to be an autonomous actor, the network members have to show they are aware of the existence of their network. This self-consciousness can be seen from their common attitude and their ability to organise themselves in such a way that they are complementary to one another. If network members are shown to have a common attitude translated into various roles they take on, it is a case of self-consciousness of the collective.

I conclude by combining the feature of the autonomous network organisation being the *closed character,* with the network feature *harming the rights of outsider* because the closure is the reason third parties are harmed (insiders vs. outsiders) and distinguishing this meaning of the closed character from networks which can be just *strong bonds and inward-looking*. Network literature distinguishes the 'bonding' and 'bridging' networks to illustrate that networks can be internal looking and external looking, making them vary in terms of openness. If a social network cooperates in such a way that the effect is that only insiders gain from the network and outsiders are left empty-handed and without a fair chance to strive for their interests, this in fact means that their right to equal treatment was harmed. Corruption literature presents corruption as distorting equal opportunities, excluding (legal) persons from fair and honest chances in competing in politics, the economy or other areas.

These features are used to evaluate the facts from the case studies, to see whether the characteristics found in both bodies of literature also appear in real life case studies. Each of the four features can take on two forms. A social network meets the features of network deterioration (corruption) only if it entails the second meaning of each feature. Therefore each feature needs to be checked. The way a network functions can only be labelled as 'network corruption' if all four features are fulfilled. Other configurations do not lead to network corruption. It is beyond the scope of this research to describe all configurations, but the table in Chapter 8 differentiates between the most common forms of networks.

Table 1 The features of networks which can bear responsibility for their deterioration (network corruption)

1. An informal collective cooperation	cooperation
	misuse of professional roles for network interests
2. Shared interest	helping one another
	generalised reciprocity (previous, present or future favour from the network)
3. Common attitude	self-consciousness of the individuals
	self-consciousness of the collective
4. Closed character	strong bond
	exclusion (harming the rights of outsiders)

Chapter 4 dealt with the body of knowledge on networks. Paragraph 4.2.2 provided a description of social networks and their main characteristics. Paragraph 4.7 dealt with the question of whether networks can actually be held responsible for their collective behaviour and outcome. This question is important in the light of networks' involvement in corruption. It turned out to be possible to attribute responsibility to social networks when they met certain criteria. These criteria formed the unique features of networks which can bear responsibility (autonomous network organisations) and were presented in paragraph 5.2.2. Although Chapter 3 did conclude that little attention is given to corruption linked to networks, three features of the corruption literature were extracted and presented in paragraph 5.2.1. Together the last two sets of features led to the features of informal social networks which can bear responsibility for their deterioration. For the sake of clarity, table 2 provides a corresponding overview.

Table 2 Informal social networks (a), informal social networks which can bear responsibility (b) and informal social networks which can bear responsibility for their deterioration (c).

Features of informal social networks (a)	Features of informal social networks which can be held responsible (b)	Features of informal social networks which can bear responsibility for their deterioration (c)
(1) A social network has *an informal structure*	(1) The presence of an *informal structure*	(1) An informal collective cooperation > *misuse of professional roles for network interests*
(2) A social network does not have a formal leader or director but so-called *Centres of Influence* can be distinguished	(2) The *shared interest* of the network members	(2) Shared interest > *generalised reciprocity* (previous, present or future favour from the network)
(3) A social network is *dynamic, responsive and adaptive*, in contrast to static and bureaucratic organisations	(3) The *common attitude* of the network members	(3) Common attitude > *Self-consciousness* of the network
(4) A social network has a *purpose* which can be deduced from the behaviour of its members instead of stated or paper goals	(4) The network members' *self-consciousness* of the of the presence of the network	(4) Closed character > *exclusion* (harming the rights of outsiders)
(5) A social network coincides with self-categorisation, individuals *identify themselves with* the network to which they are a member	(5) The *closed character* of the network	
(6) A social network is *not simply the sum* of its members		

5.4 SUB-CONCLUSIONS

This chapter summarised the six general features of social networks, followed by the five features of autonomous network organisations. These last features can be used to assess whether a network is able to bear the responsibility which makes it a moral actor. As such an autonomous network organisation has responsibility in addition to the individual responsibilities individuals have. This is an important acknowledgement because most informal organisations such as networks or groups cannot bear responsibility because they are a random set of people or an aggregate in which the sum is only the total of the individuals. Only when an informal social network meets these criteria of a loosely organised collective, can responsibility be attributed to it. This implies that if such a network deteriorates, the network can be held responsible and so will its members. Thereafter, the concept of network deterioration was introduced and the way in which its four distinctive features came about was explained.

The features of network corruption are extracted from the corruption and network theory, which allows an assessment of networks to evaluate whether the networks deteriorate and whether they can bear responsibility for the deterioration. The first feature is that of 'an informal collective cooperation' in which professional roles are misused for network interests. The second feature is 'shared interest' which means that the network observes the generalised reciprocity which concerns the previous, present or future favours from the network. The third feature is that of 'common attitude' which implies that the network members are aware of the presence of the collective. The fourth feature is that of 'closed character' which concerns the closure of the network which excludes others and thereby harms their rights. These features are interdependent and reinforce one another, resulting in mechanisms which eventually contribute to the deterioration of networks. The concept of network corruption will be applied to three real case studies in Chapter 6 to assess whether this concept offers a better insight into the phenomenon of corruption and whether it contributes in a practical sense so that we can actually point out the mechanisms which allow networks to deteriorate. This also poses questions of whether networks can deteriorate from social capital into corruption or whether networks can be linked to other forms of (undue) influence. This question is answered in Chapter 8. The next chapter presents the facts of each of the three cases.

6. Case Studies: Global, National and Local Networks

6.1 Introduction

The previous chapter described the relation between networks and social capital, but also stressed the downside of networks and networking: the fact that social capital can become corrupted. Now that the topic of corruption in the sphere of networks is explored and we understand that there can in fact be such a thing as an autonomous network organisation, it is important to take a closer look at the networks in the selected case studies. A lot of time and capacity has been or will be spent on the criminal investigations and (future) court proceedings, but it is to be seen if and how the network is addressed; current anti-corruption laws do not recognise trading in influence, let alone networks. This chapter consists of a description of each of the three case studies. The facts of the three cases will be presented in this chapter. The main purpose of these case studies is to be able to distinguish when networks deteriorate, or in other words, to distinguish social capital from network corruption. These cases have not been entirely thought out, nor have there been final verdicts, therefore my research is of an explorative nature. After the facts of the cases have been summarised in this chapter, they will be analysed in depth in Chapter 7, to understand what patterns they have in common and in what way they differ, or in other words, whether they can be considered corrupt autonomous network organisations.

6.2 Case Study 1 International: The FIFA case

6.2.1 Introduction

The first case involves the Fédération Internationale de Football Association (FIFA), which is the non-governmental football governing agency located in Switzerland. The organisation has long been accused of corruption, but the corruption allegations became concrete with the indictment brought by the US Department of Justice in which several FIFA officials and corporate executives were formally accused of having committed racketeering conspiracy, fraud, corruption and money-laundering (US Department of Justice, 2015). In March 2015, Attorney General Lynch announced the indictment of 14 defendants: nine high officials from FIFA, four sports marketing executives and one intermediary (US Department of Justice, 2015). They are charged of "rampant, systemic, and deep-rooted" corruption following a major inquiry by the Federal Bureau of Investigation (FBI) and the Internal Revenue Service Criminal Investigations Division.

6.2.2 Case Presentation

Although this case is presented as the FIFA case, we will learn that the corruption did not only involve FIFA officials. All officials abused their positions of trust for personal gain, often through an alliance with sports marketing executives and intermediaries, who shut out competitors and kept highly lucrative contracts for themselves through the systematic payment of bribes and kickbacks.

The racketeering charges in the FIFA indictment described an "enterprise" constituted by various legal entities including FIFA itself, its six constituent continental confederations[1], 211 member associations, affiliated regional federations and sports marketing companies (US Department of Justice, 2015). These legal entities were "associated in fact" and constituted an "ongoing organisation" whose members "functioned as a continuing unit" for purposes of achieving the common business aims of the enterprise (US District Court Eastern District of New York v. Webb *et al.*, 2015: 1). FIFA's main goal is the continuous improvement of football (FIFA, n.d. b). Amongst other things, the organisation is responsible for overseeing the World Cup football competition and other international competitions. In doing so, it has jurisdiction over international football. One key way the enterprise derives revenue is through the commercialisation of the media and marketing rights of football events and tournaments (US Department of Justice, 2015). FIFA and its confederations sell these rights to sports marketing companies, which often come down to multi-year contracts covering multiple editions of the tournaments (US Department of Justice, 2015). These companies, in turn, sell these rights to TV and radio broadcast networks, major corporate sponsors and other sub-licensees who want to broadcast the matches or promote their brands (US Department of Justice, 2015). The revenue generated from these contracts is substantial; according to FIFA:

Most of its revenue comes from the FIFA World Cup, the financial success of which provides global football with a solid foundation from which to flourish. Bidding for a World Cup is an extensive and expensive process, which depends entirely on the votes of FIFA's Executive Committee (Youd, 2014: 170-171).

The majority of this revenue is redistributed back into football through investment in development programmes, international football tournaments, football governance and the organisation of the World Cup (FIFA, 2015b: 7).

---

1 The six constituent continental confederations are: the Confederation of North, Central American and Caribbean Association Football (CONCACAF), the Confederación Sudamericana de Fútbol (CONMEBOL), the Union des Associations Européennes de Football (UEFA), the Confédération Africaine de Football (CAF), the Asian Football Confederation (AFC) and the Oceania Football Confederation (OFC), to be found on: http://www.fifa.com/associations/.

The US indictments against FIFA officials can be seen as the first major step in the legal proceedings of the FIFA corruption case. Some key figures of FIFA are still being investigated by US and Swiss authorities and more indictments are expected. However, the case can also be seen as the 'final' episode in a series of events surrounding corrupt practices related to FIFA. The five-term president of FIFA, Sepp Blatter, has been accused of corruption ever since his election. In June 1998 Sepp Blatter won his first presidential election. In 1999 the first allegations were heard about the possible rigging of his election. FIFA executives are believed to have received tens of thousands of dollars in exchange for their votes. The allegations were dropped and no evidence was delivered (*The New York Times*, 2015). In 2002 Blatter was accused of financial mismanagement and corruption by FIFA Secretary General Michel Zen-Ruffinen (total USD 500 million). Again, Blatter denied the corruption allegations and acknowledged that he ended an investigation into FIFA's finances to preserve the confidentiality of several members accused of wrongdoing. Zen-Ruffinen submitted a dossier to the Swiss authorities on behalf of other Executive Committee members who accused Blatter of financial mismanagement, conflict of interest and abuse of power (*The New York Times*, 2015). Zen-Ruffinen lost the power struggle and left FIFA.

In 2006, FIFA's vice president Jack Warner and his family were accused of illegally selling World Cup tickets, through which they are believed to have made USD 1 million in profits (BBC Panorama, 2010). A travel company controlled by Warner's family served as the intermediary in the enormous fraud scheme. FIFA expressed disapproval of this action, but Warner retained his position (*The New York Times*, 2015).

The bidding process to award the 2018 and 2022 World Cups brought out more corruption. The decision to award two World Cups was criticised and believed to be flawed from the start because of large-scale vote trading. In 2010, investigative journalists from the British newspaper *The Sunday Times* revealed corrupt practices by FIFA officials as part an undercover operation. Six officials were suspended for trying to sell their World Cup votes, including executive committee members Amos Adamu (Nigeria) and Reynald Temarii (Tahiti), both of whom were caught on tape asking for payments in exchange for their support (*The New York Times*, 2015).

In 2010, three FIFA officials were accused of accepting bribes from the International Sports and Leisure marketing company in return for votes for hosting elections in the 2018 (Russian Federation) and 2022 (Qatar) World Cups. The announcement of the hosting states was followed by allegations of rampant corruption and bribery (*The New York Times*, 2015). In particular, the vote for Qatar was met with surprise. It appeared to be an illogical choice because of the soaring temperatures in the summer, the large-scale human rights violations and lack of existing football facilities (Youd, 2014: 171). Besides the bribery allegations which would become known later on, Blatter admitted that politically motivated collusion had taken place during the voting process. The Spanish and Qatari World Cup bid teams traded their votes in the respective 2018 and 2022 bids

(Youd, 2014: 172). Phaedra Almajid, the media officer involved in Qatar's 2022 World Cup bid team, would later blow the whistle when reporting that FIFA executives received money for their votes (*The Guardian*, 2014a).

In 2011, former chairman of the English Football Association Lord Triesman alleged four executive committee members – Jack Warner (Trinidad and Tobago), Nicolas Leoz (Paraguay), Ricardo Teixeira (Brazil) and Worawi Makudi (Thailand) – of attempted bribery in exchange for their World Cup vote (BBC, 2015d). Before a British parliamentary inquiry into the governance of football in England and the country's failure to secure the right to host the 2018 World Cup finals, Triesman admitted that, looking back, his bid team should have reported the four right away. Triesman confessed that the Football Association chose not to complain at the time for fear it would jeopardise England's bid (BBC, 2015d).

FIFA's vice president Jack Warner resigned after bribery accusations were made related to former Asian Football Confederation President Mohammed bin Hammam, who was later found guilty by FIFA's Ethics Committee for his role in planning a USD 40,000 payment to the Caribbean Football Union to collect votes in the FIFA presidential election (Youd, 2014: 182-183). One of the executive committee members who resigned after the bribery allegations was Chuck Blazer, a former general secretary of the Confederation of North, Central America and Caribbean Association Football (CONCACAF). One of its key roles is helping to arrange World Cup TV and sponsorship deals in the US (BBC, 2015b; *The New York Times*, 2015). Jeffrey Webb is the head of CONCACAF and successor of Warner. Webb has been extradited to the US amidst the corruption allegations. Blazer became an informant to the US government and helped the US with their investigation of the FIFA case, which led to the incrimination of many individuals. He opened up about the wrongdoings which took place between 2004 and 2011. He confessed that he and others of FIFA's executive committee agreed to accept bribes in connection with the selection of South Africa as the host of the 2010 World Cup. Here the US prosecutors focussed on a USD 10 million deal that was a bribe to secure this 2010 World Cup for South Africa (BBC, 2015b). One of his co-conspirators received a bribe in Morocco for its bid to host the 1998 tournament, which was eventually awarded to France (BBC, 2015b). Together with others, he also accepted bribes in connection with broadcast and other rights to five CONCACAF Gold Cup tournaments. Most senior figures accused are football powerbrokers in North America, Latin America and the Caribbean (BBC, 2015b). An email obtained by a South African newspaper appears to show that the then South African President, Thabo Mbeki, and Sepp Blatter agreed to the deal. In the email, FIFA Secretary General Jerome Valcke wrote to a South African minister asking when the transfer could be made, and saying that both Blatter and Mbeki had discussed the matter previously (BBC, 2015b). The South African government insists it was a legitimate payment to promote Caribbean football, but documents seen by the BBC suggest then FIFA vice president Jack Warner used the payment for cash withdrawals and personal loans and to launder money (BBC, 2015b).

In 2012, FIFA appointed former US federal prosecutor Michael Garcia to investigate allegations of foul play related to the 2018 and 2022 World Cup bidding processes. Phaedra Almajid provided evidence of wrongdoing surrounding the Qatar bid to Garcia's independent inquiry into the 2018 and 2022 World Cup bids. Her evidence was given on condition of anonymity (*The Guardian*, 2014a). FIFA gave a second life time ban to Bin Hammam after his "repeated violations" of international soccer's code of ethics. FIFA's ethics committee announced Bin Hammam was suspended due to allegations he had bribed 25 Caribbean Football Union (CFU) members with USD 1 million in total. One delegate, Fred Lunn of the Bahamas, received such an envelope and reported the offer after having taken a picture of the money before returning it. Nearly three dozen officials were later either barred or suspended by FIFA as a result of the payments (*The New York Times*, 2015). The money, USD 40,000 in unmarked envelopes, was distributed by Jack Warner, then a member of FIFA's executive committee (*The Guardian*, 2014c).

In 2013, FIFA acknowledged that its executives received several million dollars through partnerships with marketing company International Sport and Leisure (ISL). ISL was FIFA's media and marketing partner at the end of the 1990s, responsible for handling TV rights negotiations for the World Cup. The company went bust in 2001 owing millions of pounds to creditors. Investigators found evidence that bribes had been paid to senior FIFA officials in return for their help in securing lucrative TV deals, mostly in South America (BBC, 2013; BBC Panorama, 2010).

In 2015, a letter (dd. 2008) was leaked to the media in which Oliphant, the president of the South African Football Association, requests FIFA's secretary general Jerome Valcke to place USD 10 million in accounts controlled by Warner as a bribe for votes to host the 2010 World Cup in South Africa. Valcke is known to be Blatter's long-time closest ally and fixer (Gibson, 2015).

In December 2014, FIFA chose not to release its own investigation into corruption, but instead released an executive summary which it said exonerated the bidding process. The report's independent author and head of the investigative arm of its ethics committee, American lawyer Garcia, resigned in protest (Gibson, 2014b). FIFA's appeals committee had rejected a claim from Garcia that the head of the adjudicatory arm, Eckert, had fundamentally misrepresented his 430-page report. Eckert's 42-page summary effectively cleared 2018 host Russia and 2022 host Qatar of serious wrongdoing despite admitting the former had refused to cooperate, having insisted all their emails had been lost. The summary determined various incidents which might have occurred did not compromise the integrity of the voting process. Phaedra Almajid believes the guarantee that her report would be included anonymously was deliberately breached in a summary of Garcia's report published by Eckert (*The Guardian*, 2014a). An hour after the summary was published, Garcia reported his colleague Eckert, claiming his summary contained "numerous materially incomplete and erroneous representations." (Gibson, 2014b). However, the appeals committee found Garcia had nothing to appeal against since the summary only voiced an opinion, and declined to hear his appeal. That same day, FIFA's disciplinary committee had ruled that complaints from two whistle-blowers that their confidentiality had been breached also had no merit (Gibson, 2014a).

In 2015, Temarii, one of FIFA's executive committee members, was banned from soccer's governing body for eight years after allegations that he accepted money from Bin Hammam to help cover legal costs related to an appeal of a separate FIFA ban back in 2010 (*The Guardian*, 2015). 2015 is the year of the US indictment. Swiss authorities raided a Zurich hotel and took seven FIFA officials into custody after receiving this request from the U.S. Justice Department. The US Justice Department unsealed the 47-count indictment (US District Court Eastern District of New York v. Webb *et al.*, 2015) that included the 14 defendants listed above (nine FIFA officials and five corporate executives), indicted among others for racketeering, wire fraud and money laundering conspiracies in connection with the individuals' participation in a 24-year scheme to enrich themselves through the corruption of international soccer (US Department of Justice, 2015). Seven of the defendants (Jeffrey Webb, Eduardo Li, Julio Rocha, Costas Takkas, Eugenio Figueredo, Rafael Esquivel and José Maria Marin) were taken into custody by Swiss authorities (US Department of Justice, 2015).

Despite the wide-reaching corruption allegations related to FIFA, Blatter won the FIFA presidency for the fifth time but resigned a few days later, saying that FIFA "needs a profound restructuring". In the meantime, Blazer admitted he accepted bribes during the bidding processes of the 1998 and 2010 World Cups. *The Sunday Times* uncovered secret video tapes that reportedly show former executive committee member Ismail Bhamjee claiming the 2010 World Cup votes were "deliberately miscounted" (*The Sunday Times*, 2015). In the meantime FIFA announced that as corruption investigations continue, it will suspend the voting process for the World Cup in 2026. Valcke acknowledged that he approved the transfer but maintains he has done nothing wrong. Swiss authorities announced that they are investigating 53 banking relations related to FIFA and 104 suspicious incidents in Swiss bank accounts related to FIFA. Harold Mayne-Nicholls, who assessed the bids for the 2018 and 2022 World Cups, was suspended from FIFA for seven years. He had previously admitted to speaking with Qatari officials about job positions at the country's Aspire youth academy for three of his relatives (BBC, 2015b) Blazer received a lifetime ban from FIFA for his involvement in "schemes involving the offer, acceptance, payment and receipt of undisclosed and illegal payments." Swiss authorities investigate Blatter as a suspect of criminal mismanagement and misappropriation, as well as making a "disloyal payment" to UEFA President Michel Platini. Through his lawyer, Blatter maintains his innocence. Warner is accused of many instances of bribery and corruption and received a lifetime ban from football. FIFA's ethics committee banned Blatter and Platini from all football-related activities for eight years

(FIFA, 2015b). They were found guilty of breaches surrounding a £ 1.3 million ($ 2 million) "disloyal payment" made to Platini in 2011 (BBC, 2015b). Blatter, in his position as President of FIFA, authorised the payment to Platini, which had no legal basis in the written agreement signed between both officials on 25 August 1999. Neither in his written statement nor in his personal hearing was Mr Blatter able to demonstrate another legal basis for this payment (FIFA, 2015b). FIFA's ethics committee stated that:

> The evidence available (...) in the present case was not sufficient to establish, (...) that Mr Platini obtained the payment for the execution or omission of an official act within the meaning of article 21 paragraph 1 of the FCE (Bribery and corruption). Nevertheless, the conduct (...) constituted a breach of article 20 paragraph 1 of the FCE (Offering and accepting gifts and other benefits). Furthermore, Mr Platini found himself in a situation of conflict of interest, despite which he continued to perform his related duties, failing to disclose said situation and the existence of personal interests linked to his prospective activities in violation of article 19 paragraphs 1, 2 and 3 of the FCE (Conflicts of interest). By failing to place FIFA's interests first and abstain from doing anything which could be contrary to FIFA's interests, Mr Platini also violated his fiduciary duty to FIFA and breached article 15 of the FCE (Loyalty). In addition, Mr Platini failed to act with complete credibility and integrity, showing unawareness of the importance of his duties and concomitant obligations and responsibilities. His actions did not show commitment to an ethical attitude, failing to respect all applicable laws and regulations as well as FIFA's regulatory framework to the extent applicable to him and demonstrating an abusive execution of his position as Vice-President of FIFA and member of the FIFA Executive Committee, hence violating article 13 of the FCE (General rules of conduct) (FIFA, 2015b). Swiss authorities are conducting criminal investigations into these two men. Platini had hoped to run as a candidate to replace Blatter but the ban on him will halt these ambitions (BBC, 2015b). He also stepped down as the head of the European football association (UEFA) (BBC, 2015b).

Following the US indictment, Swiss authorities opened criminal investigations into irregularities in the bidding process of the 2018 World Cup, to be played in Russia, and the 2022 World Cup, to be played in Qatar. Germany's hosting of the 2006 World Cup is also under scrutiny over a large payment to FIFA. The criminal investigations into FIFA's corruption are ongoing and it is suspected that many more individuals and companies will be formally accused. Blatter's successor Gianni Infantino has allegedly violated FIFA's code of ethics when he gave advice on who should be elected as the new president of UEFA. It is believed that in May 2016, Infantino sent an 'advisor' to a meeting with the northern European football associations in Milan to tell them that Aleksander Ceferin should become the next president of UEFA (Feenstra & Misérus, 2016). A few days later, Sweden, Denmark, Norway and Finland announced their support for Ceferin. Infantino's integrity is being doubted as a result of accusations of unlawfully appointing and firing employees, the unauthorised use of private jets and declaring private expenses. Infantino has tried to expand his power as the head of world football (Feenstra & Misérus, 2016). A newspaper reported that he created a plan to remove Domenico Scala as the head of FIFA's audit and compliance committee, and considered the installation of Ceferin, a young lawyer who is close to Infantino, to be another step to increase his power (Feenstra & Misérus, 2016).

6.2.3 *Official Investigations*

According to the indictment (US District Court Eastern District of New York v. Webb *et al.*, 2015), the defendants and their co-conspirators are responsible for the corruption of the FIFA enterprise by engaging in various criminal activities, including fraud, bribery and money laundering, in pursuit of personal and commercial gain (US District Court Eastern District of New York v. Webb *et al.*, 2015: 29). The football officials are charged with conspiring to solicit and receive well over USD 150 million in bribes and kickbacks in exchange for their official support of the sports marketing executives who agreed to make the unlawful payments (US Department of Justice, 2015).

The defendants and their co-conspirators have been divided into three categories. The first category includes the football officials acting in a fiduciary capacity within FIFA and its associations. The second category includes the sports media and marketing company executives. The third category involves the trusted intermediaries who laundered illicit payments (businessmen, bankers and others) (US Department of Justice, 2015).

The following nine defendants are FIFA officials:

- Jeffrey Webb: FIFA vice president and executive committee member, CONCACAF president, Caribbean Football Union (CFU) executive committee member and Cayman Islands Football Association (CIFA) president (US District Court Eastern District of New York v. Webb *et al.*, 2015: 21)
- Eduardo Li: FIFA executive committee member-elect, CONCACAF executive committee member and Costa Rican soccer federation (FEDEFUT) president (18-19).
- Julio Rocha: FIFA development officer. Former Central American Football Union (UNCAF) president and Nicaraguan soccer federation (FENIFUT) president (20).
- Costas Takkas: attaché to the CONCACAF president. Former CIFA general secretary (20).

- Jack Warner: former FIFA vice president and executive committee member, CONCACAF president, CFU president and Trinidad and Tobago Football Federation (TTFF) special adviser (21).
- Eugenio Figueredo: FIFA vice president and executive committee member. Former CONMEBOL president and Uruguayan soccer federation (AUF) president (16-17).
- Rafael Esquivel: Current CONMEBOL executive committee member and Venezuelan soccer federation (FVF) president.
- José Maria Marin: member of the FIFA organising committee for the Olympic football tournaments. Former CBF president (19).
- Nicolás Leoz: former FIFA executive committee member and CONMEBOL president (18).
- Four of the defendants were sports marketing executives:
- Alejandro Burzaco: controlling principal of Torneos y Competencias S.A., a sports marketing business based in Argentina, and its affiliates (14-15).
- Aaron Davidson: president of Traffic Sports USA Inc (15-16).
- Hugo (Sr.) and Mariano Jinkis (Jr.): controlling principals of Full Play Group S.A., a sports marketing business based in Argentina, and its affiliates (17-18).
- One of the defendants was in the broadcasting business but allegedly served as an intermediary to facilitate illicit payments between sports marketing executives and soccer officials:
- José Margulies: controlling principal of Valente Corp. and Somerton Ltd. (19).
- The following individuals and corporations previously pleaded guilty under seal:
- Daryll Warner, son of defendant Jack Warner and a former FIFA development officer, waived indictment and pleaded guilty to a two-count information charging him with wire fraud and the structuring of financial transactions (dd. 15 July 2013) (US Department of Justice, 2015). Daryan Warner, also a son of defendant Jack Warner, waived indictment and pleaded guilty to a three-count information charging him with wire fraud conspiracy, money laundering conspiracy and the structuring of financial transactions. (25 October 2013) Daryan Warner forfeited over USD 1.1 million around the time of his plea and has agreed to pay a second forfeiture money judgment at the time of sentencing (US Department of Justice, 2015).
- Charles Blazer, the former CONCACAF secretary general and a former FIFA executive committee member, waived indictment and pleaded guilty to a 10-count information charging him with racketeering conspiracy, wire fraud conspiracy, money laundering conspiracy, income tax evasion and failure to file a Report of Foreign Bank and Financial Accounts. Blazer forfeited over USD 1.9 million at the time of

his plea and has agreed to pay a second amount to be determined at the time of sentencing (dd. 25 November 2013) (US Department of Justice, 2015).[2]

- José Hawilla, the owner and founder of the Traffic Group, the Brazilian sports marketing conglomerate, waived indictment and pleaded guilty to a four-count information charging him with racketeering conspiracy, wire fraud conspiracy, money laundering conspiracy and obstruction of justice. Hawilla also agreed to forfeit over USD 151 million, USD 25 million of which was paid at the time of his plea. (dd. 12 December 2014) (US Department of Justice, 2015)
- Corporations Traffic Sports USA Inc. and Traffic Sports International Inc. pleaded guilty to wire fraud conspiracy (dd. 14 May 2015)

The indicted and convicted individual defendants face maximum terms of imprisonment of 20 years for the RICO conspiracy, wire fraud conspiracy, wire fraud, money laundering conspiracy, money laundering and obstruction of justice charges (US Department of Justice, 2015). In November 2017, in total 23 former football administrators and marketing executives admitted guilt to crimes of financial corruption (Conn, 2017a).

At least 24 other individuals were referenced anonymously in the same indictment as unindicted co-conspirators. The defendants, together with these co-conspirators, conspired with one another to use their positions within the enterprise to engage in schemes involving the solicitation, offer, acceptance, payment and receipt of undisclosed and illegal payments, bribes and kickbacks. Although they also helped pursue the principal purpose of the enterprise, the defendants and their co-conspirators corrupted the enterprise by engaging in various criminal activities, including fraud, bribery and money laundering, in pursuit of personal and commercial gain. Additionally, the defendants "participated in the corruption of the enterprise by conspiring with and aiding and abetting their co-conspirators in the abuse of their positions of trust and the violation of their fiduciary duties." (US District Court Eastern District of New York v. Webb *et al.*, 2015: 28-29).

The indictment makes mention of the damage inflicted by the defendants and co-conspirators. By conspiring to enrich themselves by means of bribes and kickbacks related to media and marketing rights, they firstly deprived FIFA and all its related associations and teams and development programmes from important financial support and the full value of the media and marketing rights (US District Court Eastern District of New York v. Webb *et al.*, 2015: 30). Secondly, the schemes distorted the market for commercial rights in the football branch to the detriment of honest sports marketing companies competing for these rights. As such the conduct has far-reaching anti-competitive effects (US District Court Eastern District of New York v. Webb *et al.*, 2015: 30). The indictment

2 In July 2017 Charles Blazer passed away. Longman, R. & Ruiz, R.R. (2017). Chuck Blazer, Central Figure in FIFA Scandal, Dies at 72. *The New York Times*, 13 July 2017 Available from: https://www.nytimes.com/2017/07/13/sports/soccer/chuck-blazer-central-figure-in-fifa-scandal-dies-at-72.html (Accessed 25/10/17).

continues by referring how the "aggregate" deprived FIFA, the confederations and their constituent organisations of their right to the honest and loyal services of the football officials involved. This inflicted "significant reputational harm on the victimised institutions, damaging their prospects for attracting conscientious members and leaders." (US District Court Eastern District of New York v. Webb *et al.*, 2015: 31).

In chapter V of the indictment, the overview of the Racketeering Conspiracy is described. Here one can read that the federal grand jury alleged that over a period of 25 years, the defendants and their co-conspirators obtained positions of power and influence within the football world. During this time and sometimes with the help of the defendants and their co-conspirators, "a network of marketing companies developed to capitalise in the expanding media market for the sport, particularly in the United States." (US District Court Eastern District of New York v. Webb *et al.*, 2015: 31). The organisations in charge of promoting and governing football were formed over time but "became increasingly intertwined with one another and with the sports marketing companies that enabled them to generate unprecedented profits through the sale of media rights to soccer matches. The corruption of the enterprise arose and flourished in this context." (US District Court Eastern District of New York v. Webb *et al.*, 2015: 31). The corruption is referred to as "endemic" (US District Court Eastern District of New York v. Webb *et al.*, 2015: 32). The individuals rose to power and enriched themselves through these fraudulent practices. In some cases, and after the practices were exposed, they were expelled or forced to resign (US District Court Eastern District of New York v. Webb *et al.*, 2015: 32). When the scandal emerged, other defendants and co-conspirators were appointed, promising reform. Instead of sorting out the wrongdoing, they quickly engaged in the same unlawful practices as their predecessors (US District Court Eastern District of New York v. Webb *et al.*, 2015: 32).

The Jury's Verdict

More than 20 defendants had pleaded guilty as a result of the criminal investigations. Three officials fought against the accusations, two of whom have now been convicted (Ruiz, 2017). On 22 December 2017, the jury in federal court in Brooklyn convicted the former top football official of Paraguay, Juan Ángel Napout, who was accused of accepting $10.5 million in bribes since 2010.[3] He was found guilty on three counts, of racketeering conspiracy and wire fraud conspiracy. He was found not guilty on two counts of money laundering conspiracy. The former top football official of Brazil, José Maria Marin, was accused of accepting $6.55 million. Marin was a member of the FIFA organising committee for the Olympic football tournaments and former CBF president. He was found guilty on six counts, of racketeering conspiracy, wire fraud and money laundering conspiracy. He was found not guilty on one count of money laundering conspiracy (Ruiz,

3 Mr Napout was not listed on the first indictment of 2015.

2017). The jury considers both men to have played a role in a web of corruption that extended across several continents and ensnared dozens of men who control the world's most popular sport (Ruiz, 2017).

FIFA responded to the verdict by asserting that it is the main victim in the case and restating the organisation's intention to reclaim tens of millions of dollars that the United States has ordered the convicted criminals to forfeit. Its statement said:

"FIFA strongly supports and encourages the U.S. authorities' efforts to hold accountable those individuals who abused their positions and corrupted international football for their own personal benefit. (…) As the jury has found a number of defendants guilty of the charged crimes, FIFA will now take all necessary steps to seek restitution and recover any losses caused by their misconduct." (AP News, 2017).

6.2.4 *Other Research*

The 2015 US prosecution announcement was no surprise, because for years NGOs and investigate journalists had reported on the corrupt practices of FIFA. There are so many individuals and companies involved in the FIFA corruption scandal that it is impossible to name them all. Besides key figures from FIFA such as Blatter and UEFA's Platini, many executives from national football bodies, businessmen, politicians and former football players are believed to be involved.

Even when the corruption accusation unfolded, Blatter was reappointed as FIFA's President in May 2015. According to the *Washington Post* this was not a surprise (Thahoor, 2015). Their journalists point out the fact that for years Blatter has secured his power through strong backing from associations in Asia, Africa and Latin America. In the election for FIFA's presidency, each of FIFA's members gets an equal vote – whether you're a small island or territory or a large country such as Brazil or France. Blatter has strategically favoured the non-Western part of his administration, by bringing the World Cup to Asia in 2002, and then to Africa in 2010 (Thahoor, 2015). He made favouring the norm and "placed himself at the top of networks of patronage that run down into the local levels of the sport in the developing world, where many countries need FIFA's funds to develop soccer at the grass roots. (Thahoor, 2015).

British investigative journalist Andrew Jennings writes articles and books on power relations in world sport. According to Jennings ever since he started writing about FIFA President Sepp Blatter paying himself secret bonuses, FIFA's agents reacted by stealing his phone records and intimidating people who FIFA believed to be Jennings informants. Also, FIFA used its funds to hire lawyers to file law suits against Jennings, but they never sued him (Jennings, 2011: 389-390; BBC Panorama, 2010). Jennings has investigated FIFA for more than fifteen years. He describes how Blatter recruited loyalists by means of money and full VIP treatment (2011: 395). Critics were banned, intimidated and threatened by all means available. Jennings and other journalists have often contacted FIFA to provide evidence of corrupt practices, for instance the evidence proving Jack Warner's black market ticket scheme, but FIFA and/or Blatter took no action. Instead they reacted in defence (BBC Panorama, 2010). According to Jennings, most FIFA officials started to believe that their practice was a privilege given by God, as were the business class chairs and the company of presidents, prime ministers and royals (2011: 15). In the meantime, children still have to play football without shoes, showering or decent equipment. The money is gone to be laundered in the Cayman Island (2011: 17). Jennings explained that serious intimidation took place in the form of DDOS attacks which paralysed Internet traffic in the UK (2011: 18-19).

According to Jennings, the FIFA network has all the characteristics of a mafia. Blatter's higher management shows all elements of a crime syndicate: a strong remorseless leader, a hierarchy, a strong code for members' behaviour and, as a main goal, power and profit by means of illegal and immoral activities (2011: 308). There was never criticism of those who did wrong. Weber was still welcome at a conference even though he gave bribes (2011: 308). When Valcke was 'fired', he went to work for Teixeira in Brazil, selecting cities and stadiums, and did business with politicians and business partners regarding World Cup contracts (2011: 308-309). Thereafter, Valcke went to Zurich and was promoted as secretary general of FIFA. After all the evidence of corruption and criticism by fans, politicians and reporters, Blatter remained inviolable (2011: 310). He governed six families across the globe; these are continental bonds. He is favoured by many and used the 209 national bonds so they voted for him. The interesting question is why brands such as Coca-Cola never reacted to the corruption allegations, while their money had gone into the pockets of FIFA officials (2011: 307-308).

David Conn (*The Guardian*) has spent years writing about corruption at FIFA and in 2017 he interviewed Blatter. In this interview, Blatter blames Platini (Conn, 2017b). According to Blatter, Platini took away the crucial votes from the US after he met the then French president Nicolas Sarkozy, and the emir of Qatar, for, as Blatter saw it, the disastrous vote to take the World Cup to Qatar (Conn, 2017b). Blatter argues that it is a distraction to look for bribery when it comes to World Cup votes: "The World Cups are not bought; they are influenced by political pressure (…) Sarkozy changed everything. He asked Platini to look for the interests of France and vote with his colleagues." (Conn, 2017b). Blatter accepts that the US' investigators appeared to have found major corruption, mentioning kickbacks on Copa America TV deals, but he argues that this has nothing to do with FIFA itself. On the contrary, it involved the confederations, over which he had no control. Blatter reacts to the US indictment by saying, "So why the hell then should the FIFA president bear all the charges, the responsibility and the blame?" (Conn, 2017b).

6.3 CASE STUDY 2 UNITED KINGDOM: NOW INTERNATIONAL PHONE-HACKING SCANDAL

6.3.1 *Introduction*

This second case concerns a phone-hacking scandal in which employees of the *News of the World* newspaper engaged in phone hacking, police bribery and exercising improper influence in the pursuit of stories. Three major operations investigated separate aspects of the scandal. In 2011, the UK's Metropolitan Police launched Operation Weeting, an investigation into the phone hacking by employees of the *News of the World* (NoW) newspaper. Its main focus was on the interception of mobile telephone messages. The investigation widened to include police bribery and exercising improper influence in the pursuit of stories (Crown Prosecution Service 2015). Operation Weeting was closely linked to Operation Elveden in which inappropriate payments by the press to police officers, and others holding public office or position, were investigated. Operation Tuleta investigated various forms of computer hacking on behalf of journalists (The Right Honourable Lord Justice Leveson, 2012: 10). In July 2011, the Prime Minister announced a two-part inquiry by the Leveson Committee, investigating the role of the press and police in the phone-hacking scandal (Leveson Inquiry, n.d.). This case concerned the connections between senior politicians, London's Metropolitan Police Service and media tycoons. Through these connections, power and influence were exchanged in the interests of the key figures involved, thereby sacrificing the rights of ordinary citizens.

6.3.2 *Case Presentation*

The Leveson Inquiry Part 1 focused on the culture and ethics of the British newspaper industry and its connections with London's Metropolitan Police Service (MPS) and politicians. The Inquiry highlighted the fact that "the owners of newspapers – not inaccurately described as 'press barons' – exercised very real influence on public affairs" (Leveson Inquiry, 2012: 6). Part 2 of the Inquiry will examine the unlawful and improper conduct of the actors involved (including corruption and complicity in misconduct, with the question "who did what to whom") but cannot commence until the current police investigations and any subsequent criminal proceedings have been completed (The Right Honourable Lord Justice Leveson, 2012: 10).

The Leveson Inquiry Part 1[4] examined the culture, practices and ethics of the press and, in particular, the connections of the press with the public, London's Metropolitan

4 Part 2 of the Inquiry will examine the unlawful and improper conduct of the actors involved (including corruption and complicity in misconduct) but cannot commence until the current police investigations and any subsequent criminal proceedings have been completed.

Police Service and politicians. Many believed that, through these connections, power and influence were exchanged in the interests of the key figures involved, thereby sacrificing the rights of ordinary citizens. The Leveson Inquiry published Part I of its Inquiry in November 2012. This part already consisted of approximately 2000 pages (The Right Honourable Lord Justice Leveson, 2012). The Terms of Reference of the Inquiry Part 1 were:

> "1. To inquire into the culture, practices, and ethics of the press, including:
> 1. contacts and the relationships between national newspapers and politicians, and the conduct of each;
> 2. contacts and the relationship between the press and the police, and the conduct of each;
> 3. the extent to which the current policy and regulatory framework has failed including in relation to data protection; and
> 4. the extent to which there was a failure to act on previous warnings about media misconduct.
>
> 2. To make recommendations:
> 1. for a new more effective policy and regulatory regime which supports the integrity and freedom of the press, the plurality of the media, and its independence, including from Government, while encouraging the highest ethical and professional standards;
> 2. for how future concerns about press behaviour, media policy, regulation and cross-media ownership should be dealt with by all the relevant authorities, including Parliament, Government, the prosecuting authorities and the police;
> 3. the future conduct of relations between politicians and the press; and
> 4. the future conduct of relations between the police and the press." (Honourable Lord Justice Leveson, 2012: 4-5).

According to Leveson, the problem revolves around one principal public concern and he puts it simply as "that the relationship has become 'too close'." Although the term 'too close' is not further specified, the question has boiled down to this issue: have there been unaccountable exchanges in influence and favours, trading political support and advancement (or the avoidance of political damage) for policies which favour the commercial interests of the press, or the abstention from policies which would disfavour those interests? Leveson focussed on whether there are aspects of the close relationship between politicians and the press which should just be less close, or which the public should be able to know more about so that they can make their own minds up about it. (Honourable Lord Justice Leveson, 2012: 1429).

The Report refers to the relationship between the press and the police. And the allegations are "that the two have become far too close, involving the payment of money or the provision of other favours for inside information, prior notice of newsworthy incidents or participation in high profile operations." Additionally it covered "the cross fertilisation of employment with retired senior police officers being engaged as newspaper columnists and journalists being employed in PR departments or as PR advisers by police services." (Honourable Lord Justice Leveson, 2012: 11). Part 1 also dealt with the relationship between the press and politicians including, the public perception that " in return for political support, politicians have been too ready to allow undue influence to be exercised in relation to policy and that, in any event, the relationship between the two has not been transparent." (Honourable Lord Justice Leveson, 2012: 11).

The Leveson Report part 1 does briefly refer to bribery and corruption in relation to Operation Elveden (Honourable Lord Justice Leveson, 2012: 475). "As of 31 October 2012 (…) a total of 52 individuals had been arrested by officers working on Operation Elveden; of these, 27 were current and former journalists (including journalists from The Sun; the Daily Mirror and its sister paper, the Sunday Mirror; and the Daily Star Sunday)." (Honourable Lord Justice Leveson, 2012: 475). It stresses that these arrests are not direct proof that an "unlawful and unethical practice existed within the press of inducing, or seeking to induce, public officials to disclose confidential information about individuals or organisations; given the test required to justify arrest in the first place, it merely raises reasonable grounds to suspect that various offences may have been committed." (Honourable Lord Justice Leveson, 2012: 475). The ongoing criminal investigation hampered the ability of the Inquiry to explore the available evidence. The Inquiry heard of all sorts of abuse by the media, such as harassment, intrusion into grief or shock and deliberately reporting inaccurate information. However, most damage was done through the phone hacking, which led to the situation in which details of the private lives of many individuals, and of their most trusted confidants and friends, became the subject of articles in the press (Honourable Lord Justice Leveson, 2012: 484).

Some of the practices of NoW are presented in Chapter 4 of the Leveson Report Part 1. Robert Jay QC, the leading counsel in the Leveson Inquiry, who cross-examined David Cameron and Rupert Murdoch, said in opening the Inquiry:

> "In most institutions, cultural problems of this nature will usually emanate from high up within the organisation, but this will not always be the case. They will not always be the product of a deliberate policy decision made by those with power within the organisation to make them. Sometimes the existence of a culture derives from the operation of more subtle and complex forces, from historical trends, from what is condoned and not stamped upon, leading to insidious evolution and perpetuation, from complacency leading to

arrogance and purblindness [sic]. There is clearly a range of possibilities." (Honourable Lord Justice Leveson, 2012: 493).

One driving force which determined the practice of the NoW was the strong focus on circulation. Many of the former employees of the newspaper voiced that the newsroom at NoW was a high-pressure environment and that reporters were under pressure to deliver stories, preferably exclusive ones. Most evidence points in the direction of a pressure on staff to use all means possible, whether or not they were ethical or legal, to get a story (Honourable Lord Justice Leveson, 2012: 504). Also, witnesses described a culture of bullying. In a previous dismissal case concerning an employee of the NoW, the Employment Tribunal hearing found that then editor of the NoW, Andy Coulson, had "presided over a culture of bullying" as well as specifying particular instances of behaviour by the editor that it considered to constitute bullying." (Honourable Lord Justice Leveson, 2012: 498). The NoW's approach to discipline was soft. Former editor Mr Myler (2007-2011) could only recall one written reprimand to a member of staff who committed breaches of the Editors' Code (Honourable Lord Justice Leveson, 2012: 502-504). The Leveson Report states that it identified that the culture, practices and ethics of the press in a broader sense had a single focus on legal risk and not on ethical risk and the rights of the individuals (Honourable Lord Justice Leveson, 2012: 509). Mr Chapman, the Company Secretary, told the Inquiry that his compliance function "would have related to the commercial side of the business". His responsibility was limited to commercial and business support functions and did not include editorial functions. Mr Chapman felt that responsibility for compliance on the editorial side of the business would lie with the editorial legal team; in other words, with Mr Crone, who was the Legal Affairs manager of News International. Mr Crone claimed that ethical compliance might be a matter for Mr Chapman, the head of corporate and legal affairs at News International, when he became aware of serious ethical and legal wrongdoings. For his part, Mr Myler accepted ultimate responsibility for governance at the NoW, but said that he sought to instil "a culture of individual and collective responsibility for ensuring compliance with the PCC code and the law." (Honourable Lord Justice Leveson, 2012: 529-530). The Leveson Report found that:

> "It is at least possible that this systematic failure to hold anyone to account for breaches of the Code might have led to a sense among journalists at the NoW, that compliance was not, in fact, particularly highly rated and that breaches of the Code would go unpunished. If breaches of the Code lead to more, or better, stories, then systematic failure to penalise anyone for breaching the Code could be seen as indirect encouragement to do so. The fact that Mr Goodman (the NoW's royal editor) was dismissed does at least suggest that the company was aware that it needed to appear to the outside world as though it took criminal activity seriously. The terms on which he parted from the company, however,

> and the discussions that preceded his departure, suggest that this was not altogether the case. The persistent failure of the company to properly investigate Mr Goodman's allegations that methods of unlawful interception were both widely in use and approved by management within the organisation was a significant failure of governance." (Honourable Lord Justice Leveson, 2012: 536).

The report found that the practices of journalists in relation to expenses were fraudulent and illegal. Outrageous expense claims were not debated but laughed at. They were justified by reference to the fact that it was not the taxpayer who paid for them and after all the tasks performed were sometimes impossible and a heavy burden (Honourable Lord Justice Leveson, 2012: 534-535). Given the police investigations into bribery of police and public officials, the report did not go into detail on any specific corruption allegations. However, it concluded "that there is, at least, a real possibility that there was a culture of payments at the NoW for information of the type discussed, facilitated or overlooked by management control of financial authorisations." (Honourable Lord Justice Leveson, 2012: 535).

The report stated that, based on the evidence which has emerged from the prosecution of Mr Goodman and others, the admissions made by News International in the context of civil claims founded upon allegations of phone hacking and what the Inquiry has been told by former employees, there is clear evidence that voicemail interception occurred at NoW from approximately 2000 until 2009. It is also clear that the misconduct of phone hacking was committed by several journalists. It describes the practice of voicemail interception within parts of the NoW as cultural (Honourable Lord Justice Leveson, 2012: 611). According to Leveson, it is "striking and of serious concern that despite that knowledge and the rumours circulating through Fleet Street, nothing public was said or done about this issue beyond a series of 'in-jokes' at award ceremonies and unguarded references in memoires." (Honourable Lord Justice Leveson, 2012: 619). He continues that after the first convictions proved that phone hacking had occurred, "minimal steps were taken within the industry to identify whether phone hacking had occurred elsewhere or to investigate the extent of these practices." (Honourable Lord Justice Leveson, 2012: 619).

The Leveson Inquiry also investigated the way the press would deal with criticism. According to the report, the Phone Hacking Scandal as a whole revealed that large parts of the press showed a complete unwillingness to engage with those who voiced criticism by pointing out unethical practices. To the contrary, much of the press subjected them to intense scrutiny, not rarely consisting of intimidation (Honourable Lord Justice Leveson, 2012: 704). This involved the intimidation of lawyers, MPs and those investigating the conduct by the press.

6.3.2.1 The Relationship Between the Press and the Police

In an earlier report entitled *The Ethical Issues Arising from the Relationship Between Police and Media*, Mrs Filkin said that "it is clear both from what appears in the media, and from what I have been told, that there is contact - which is neither recorded nor permitted - between the media and police officers and staff, at all levels. This results in improper disclosure of information which is damaging to the public, the Metropolitan Police Service (MPS) and to the policing of London." (Honourable Lord Justice Leveson, 2012: 808).

The leading counsel in the Leveson Inquiry, Robert Jay QC, started the opening of Module Two of the Inquiry as follows:

> "Public concern hereabouts may be expressed in just one sentence: the relationship between the police and the media, and News International in particular, was, at best, inappropriately close and if not actually corrupt, very close to it. Furthermore, the nature of this relationship may explain why the police did not properly investigate phone hacking in 2006 and subsequently in 2009 and 2010, preferring to finesse the issue on these later occasions by less than frank public statements." (Honourable Lord Justice Leveson, 2012: 734).

He described some of the inherent risks engaged when individual members of two powerful institutions or groups of institutions, in this case the press and the police, come into contact

> "... As so often happens in human affairs, the difference between healthy and dysfunctional behaviours does not have to be vast. By this, I mean at least two things: first, that it does not necessarily take many rotten apples to undermine the whole body politic, and secondly, that very often it does not take many adjustments in behaviours, objectively measured, to turn what is good into what is bad and vice versa. More precisely, the potential for abuse on both sides of this bilateral equation is significant, leading to the risk, if not the reality, of unhealthy, over-cosy and overly close relations between the two ... Ultimately, the vice here is lack of democratic accountability and the perception, if not the reality, of personal gain. The noun "gain" in this context needs, of course, to be broadly interpreted and should certainly be apt to accommodate the enhancement of an individual's professional or personal profile." (Honourable Lord Justice Leveson, 2012: 851).

Lord Blair expressed a similar view: "I believe that where that problem may have become significant is that a very small number of relatively senior officers increasingly became too close to journalists, not I believe for financial gain but for the enhancement of their reputation and for the sheer enjoyment of being in a position to share and divulge confidences. It is a siren song …" (Honourable Lord Justice Leveson, 2012: 851).

Although some police officers and journalists described that only "work-related professional contacts" had derived from their networking activities, others clearly thought that close friendships had derived from the extensive networking (Honourable Lord Justice Leveson, 2012: 856). For example, Michael Sullivan, crime reporter for *The Sun*, suggested that he considered himself to have been part of Mr Fedorcio's (MPS) 'inner circle' of favoured journalists.

> "I think Dick, if I can call him that since he's a friend as well as professional contact, over a period of time you get to know someone well and therefore you would normally expect to perhaps have more contact with that person, not just Dick, but with plenty of others, rather than someone arriving – say, for instance, another newspaper has appointed a crime reporter (…) it does take a number of years to build up a good working relationship, so I think that would – "favour" is perhaps not totally applicable but perhaps I would regard myself as part of a group of … long serving crime reporters who would have been in a circle of trusted journalists for Mr Fedorcio to talk to." (Honourable Lord Justice Leveson, 2012: 856).

This notion of a favoured grouping or 'inner circle' of journalists appears to be recognised by others of the press reporting on the MPS at the time. Former *Guardian* crime reporter Sandra Laville stated:

> "I think there was something of an inner circle that was created, but to my perception that was more about the length of time certain individuals had been covering crime and they had built relationships over many years; in fact, you know, seven or eight years, and they knew each other very well (…). It's our job to go to the source of the information and find it out … it never struck me as anything dodgy, it just struck me as these people were good at their jobs and, you know, they'd managed to make a very good contact over many years." (Honourable Lord Justice Leveson, 2012: 857).

The Leveson Report uses the terms "closeness" and "cosiness" to describe the nature of the relationship between some of the MPS' senior officers and NoW staff (Honourable Lord Justice Leveson, 2012: 862-863). One relationship which stands out from the others is that of Dick Fedorcio (chief communications at the MPS) and Neil Wallis (ex NoW deputy editor and later director of a PR firm). This long standing friendship is believed to have influenced the appointment process. However, Leveson did not find any evidence "to suggest that the process itself, once instituted, was not conducted fairly, but whatever its adequacy, the fact remained that there was an appearance of bias, particularly given that Mr Wallis had already completed work for the MPS." (Honourable Lord Justice Leveson, 2012: 886). Mr Wallis's company, Chamy Media, was paid £24,000 by the MPS for PR advice between October 2009 and September 2010.

On 27 January 2009 Mr Wallis, then in the position of Executive Editor of the NoW, sent an email to Mr Yates with the CV of his daughter attached. Mr Wallis explained that he had sent the email because he did not know the head of HR at the MPS and said that asking a friend or a contact to pass on a CV of your child was "the way of the world", noting that on occasions he had given work experience to the children of journalists from other newspapers. (Honourable Lord Justice Leveson, 2012: 886). The Leveson Report concluded that, "Rightly or wrongly, the practice of referring friends and relatives for appointment on a temporary or permanent basis within the MPS would appear to be fairly commonplace although there may be an important difference between paid (even temporary) employment and unpaid work experience (…)."(Honourable Lord Justice Leveson, 2012: 886-887). Mr Tiplady sent an email to Mr. Yates stating:

> "Bit of advice plse [sic] – the attached CV belongs to the daughter of Neil Wallis, the Dep Editor of the NoW. You probably know that Neil has been a great friend (and occasional critic) of the Met in past years and has been a close advisor to Paul [Stephenson] on stuff/tactics in respect of the new Commissionership. Mr Wallis' daughter is looking for a change of direction and something steady – a bit along the lines of the work that my son did recently – although she looks eminently qualified to do something more demanding. I have met her on several occasions and although would not claim to know her well she is clearly bright, very personable and presents well. Clearly there is a vetting issue which would prob [sic] have to go through normal channels unless you advise me otherwise. Be grateful for an early response so I can manage expectations with both Neil and his daughter." (Honourable Lord Justice Leveson, 2012: 887).

The IPCC and the Leveson Report stressed there was no evidence found that Mr Yates directly influenced the appointment of Ms Wallis and concluded that there was no evidence that his actions and involvement amounted to misconduct. However, both concluded that there is an appearance of favouritism. Yates and Tiplady should have foreseen that any junior staff member would see this as a direct instruction and Yates' reference to his role as a "post box" should be read along with the reference to the friendship with the other key figures (Honourable Lord Justice Leveson, 2012: 888).

In the Leveson Report, Chapter 3 of part G, paragraph 5 is named 'The problems of friendship". Paragraph 7 deals with the corruption issue. Lord Stevens, who had been appointed Deputy Commissioner of the MPS in 1998, explained that the MPS, given its size, had always been vulnerable to the bribing of personnel by the media and suggested that fighting this form of corruption was a continual battle (Honourable Lord Justice Leveson, 2012: 933). It is believed that the corruption in Police Service relationships was not endemic. However, her Majesty's Chief Inspector of Constabulary on police integrity (HMIC) identified as specific weaknesses the "absence of clear boundaries" regarding outside relationships (Honourable Lord Justice Leveson, 2012: 939). The report refers to an earlier review of undue influence, inappropriate contractual arrangements and other abuses of power in police relationships with the media and other parties, which had been conducted a year before by HMIC at the request of the Home Secretary (Honourable Lord Justice Leveson, 2012: 950). The report '*Without Fear or Favour – a review of police relationships*' distinguished the "frank corruption", money passing hands, which was relatively rare, from that of "soft corruption", doing favours, and treating something or someone much more favourably, which was a bigger concern (Honourable Lord Justice Leveson, 2012: 953). The recommendations given in this report come down to "a significant revision in the way the relationship operates." (Honourable Lord Justice Leveson, 2012: 956). It continues to stress that "the relationship between the police force and the media should foremost serve a legitimate policing purpose (...) and it should be more than relationship-building and relate to the core values and standards of policing." (Honourable Lord Justice Leveson, 2012: 956). It also pays attention to "the manner in which the relationship is conducted. In essence, I think it should operate without favouritism and with integrity, and I say this is about integrity of the mission policing. So that kind of questions exclusive contact. It doesn't eliminate it, but it questions it." (Honourable Lord Justice Leveson, 2012: 956-957). The police have to avoid a conflict of interest at all times, particularly because of their confidentiality obligations (Honourable Lord Justice Leveson, 2012: 957).

Mrs Filkin was appointed to conduct a review of the relationship between the MPS and the media after the phone-hacking scandal was disclosed in July 2011, but concerns were raised about the MPS had thoroughly investigated the matter, now that it had become known that the practice had been more widespread than initially perceived (Honourable Lord Justice Leveson, 2012: 960).

> "Mrs Filkin has described the key problems around the perception of leaks from the MPS to the media, interlinked with the 'cosy' relationships which have developed between the two. She concluded that this disclosure of information; the context of the relationship which fosters this disclosure; and the extent to which these relationships are regulated, should be addressed by the MPS in order to ensure complete oversight of an ethical practice, which would restore any damage to the public trust." (Honourable Lord Justice Leveson, 2012: 962).

6.3.2.2 The Relationship Between the Media and Politicians

After having examined the relationship between the MPS and the media, the Leveson Report examined the relationship between national newspapers and politicians and the conduct of each (Honourable Lord Justice Leveson, 2012: 1117). The Report considers the "closeness which may have, or appear to have, impacted on the willingness or ability of the politicians to decide matters of public policy about the media, and specifically of policy on press standards, fairly and impartially in the public interest." (Honourable Lord Justice Leveson, 2012: 1118). The Inquiry began its focus on the relationship with evidence about the acquisition in 1981 by Rupert Murdoch of *The Times* and *The Sunday Times* and it has reflected on events from then to the present (Honourable Lord Justice Leveson, 2012: 1118). According to Leveson, "a clear pattern emerged about the relationship between the press and the politicians in recent years at the most senior levels of influence." (Honourable Lord Justice Leveson, 2012: 1119). There is no evidence of explicit, covert deals between senior politicians and newspaper proprietors or editors. However, the powerful relationships "are more subtle than that, the extent to which interests coincide or diverge is more complicated, and the dialogue more sophisticated. But there can be no doubt that within these relationships, some of them having the quality of personal friendships (and some of active hostility), there have been exchanges of influence on matters of public policy which have given rise to legitimate questions about the trust and confidence the public can have that they have been conducted scrupulously in the public interest." (Honourable Lord Justice Leveson, 2012: 1119).

The Report provides an overview of the last five prime ministers and characterisations of their relationships with the newspapers. Leveson concludes that the close relationships are "not unique to any individual politician or any one political party. It has affected previous administrations, both in office and whilst seeking power." (Honourable Lord Justice Leveson, 2012: 1232). The evidence does not establish anything resembling a 'deal' whereby News International's support was traded for the expectation of policy favours (Honourable Lord Justice Leveson, 2012: 1232). Former Prime Minister Cameron had close contact with the media throughout his career, and in his private life, which led to many friendships with people in the media. When asked by Leveson to compile a list "of those media figures with whom he had had contact both as Leader of the Opposition and in Government, there are some whom he had met so often that it was impractical to list contacts individually. Instead he identified them." (Honourable Lord Justice Leveson, 2012: 1214). "The number of such friends demonstrates that Mrs Brooks was not alone amongst media figures with whom Mr Cameron socialised." (Honourable Lord Justice Leveson, 2012: 1214). Leveson: "It is about the way in which what the politicians have described as 'overly close' relationships can impact on policy and the needs of transparency to ensure that this becomes apparent." (Honourable Lord Justice Leveson, 2012: 1214). "As Prime Minister, he took deliberate steps to reduce his personal contact with the media but, at a different level, the approach of maintaining wide and deep contacts with the media remained and was continued in Government." (Honourable Lord Justice Leveson, 2012: 1231). "Both Mr Cameron and Mr Osborne have, with hindsight, expressed regret at their decision to appoint Mr Coulson to that post. Mr Coulson's own assurances played an important part in that decision." (Honourable Lord Justice Leveson, 2012: 1231).

> "The results of Mr Cameron's media strategy in Opposition were successful in winning the support of the centre right press and the endorsement of News International. The circumstances in which Rupert Murdoch and his close advisers decided to endorse Mr Cameron are complex. Mr Cameron went to great lengths to secure meetings face-to-face with Mr Murdoch and other News International executives and editors. The benefits of this may have played some part in the outcome but should not be overestimated. As Mr Osborne fairly observed, the Conservatives were not the only politicians dining with the Murdochs and their executives. There were many factors other than personal contact." (Honourable Lord Justice Leveson, 2012: 1232).

Leveson does not explain what these factors are.

The Leveson Report provides an insight into the involvement of the press to influence the political agenda related to press standards and privacy matters (Honourable Lord Justice Leveson, 2012: 1246-1270). "Not merely did representatives of the press make strong public representations against the introduction of a custodial sentence, but a number of significant meetings took place behind the scenes. The issue was clearly one which the press had taken to heart, and the nature of the relationship of a number of key players with politicians was such that ready access was available." (Honourable Lord Justice Leveson, 2012: 1273). The report also mentions how key figures from the press influenced decisions on acquisitions such as that of the iconic titles *The Times* and *The Sunday Times* by Rupert Murdoch's News International (Honourable Lord Justice Leveson, 2012: 1233-1245). One paragraph discusses in detail the lobbying behind the scenes to influence decision making concerning the British Sky Broadcasting (BskyB) bid in 2010.[5] Culture Secretary Jeremy Hunt had invited interested parties to make their submissions. In addition to the responses to this invitation, a remarkable amount of additional unsolicited communication took place (Honourable Lord Justice Leveson, 2012: 1373; Rayner, 2012). The Alliance had its solicitors and public relations advisers actively trying to influence the Secretary of State through correspondence by means of email and formal correspondence. However, this communication paled in comparison with the behind-

5 This full takeover would have allowed integration with other entities such as Sky Deutschland and Sky Italia. News Corporation had 39 per cent of the shares at the time. Info available from: Pratley, N. (2011). News Corp needs all of BSkyB. Available from: https://www.theguardian.com/business/2011/jul/11/view-point-news-corp-bskyb-takeover (Accessed 04/10/16).

the-scenes contact between Mr Fredric Michel, the News Corp head of public affairs, and people at the Department for Culture Media & Sport (DCMS) such as Hunt's special adviser Adam Smith (Honourable Lord Justice Leveson, 2012: 1373; Rayner 2012). It was Mr Michel who had a great deal of contact with Mr Smith via email, text and telephone (Honourable Lord Justice Leveson, 2012: 1373, 1376). The Leveson Report reads:

> "It is conspicuous that all of the exchanges during this period were initiated by Mr Michel. All were brief. The bid was barely touched upon and there was no substantive communication either about the substance of the bid or the process. It was all about making the connection at the personal level. Mr Hunt was careful to put off any social arrangements until after the bid. His responses were consistent with the general approach which he took to those in the media industry with whom he came into contact during the bid." (Honourable Lord Justice Leveson, 2012: 1378).

Mr Smith was usually formal and brief in the way he replied, but there were times when Mr Smith succumbed to Mr Michel's tactics and appeared to have been responsive to these tactics. "On one occasion he found himself joking with Mr Michel about an opponent of the bid. On another, he joined in criticism of Ofcom. He passed on information about the progress of the bid that would have been more properly communicated in a much more formal manner. He did not make formal notes of the communications." (Honourable Lord Justice Leveson, 2012: 1393).

The startling opening to Mr Michel's email report of a conversation with Mr Smith to James Murdoch dated 24 January 2011 and time-stamped at 15:21 hrs reads: "Managed to get some infos on the plans for tomorrow [although absolutely illegal..>!]" (second brackets original). The substance of the report concerned an early indication in outline of what was to happen the following day when Mr Hunt announced that he was minded to refer the bid but was going to take advice on News Corp's UIL. "In fact communicating this information was not, in itself, illegal but the report does, put at its lowest, convey a sense that information was surreptitiously being provided." (Honourable Lord Justice Leveson, 2012: 1395).

Leveson considers that at a certain stage communications were unacceptable in the context of Mr Smith's principal making a quasi-judicial decision (Honourable Lord Justice Leveson, 2012: 1396). Mr Smith explained that he did not call a halt to the exchanges, because he felt that it was his job to remain as the point of contact (Honourable Lord Justice Leveson, 2012: 1396). Leveson concludes by pointing out the fact that in any judicial review of case, the risk of judicial bias would not have been discovered because there was great transparency in the way formal documents were exchanged and documented. The main concern, according to Leveson, is the hidden problem of voluminous "private" (unrecorded) communications by text and email (Honourable Lord Justice Leveson, 2012: 1405). The risk of bias is created by communication which is informal and unrecorded, and which contains some mixture of the personal, the political or the presentational (Honourable Lord Justice Leveson, 2012: 1405). Mr Michel's advice to his principal not to meet with the decision-maker on the grounds of counter-productivity, but advising in terms that he "could have a chat with him on his mobile which is completely fine and I will liaise with his team privately as well" is given by Leveson as an example:

> "This example in microcosm of a practice where the informal, 'off record' and 'personal' is seen as an obvious and effective means of conducting lobbying on matters of media policy is symptomatic of a problem evidenced more widely to the Inquiry; the fact that such practices have a side-effect (I say no more than that) of placing the conduct of public policy issues outside the mechanisms of transparency, accountability and public record cannot but give rise to perceptions and questions which are corrosive to public trust and confidence. I underline this point because it is in this respect that I consider the conduct of the BSkyB bid to have important characteristics, as part of a much wider issue about the relationship between the politicians and the press, which I consider in some detail in the conclusions I draw at the end of this Part of the Report." (Honourable Lord Justice Leveson, 2012: 1405).

The Lord Justice summarises the problem at stake by citing the former Prime Minister: "we all got too close to News International" (Honourable Lord Justice Leveson, 2012: 1430). Leveson confirms in his findings that the evidence clearly demonstrates that in the last thirty-five years, the political parties of the UK national government and of the UK official opposition have had or developed too close a relationship with the press (Honourable Lord Justice Leveson, 2012: 1430). Over this period, the relationship became closer. He explains having noticed a misbalance between the amount of time, attention and resources politicians spent on this relationship in comparison to, and at the expense of, other legitimate claims in relation to their conduct of public affairs. Also, he deemed that politicians, in their relationship with the press, have not always observed appropriate boundaries between conducting public affairs and their personal or private interests. Neither was there sufficient transparency and accountability in the way politicians maintained these relationships (Honourable Lord Justice Leveson, 2012: 1439). Lord Justice Leveson highlighted the inevitable "trading" element in these relationships:

> "The politicians have exclusive news and exclusive relationships, private advocacies and personal titbits to offer; and, in return, the press has partisanship, personal favours, the protection of sources and not holding to account. Potential promises and threats hang in the air. It all means, in short, that politicians

have a particular susceptibility to being lobbied when they get close to the opinion-makers of the press." (Honourable Lord Justice Leveson, 2012: 1446).

6.3.2.3 Regulators

Leveson concludes his report by explaining why complaints about breach of privacy by the press and complaints concerning the way the press cooperated with politicians and the police did not lead to investigations. One reason was, that the relationship between the Press Complaints Commission (PCC) and the entities that it was supposed to be regulating depended on the element of consent and collaboration between these parties (Honourable Lord Justice Leveson, 2012: 1555). "Although collusion would be too strong a term, the terms of engagement lack an appropriate deference; the concern to achieve collaboration should not be the order of the day, but rather the press should respect those who are regulating it." (Honourable Lord Justice Leveson, 2012: 1555).

6.3.3 *Official Investigations*

The criminal investigations into Brooks' conduct lasted eight months but, in 2014, she was cleared of all accusations including those of bribery and planning phone hacking. Several journalists, including former NoW features editor Stenson and former NoW editor Coulson, were convicted for their part in the UK phone-hacking scandal (BBC, 2015c; *The Guardian*, 2014b). Coulson was jailed in 2014 following an eight-month trial. He had denied all charges against him, but was found guilty of plotting to intercept voicemails between 2000 and 2006 (BBC, 2014). Five others had pleaded guilty to conspiracy to hack phones before the trial began: private investigator Mulcaire, news editors Weatherup and Miskiw and reporters Thurlbeck and Evans. Mulcaire performed thousands of hacks for the newspaper under the instruction of news editors. (BBC, 2014). Former managing editor Kuttner was cleared of any wrong-doing in the Phone Hacking Trial. Brooks' husband Charlie Brooks, her former personal assistant Cheryl Carter and News International's head of security Mark Hanna were accused of a conspiracy to hide material from the police. They were cleared of all charges against them. The jury was discharged after failing to reach verdicts on charges that Coulson and Goodman conspired to commit misconduct in a public office by paying police officers for two royal directories. On 11 December 2015, the Crown Prosecution Service announced no further action will be taken in their investigation of the phone hacking. It said there was "insufficient evidence" to bring corporate liability charges against News Group or charges against 10 individuals at Mirror Group. A total of 12 prosecutions for offences relating to phone hacking were brought, of which nine led to a conviction (BBC, 2015a).

6.3.4 *Other Research*

The owner of NoW, Murdoch, is the founder, chairman and CEO of the global media holding company News Corporation. Newspapers with a strong reputation, such as *The Wall Street Journal* and *The Times*, have been accused of becoming 'instruments' to help politicians favoured by Murdoch. Brooks, the editor of the NoW between 2009 and 2011, became close friends with Murdoch. The social network with Murdoch and Brooks at its centre allegedly became intertwined with the highest levels of government (Hanning & Bell, 2011). Brooks was seen as very influential in gaining access to the political contacts that Murdoch sought. She started as a secretary for one of Murdoch's newspapers and rose through his news empire. She was the editor of the NoW between 2009 and 2011. The two became close friends, and the network with Murdoch and Brooks at its centre became intertwined with the highest levels of government. The media reported Brooks to be a friend of former prime ministers, Cameron, Brown and Blair and their wives (Hanning & Bell, 2011). Cameron's then director of communications, Coulson, had preceded Brooks as editor of NoW. Hall, a former NoW editor, described Brooks as an "arch-networker" (Lyall & Becker, 2011). Although the interactions between journalists and police officers involved more conventional forms of bribery, it was particularly the close social network surrounding Murdoch that led to infringements of the privacy and confidentiality rights and violated the freedom of speech of those outside the network. In January 2016 Coulson announced, after having been released from prison, that he set up a PR firm which offers discreet corporate strategy and communications advice to clients. According to *The Guardian* an official statement hinted that, nearly five years after he left Downing Street, Coulson is planning to return to the political arena. "With Andy's extensive experience across media and politics, and a growing demand from CEOs, companies and organisations for strategic corporate and communications advice, we feel there is a real opportunity to establish a new agency in the marketplace." (Rawlinson, 2016).

Leveson Part 2 was commissioned in July 2011 when its terms of reference were set out. The prime minister promised publicly then, and again in November 2012, that it would take place when prosecutions were over. Although the Leveson Inquiry Part 2 has not started, the general impression is that politicians gave journalists scoops (which would help sell more copies) in return for favourable stories about the politicians and their political parties in the newspaper. Journalists and Labour MPs have expressed their fear that government will decide to call off the second part of the Inquiry. This political decision would imply that there will not be an investigation into how the corruption came about and was able to thrive for so long (BBC, 2016; Greenslade, 2015).

In November 2016, the government published a consultation seeking views on two issues relating to the Leveson Inquiry (Department for Culture, Media & Sport, Home Office and The Rt Hon Karen Bradley MP, 2016). Public views were asked on the implementation of two aspects of the Leveson reforms. The first concerns section 40 of the Crime and Courts Act 2013, which will create a new right of access to affordable justice in libel and privacy and which gives news publishers incentives to join a recognised independent regulator. The second is whether proceeding with Part 2 of the Inquiry is still appropriate, proportionate and in the public interest, because the scope and terms of this inquiry had been set in 2011. The proposition to abandon both faced a lot of criticism from the public and academia. "The consultation appears (…) to serve the interests of the big newspaper corporations that it obscures the fundamental point of the Leveson reforms: to bring news publishers into a system of independent, effective self-regulation that will encourage high ethical standards, while protecting the public from the consequences of unethical behaviour." (*The Guardian*, 2016). There are various public initiatives which seek to put pressure on the MPs to go forward with the Leveson Inquiry Part 2.[6]

6.4 Case Study 3 The Netherlands: the Dutch City of Roermond

6.4.1 *Introduction*

The third case concerns a corruption scandal in the municipality of Roermond, which has about 57,000 inhabitants and is located in the south of the Netherlands (Roermond, 2016: 2). In 2012, Dutch citizens were informed about ongoing criminal investigations into allegedly large-scale corruption in Roermond. One of the two main suspects was senior council officer Jos Van Rey, who was responsible for economic affairs, real estate planning and housing. Van Rey was a member of the political party VVD (Volkspartij voor Vrijheid en Democratie – People's Party for Freedom and Democracy) and at that time combined the position of senior council officer with that of MP in the province of Limburg and that of Senator (First Chamber). The second major suspect was the city's largest project developer and Van Rey's friend, Piet van Pol (Goossen & Sniekers, 2014). It was believed that, between 1998 and 2012, Van Rey took bribes from the project developer (in the form of cash and spending holidays in Van Pol's home in France) in return for leaking information and making favourable decisions concerning real estate developments. The project developer is thought to have realised projects estimated to be worth a total of hundreds of millions of euros by paying bribes. Some projects were assigned to him without public procurement procedures having been used, because he was already the owner of the land. Besides these allegations, other forms of abuse of power, conflicts of interest and corruption were reported, involving many other individuals.

6 One of these initiatives is Hacked Off, the campaign for a free accountable press. Its website is: http://hackinginquiry.org/levesonpart2pledge/ (Accessed 17/02/17).

6.4.2 *Case Presentation*

6.4.2.1 Sorgdrager/Frissen Investigative Commission

In 2011 regional newspaper *De Limburger* first reported on the conflicts of interest concerning Van Rey (Frissen *et al.*, 2012: 3) The allegations included the conflicts of interest arising out of the relationship between senior council officer Van Rey and his friend and project developer Van Pol. Their trips and holidays together were believed to damage the objective decision-making by Van Rey. *De Limburger* had reported on several real estate and building projects in which Van Rey had a conflict of interest because of the involvement of the project developer and friend Van Pol (Frissen *et al.*, 2012: 3). His objectivity as senior council officer was also being scrutinised due to his other activities concerning his possession of real estate. The decisions made concerning the real estate in Roermond are believed to have been detrimental to the municipality (such as overly high taxation of real estate which Van Rey and his friends benefitted from, while the municipality paid too much for this real estate). These allegations raised concerns about the way the Roermond Municipality Council and the Mayor and City Council Members were functioning (Frissen *et al.*, 2012: 3). The Roermond Municipal Council and Mayor and City Council members distanced themselves from these allegations. The Mayor of Roermond, Van Beers, requested the Sorgdrager/Frissen Commission to investigate the alleged violation of the code of conduct by Van Rey and his alleged conflicts of interest (Frissen *et al.*, 2012: 3). The list with the reports made by Van Rey concerning his trips and gifts were open for access to the City Council members but in reality only one of Van Rey's faction members did check it.[7]

In March 2012 the Sorgdrager/Frissen Commission published its report with the title *De schijn en de feiten. Een onderzoek naar mogelijke belangenverstrengeling in de gemeente Roermond* ('The appearance and the facts. An investigation into the possible conflict of interest in the municipality of Roermond') (Frissen *et al.*, 2012). The Commission carried out its investigation and spoke with 37 persons, including Van Rey and Van Pol. Its conclusion was that Van Rey had consistently taken on the appearance of conflicts of interest because of his friendship with Van Pol. In two instances there was proof of conflicts of interest (Frissen *et al.*, 2012: 46-47). Their friendship was widely known and the reporting by *De Limburger* was factually correct. However, the Commission did not agree with all of the newspaper's findings. Van Rey had reported about all of his contacts with Van Pol and the Roermond Municipal Council and the Mayor and City Council members had known about these. The Municipal Council had always supported Van Rey's policy as well as his position (Frissen *et al.*, 2012: 45). The Commission concluded that the way Van Rey and Van Pol expressed their friendship in fact led to an evident and ongoing appearance of conflict of interest. This has led to the impression that Van Pol had benefitted from this friendship by gaining a preferential position which

7 Information provided by an investigative journalist.

violated the principle of fair competition. Their trips to real estate fairs were a violation of the local code of conduct and appeared to have violated the level playing field (Frissen *et al.*, 2012: 45). In selecting project developers in certain municipal development projects, the appearance of conflict of interests can be noted, the more so because not all strict policies on procurement had been observed. The Commission was clear in its verdict that factual conflict of interests between Van Rey and Van Pol were not found (Frissen *et al.*, 2012: 45). There were two instances in which factual conflicts of interest were found: the fact that Van Rey bought a certain share and the fact that he still owned a sizeable amount of real estate in Roermond. Being in the position of senior council officer responsible for economic affairs, real estate planning and housing, automatically meant that any of his decision-making would have had an effect of the price of real estate.

The Commission voiced criticism concerning the fact that no explicit guidelines, policies or agreements were made by the Mayor and City Council members to prevent favourable decision-making. In particular, given the strong position of Van Rey in the local community, the Mayor and City Council members should have taken on themselves a bigger responsibility in monitoring individual integrity. The Commission concluded by stating that the municipality of Roermond was dominated by the VVD's strong position and the checks and balances were not always as strong as they should have been (Frissen *et al.*, 2012: 48). Before the Sorgdrager-Frissen Commission had spoken to individuals for their research, most of these individuals are believed to have been contacted by Van Rey on what they ought to declare. The criminal investigations found that Van Rey received several of the interviews digitally and commented on them, after which the interviewees sent them back to the Commission.[8] In 2015 the Media Groep Limburg B.V. asked the municipality of Roermond to disclose the concept report by Sorgdrager/Frissen. The journalists wanted to compare the concept report, which had been presented to Van Rey and the Mayor before being made final. The Mayor at the time refused to honour this request but in the end had to make it publicly available after a judge ruled in favour of the newspaper (ECLI:NL:RBLIM:2015:9521). A comparison between the two reports showed that there were many amendments made to the report, some which were beneficial to Van Rey and some which were not, but overall the changes are not considered to be substantive (Goossen & Sniekers, 2016). All in all the final report by the Sorgdrager/Frissen Commission concluded that besides the two instances in which conflicts of interest by Van Rey could be proven, many individuals were involved in causing the conflict of interest situation in Roermond and/or its continuation. The criminal investigations into the leaking of confidential information, the election fraud and the bribery started in 2012. The preparatory activities started in 2010 when the first information on the conduct of Van Rey and Van Pol became known to the law enforcement authorities.[9]

8 Information provided by X of the Rijksrecherche.

9 Information provided by X of the Rijksrecherche.

6.4.2.2 Case Development

In the summer of 2012, the Dutch Public Prosecution Service (Openbaar Ministerie) secretly started its own investigations into Van Rey under the code name 'San Jose' (NOS, 2016). They wiretapped his mobile phone and overheard Van Rey leaking confidential information to VVD party affiliate and candidate for the vacant position of city mayor of Roermond, Ricardo Offermanns (NOS, 2016). Van Rey told Offermanns, a party colleague and mayor of the smaller town of Meerssen, the questions and cases that would be asked by the selection committee during the interview and what answers this panel wanted to hear (Goossen & Sniekers, 2014). On the 19th of October 2012 the Rijksrecherche (a specialised unit which is part of the Public Prosecution Service that investigates corruption by top officials) raided Van Rey's home, the homes of his two children and his office at the City Hall (NOS, 2016). These raids were the start of continuous reports by locally and nationally active investigative journalists on the alleged corruption surrounding Van Rey. As part of its criminal investigation, the Rijksrecherche spoke with over 200 witnesses, including mayors, entrepreneurs, civil servants, senior council officers and citizens (Goossen & Sniekers, 2014: 14). In the meantime, the Municipal Council of Roermond had nominated Offermanns as the new Mayor of Roermond. This was the unforeseen moment in which the Rijksrecherche decided to raid the respective houses. A few weeks later Offermanns withdrew his candidacy after being considered a fellow suspect by the Rijksrecherche in the corruption case of Van Rey (*De Volkskrant*, 2016).

Besides the irregularities surrounding the selection of the mayor of Roermond and the role played by Van Rey, Van Pol was suspected of having transferred bribe money to a consultancy bureau (Liba Adviesbureau BV) owned by Van Rey's two children. This bureau financed his and others' personal election campaigns and trainings of several VVD candidates at the time of the national elections, including that of Frans Weekers, who was the State Secretary for Finance in the national government. Van Rey said it was just a "political favour to a friend" (Nieuwsuur, 2012). In 1993 and 1994, Weekers worked as a paralegal at Van Rey's assurance company and he also was Van Rey's personal assistant at the time Van Rey was an MP in the House of Representatives (Parlement, n.d.). Weekers accepted the payments from Van Pol and others[10] for which Van Rey acted as the intermediary, while a couple of months before, the integrity of Van Rey had been disputed and investigated because of the appearance of conflicts of interest (Frissen *et al.*, 2012).Van Rey indicated that the money spent on Weekers' campaign was his private money (Nieuwsuur, 2012). Weekers later admitted that it wasn't wise to accept the money and that he should have asked Van Rey where the money came from.

In March 2012 the Sorgdrager/Frissen Commission had concluded that there was a longstanding evident appearance of conflicts of interest on the part of Van Rey because of

10 Information provided by X of the Rijksrecherche shows that in total eight sponsors (among whom were Van Pol and Meulen) financed Weekers' billboard.

his long-lasting friendship with Van Pol. In two cases actual conflict of interests were found which concerned Van Rey's business interests and his position as senior council officer (Frissen *et al.*, 2012, 27). In November 2012, again allegations were voiced concerning Van Rey's continuous involvement in decision-making in which Van Pol had an interest. One of the Sorgdrager/Frissen Commission's recommendations had been to ensure Van Rey's private real estate was placed at a distance so that it wouldn't become a conflict of interest with his influential position of senior council officer (Frissen *et al.*, 2012, 49). Otherwise every decision concerning local development plans would automatically influence the value of Van Rey's own real estate. Weekers had indicated that, while being in the position of State Secretary, he had nothing to do with Roermond. However, a Dutch investigative journalistic broadcast, showed how Van Rey had been invited to the Ministry of Finance when seeking advice on the best way to set his real estate aside so as to prevent unnecessary taxation. Within ten days Van Rey got to talk to substitute director-general of the Tax Authority (Nieuwsuur, 2012; Goossen & Sniekers, 2014: 198).[11]

More and more the intertwined connections between Van Rey and his VVD party affiliates came under scrutiny. The connections between several VVD ministers, MPs and local politicians became scrutinised. According to professor Huberts, this example showed that there were already all sorts of contacts between Van Rey as a natural person, the Ministry of Finance and State Secretary for Finance Weekers (Nieuwsuur, 2012). With the conclusions of the Sorgdrager/Frissen Report, the letter sent by Van Rey to Weekers to ask for advice on his real estate taxation, and the meeting which followed this request, should have increased Weekers awareness when deciding whether or not to accept Van Rey's donation, according to Huberts (Nieuwsuur, 2012). Another direct link between Weekers and Van Rey concerned the State Secretary's decision that the regional office of the Tax Authority in Roermond would remain operational while other offices in the region would be closed. This was a deviation from the original plan, which was to close the office in Roermond. The Tax Authority, for which the State Secretary was responsible, preferred to retain its location in Roermond. Weekers said he followed up on the advice his civil servants gave him. The Minister for Housing and Central Government Sector had a final say in this decision and decided otherwise by choosing Venlo as the city in which the office of the Tax Authority would remain open (Nieuwsuur, 2012; Goossen & Sniekers, 2014: 198-200). Van Rey had publicly stated that he would do whatever it takes to ensure the local tax office would remain open. According to Van Beers, the Mayor of Roermond at the time, Van Rey used his large network for this purpose (Nieuwsuur, 2012). Suspicions arose as to whether this was in return for services and advantages granted by Van Rey (Nieuwsuur, 2012). Van Beers said that he profited

11 Information provided by another investigative journalist confirmed that the conversation between the Ministry of Finance and Van Rey on how to set aside real estate without having to pay tax, was arranged surprisingly quickly. The top civil servant referred him to the Roermond City Council in his search for a solution.

from Van Rey's network when bringing the interests of the municipality of Roermond to the attention of the State Secretary (Nieuwsuur, 2012). After fierce debates in the House of Representatives, State Secretary for Finance Weekers apologised for his behaviour and acknowledged he should have taken more consideration of his contacts with Van Rey following the Sorgdrager/Frissen Commission Report (Goossen & Sniekers, 2014: 195-199). He declared not to have known how the money for the billboard had been collected. He initially thought Van Rey would pay for it.[12] The whole issue did not have any political consequences nor did it become part of the criminal proceedings. The suspicions remained, but concrete and reliable evidence of the favour and return favour could not be found. The billboard was placed on the summons but only from the perspective that Van Pol made a donation to Van Rey (bribery) as will be discussed in paragraph 6.4.4.

Van Rey resigned from all his positions following these accusations. Other VVD senior council officers in Roermond then stood down out of solidarity. His political friends in the VVD faction then created council work for Van Rey by consulting him as an advisor. In 2014, Van Rey won the local elections with his new local political party, the LVR (Liberale Volkspartij Roermond – Liberal People's Party Roermond). Van Rey is backed by one third of the local voters but the new coalition excluded the LVR by means of a cordon sanitaire. His extensive network is still intact and most inhabitants of Roermond consider Van Rey to be the engine behind the economic growth and the flourishing of their city after years of high unemployment (Goossen & Sniekers, 2014: 12). Further, amidst the criminal investigations, the LVR asked Van Rey to be a member of the integrity commission that has the task of screening senior council officers on the aspect of integrity. Formally, the Municipal Council of Roermond could not turn his candidacy down (NOS, 2014).

'El Rey. From Hunter to Prey'

Van Rey has given several interviews to national and local media in which he expressed that he was furious about the way the Rijksrecherche carried out their investigations. He accused them of leaking confidential information to the press. Van Rey believes that it was a set-up by the Rijksrecherche to bring him down. He also blamed the local and regional media and their investigative journalists for their subjective publications and broadcasts, which contained many errors and which, according to Van Rey, are proof that the power of the other political party, the CDA (Christen Democratisch Appèl – the Call of Christian Democracy), is still present and dominant in the region of Roermond (Café Weltschmerz: 2016).[13] For decades Van Rey had fought against the dominant and persistent favouritism by the CDA network in his region, which he referred to as 'Vrien-

12 Information provided by investigative journalist.

13 The law enforcement authorities did confirm that for them it became clear that information from the criminal investigations had been leaked to the press but a separate investigation into the leaking did not result in any concrete proof.

denrepubliek Limburg' ('Limburg: Republic of Friends') (Café Weltschmerz: 2016; Goossen & Sniekers, 2014). This reference refers to a book which was published in 1996 and which described the strong presence of networks between local and regional government and the business sector in the province of Limburg and how these networks become corrupted (Dohmen, 1996). These networks were founded on the basis of associations or political parties and showed both characteristics of doing friends a favour as well as favouritism and nepotism (Dohmen, 1996: 79). The networks of politicians and entrepreneurs ruled on the basis of being closed to others and undermined the real ruling by local government. These networks were used to serve the interests of project developers and building contractors and for politicians and civil servants to make some extra money (Dohmen, 1996: 79-80).

In 2014 a book was published about Van Rey, titled *El Rey. Van jager tot prooi (*'El Rey. From Hunter to Prey') by the two journalists who were the first to report the alleged appearance of conflicts of interest surrounding the relationship between Van Rey and Van Pol (Goossen & Sniekers, 2014). Although the journalists repeatedly requested Van Rey to meet and talk to them, Van Rey refused to do so because he and his lawyer considered the reports by these journalists and the newspaper *De Limburger* to be biased and not objective (Goossen & Sniekers, 2014: 9). Not only did Van Rey himself refuse to talk to the journalists, others in the proximity of Van Rey did not want to contribute to the book either. According to the journalists, some did not want to talk to them because Van Rey had told them he wouldn't appreciate this and others were afraid of possible repercussions and only wanted to talk if it would be guaranteed that they remained anonymous (Goossen & Sniekers, 2014: 9). The book is based on at least 60 interviews with people from politics, the business sector, the civil service, the executive and academia. One of the prominent CDA politicians from Limburg described Van Rey to as a system of which everybody was part. He considered the entire city to be centred around Van Rey; all others were allowed to participate (Goossen & Sniekers, 2014: 61). Many former local politicians acknowledge that the Roermond Municipal Council and Mayor Van Beers were passive and weak and could not stand up against Van Rey and his faction (Goossen & Sniekers, 2014). Many of those who have been interviewed acknowledge that Van Rey has done many good things for the city of Roermond by managing the city as an entrepreneur, using his combination of functions to serve Roermond. Many believe that the citizens think they owe the economic revival of Roermond to Van Rey and therefore still support him despite the corruption conviction.

The book *El Rey* described several projects in which Van Pol and Van Rey were involved and which in financial terms were detrimental to the municipality of Roermond. However, similar to the findings by Sorgdrager/Frissen Commission, in most cases the favourable decision- making was directly the result of the strong position of Van Rey in local politics; the Mayor and City Council members and the Municipal Council were formally involved during several stages of the decision-making, but did not form an effective countervailing power (Goossen & Sniekers, 2014: 229). The book also referred to the attempt by the Mayor at the time, Van Beers, who acknowledged he had tried to convince the Sorgdrager/Frissen Commission to get rid of the term 'conflict of interest' in their report because that term had such a serious connotation (Goossen & Sniekers, 2014: 145). Persistent rumours that Van Rey has influenced the Sorgdrager/Frissen Commission to adapt sensitive issues in their report are denied by both Sorgdrager and Frissen (Goossen & Sniekers, 2014: 145). The Sorgdrager/Frissen Report was the subject of a discussion in the meeting of the Municipal Council, but it turned out that there was no majority in favour of taking any political decisions related to the findings. Van Rey remains in his position and no changes are being brought concerning his responsibilities (Goossen & Sniekers, 2014: 145). The only change made in the local decision-making process concerned the new rule that a second senior council officer would be involved if, for instance, a senior council officer would be responsible for a project in which an acquaintance or friend was involved.[14]

The 2012 raids by the Rijksrecherche were in fact premature because the Rijksrecherche had only just started tapping Van Rey's phone conversations as part of its larger corruption investigation. As soon as it became clear that Offermanns was to be appointed Mayor of Roermond, they had to take action (Goossen & Sniekers, 2014: 168-169). Hearing Van Rey leak confidential information to Offermanns was only a by-catch. Criminal law experts considered it likely that the premature raids harmed the overall corruption investigation. Many parts of the investigation should have taken place secretly, but now suspects were alarmed and might have had the chance to erase their tracks (Goossen & Sniekers, 2014: 169).

6.4.3 ***Official Investigations***

In 2015, Van Rey was summoned to appear before the court for suspected corruption (active public bribery, passive public bribery, and money laundering and election fraud). The project developer Van Pol and VVD senior council officer Tilman Schreurs were also summoned for suspected bribery. The former Mayor of Meerssen and candidate Mayor of Roermond had been summoned to court before.

Verdicts by Court of First Instance

During the trial, the public prosecution tried to convince the judges that Offermanns had already done Van Rey a favour in the past, namely when Offermanns nominated Van Rey in June 2012 as member of the Provincial Executive of Limburg (Goossen & Sniekers, 2014: 191). The judges were not convinced. They concluded that there were suspicions but no concrete proof that Van Rey's support of Offermanns' application was a return

14 Information provided by investigative journalist.

favour for the support Van Rey received from Offermanns months before. The court did agree that there would have been a risk that Offermanns, had he been appointed Mayor of Roermond, would have become a marionette of Van Rey. On 23 January 2014, the court convicted Offermanns on grounds of corruption with a sentence of 120 hours of community service.

In March 2015, during an appeal case, Offermanns was convicted of complicity to breaking confidentiality agreements but the court ruled that the public prosecutor had not established that Van Rey sought anything in return for the information and, therefore, bribery could not be proven (ECLI:NL:GHDHA:2015:533). He got a sentence of 60 hours of community service. The judge said that it was proven that Van Rey called Offermanns a few times to inform him of the cases which would be discussed and the questions which would be asked. Van Rey promised Offermanns that he would advise the commission to place Offermanns in the first position. Later the Municipal Council of Roermond recommended Offermanns for the position of Mayor of Roermond (ECLI:NL: GHDHA:2015:533). The Court believed that due to the information provided by Van Rey, Offermanns came out with an advantage and as such the "favour of service" was proven, but it could not be proven that Van Rey did this with the intention to receive a return favour at some point in time (ECLI:NL:GHDHA:2015:533). It is more likely, according to the court, that this way of acting by Van Rey had to do with his desire to ensure the political party VVD (of which both were members) would gain a strong position in the region, without bringing any direct benefits to himself or this party. However, this is not enough to prove the intention to receive a return favour.

Formally, Van Rey and Offermanns have breached the confidentiality agreements applicable to the selection and appointment procedures of high position in the public sector. Both were fierce when stating that *klankborden* (consulting and exchanging information about candidates) is a common practice within political parties (ECLI:NL: GHDHA:2015:533). The court opposed this view and stated that leaking confidential information to candidates was far beyond what is acceptable. In doing so, both men have not acted according to the applicable integrity norms, which are built on the idea that political office holders serve the general interest and fulfil their tasks in an unbiased and objective manner (ECLI:NL:GHDHA:2015:533).

In July 2016 three other men involved in this case heard their verdicts.

Van Rey

The public prosecutors asked for a 24-month prison term and a three year prohibition on taking on any official position in the local, provincial or national government for former senior council officer and former Senator Van Rey, who is still a local and provincial councillor. However, the court decided to give him 240 hours of community service for committing passive corruption, breach of confidentiality agreements and election fraud (ECLI:NL:RBROT:2016:5272). In the introduction of the assessment of the evidence, the court described Van Rey's conduct as "many shades of grey" (paragraph 8). "The suspect is a governor of the municipality of Roermond who in a long range of years – often because of (initial) good motives – and with an eye for the interests of the community and its citizens, seeking the boundaries, nearly always approaching these and many times, sometimes consciously, trespassing beyond them." (paragraph 8). The court continued to stress that the question whether corruption and some of the other offences were committed had to be answered within a criminal law framework. According to the court, this framework consists of a totally different and much heavier examination than the moral or governmental/administrative test which, for example society, the media and the Dutch governmental sector use to evaluate someone's conduct. Favouritism alone is not enough to prove criminal responsibility for corruption (paragraph 8).

By reference to the verdict in the Offermanns case, the court restated that by leaking the confidential information, Van Rey could have aimed to ensure someone from the VVD would become the new Mayor of Roermond and/or that Offermanns thereby owed Van Rey something in the future (ECLI:NL:GHDHA:2015:53; ECLI:NL:RBROT:2016:5272: 10.2). This second aim is essential to be able to consider this to be corruption, but the court was not convinced that Van Rey acted in this way to ensure such a preferential relation.

The donations made by Van Pol to Van Rey via the company Liba Adviesbureau BV, to pay for Weekers and others campaigns, are not seen as bribes by the Court and therefore no corruption was proven (paragraph 13.4.5). The court stated that these donations (around EUR 3,000) were not of real value to Van Rey and although the VVD benefitted from these, Van Rey himself did not.[15]

In paragraph 13.5.1 the court explained that, according to a provision in Dutch criminal law, it is not necessary to prove what the return favour of a gift or favour is. To prove corruption, passive in this case, it is already enough to prove that the civil servant should have had reason to suspect the gift was made with an intent to receive an advantage at some point in time.

The court is convinced that the projects of project developer Van Pol do stand out from others ordered by the municipality and that Van Rey played a role in this. However, it could not be proven that Van Rey was directly favouring van Pol in assigning these projects. These projects had a long project lead time with several moments in which decisions had to be made by the municipality and in which not only Van Rey being the senior council officer had a say, but the entire Municipal Council as well as the Mayor and City Council members (ECLI:NL:RBROT:2016:5272: 13.5.3).

In the verdict, the court stated that most of the trips made by Van Rey and Van Pol were a proof of their friendship and had a private nature. However, the trips which Van Rey and Van Pol undertook to watch the World Cup and European Cup matches (2006

15 Information provided by the investigative journalist showed that Weekers' billboard cost EUR 1,785.

and 2008) and to which family and friends of Van Rey were invited, should have made Van Rey more aware and conscious that they were offered to establish a preferential relationship or to attempt to get him to do something or refrain from doing something in his position as senior council officer. The court uses the same rationale to explain why the fact that Van Rey accepted the invitation to join Van Pol in his offer to visit real estate fairs abroad is considered a 'gift'. Although Van Rey was transparent about his trips to these fairs, the court maintains that Van Rey should have been aware of the nature of these gifts (13.5.9; 13.5.11). He did register his trips but did not disclose how he travelled, where he stayed or who paid for the trips.

The fact that Van Rey asked Van Pol and another project developer to transfer money via Liba to the election fund of the VVD signifies that he knowingly risked that these project developers would perceive this as establishing a preferential treatment from which they would benefit at some time (13.5.10).

The court justified the sentence of 240 hours of community service given to Van Rey by referring to the following:

> The suspect has many years of experience in national and local politics, and for years had the position of senior council officer with such important portfolio. In many of the larger projects for which he was responsible, his all-time best friend, the project developer Van Pol was involved. The court deems this clumsy. It also considers it clumsy for both suspects to make all these trips together. It also points out checks and balances failing; nobody confronted Van Rey with his conduct. Taking on the position of senior council officer together with many other positions in the local community was highlighted by the court. The court deemed it unwise to have an election fund of his own. Consulting with candidates of one's own party when one is an advisor to a confidential commission, is naive and risky.

The court continued that through these decisions the strong impression emerged that it is a matter of a "favour and return favour" fraud culture, to which favouritism and conflicts of interest were common; a culture of abuse of power and corruption (ECLI:NL:RBROT:2016:5272). The leaking of confidential information was proven and Van Rey exceeded the boundaries of the law. Proving corruption is far more complicated. Van Rey's asking for gifts from project developers with whom he had to do business as a senior council officer was wrong. It could not, however, be proven that he received millions of euros. The advantages he received were football matches and trips to international real estate fairs and the donations received for the VVD election fund.

It could not be proven that Van Rey had a decisive influence on assigning projects to Van Pol or that Van Pol made huge profits thanks to Van Rey. The impression of favouritism and conflicts of interest is what persists, but this appearance is not enough to justify a heavier penalty. What does count is that the suspect had been a top civil servant for many years, who knew which rules applied and who should have noticed that others had an interest in influencing him. Again and again he did not distance himself from those with whom he had to do business in his position as senior council officer. He did not act with integrity and damaged the public trust (ECLI:NL:RBROT:2016:5272).

Both Van Rey and the public prosecutors disagree with this verdict and have filed their appeal.

Tilman Schreurs

The second suspect who heard his verdict in July 2016 was former VVD senior council officer Tilman Schreurs. Tilman Schreurs was Finance senior council officer from 2002 to 2010 and was known as the fiduciary to Van Rey. The court stated that it was proven that Tilman Schreurs received gifts from Van Pol when he joined Van Rey, Van Pol and others when accepting the offer to watch the Dutch team play during the 2006 World Cup and 2008 European Cup (ECLI:NL:RBROT:2016:5277: 4.3.10). As a senior council officer he should have known that these gifts were made to influence his decision-making at some point as a senior council officer. Although the court considered Tilman Schreurs to have criminal responsibility for passive corruption, he did not get a sentence, because the court was not convinced that the acceptance of these gifts led to direct return favours to Van Pol. There is only an appearance of conflicts of interest. The court described this suspect as a "small fish who became part of a massive trial with all consequences that coincide with this" (ECLI:NL:RBROT:2016:5277: 4.3.10). The public prosecutors had asked for a sentence of 180 hours of community service and a two-year prohibition on taking on any official government position. Tilman Schreurs has lodged an appeal against this verdict.

Van Pol

The court stated that the large projects of project developer Van Pol did stand out from all others granted by the municipality. However, it could not be proven that due to the gifts Van Pol gave to Van Rey, Van Rey directly favoured Van Pol and his projects. Again the court stressed that the decision making related to these projects was not only in the hands of Van Rey but also in the hands of the Council and the College of Mayor and Aldermen (ECLI:NL:RBROT:2016:5280). The trips to the football matches, real estate fairs and his donations to the VVD election fund (Liba) were considered to be bribes.[16] The Court thereby distinguishes between the football matches paid for by Van Pol to Van Rey or to Tilman Schreurs. Because Van Rey has a personal and a professional relationship with Van Pol, it is not possible to determine in which capacity Van Rey joined Van Pol when visiting the matches. This is different in the case of Tilman Schreurs, who only

16 Investigative journalist: Van Pol donated money four times (total EUR 16,000).

had a professional relationship with Van Pol. The court therefore considers it proven that Van Rey and Tilman Schreurs accepted bribes, but it could not prove that Van Pol intentionally bribed Van Rey in his capacity as senior council officer. The fact that Van Pol earned millions due to preferential decision-making that was undertaken in return could not be proven. Only the appearance of favouritism and preferential treatment remains. Van Pol was sentenced to 100 hours of community service (ECLI:NL:RBROT:2016:5280: 4.8). The public prosecutors had asked for a 24-month prison sentence. Both Van Pol and the public prosecutors disagree with this verdict and have filed their appeal.

Verdict Court of Appeal

On 20 December 2017, the Court of Appeal sentenced Van Rey to a suspended prison sentence of 12 months because he was found guilty on three counts, namely corruption, ballot box fraud and violation of his civil servant's secrecy. He is also not allowed to hold a position of public office. The court expressed that a real imprisonment for a longer timespan would have been the right sentence, but the Court refrained from doing so because of Van Rey's seniority and the fact that Van Rey had also done good things for the municipality of Roermond. It also considered the fact that Van Rey had already been seriously punished by having to step down as a Senior Council Officer and Senator. Contrary to the Court of Instance, the Court of Appeal did not want to distinguish between trips and gifts accepted by Van Rey in his professional capacity and those accepted as a friend of Van Pol. Just because Van Rey and Van Pol were friends, Van Rey should have been more cautious of what to accept. The Court of Appeal considered it proven that Van Rey used his influence to arrange official decisions during informal talks. This concerns not only the informal talks Van Rey held to ensure Van Pol won the local procurement bids, but also the informal influence he used to arrange the billboard for the other VVD candidate, thereby transferring Van Pol's money to Liba Adviesbureau B.V. (ECLI:NL:GHDHA:2017:3702). In 2018 Van Rey announced his appeal in cassation before the Dutch Supreme Court. Additionally, the Court of Rotterdam advised the public prosecution service to try to seek an out-of-court settlement with Van Rey in its claim to confiscate EUR 300,000. (Binnenlands Bestuur, 2019).

The Court of Appeal sentenced Van Pol to a suspended prison sentence of nine months and he received a fine of EUR 40,000 or 235 in jail (Van der Steen, 2017) because he was found guilty of bribing two Senior Council Officers.

6.4.4 ***Other Research***

El Rey, the book written about this scandal by the two regional investigative journalists Goossen and Sniekers (2014) described the scandal as part of a world full of clientelism. The newspapers and the requisitory of the three public prosecutors referred to Van Rey as living in "a world of favouritism, bribery and corruption." (De Stentor, 2016). According to them, "Van Rey was dragged along in his own success and lost a sense of what is accepted and what isn't." (De Stentor, 2016; Van der Steen & Dohmen, 2016). The public prosecutors characterised the local government culture as "one of favouritism, in which things were arranged between parties and in which the democratic decision-making process has become a theatre play, of which few see through that it is being performed." (Van der Steen & Dohmen, 2016). The public prosecutors stated that Van Rey received bribes from Van Pol in all forms: trips to real estate fairs, football matches (World Cup and European Cup). The more than 20 times Van Rey stayed over at Van Pol's apartment in France were in themselves not considered to be gifts, but the travel he made to get there, including occasionally being picked up from the airport with a private helicopter, were seen as gifts paid for by Van Pol. Van Pol also paid money to Liba Adviesbureau B.V., a consultancy firm owned by Van Rey's children, which financed the training of young VVD candidates and which also financed Van Rey's own campaign. Various other entrepreneurs have paid money to Liba Adviesbureau B.V. Additionally, he was suspected of leaking confidential information about the cases and questions asked in the application procedure for becoming mayor. This suspect (candidate Offermanns) was the first to be tried in court. Van Rey was also suspected of election fraud and money laundering. On several occasions the public prosecutors referred to others involved (De Limburger, 2016; De Stentor, 2016; Van der Steen & Dohmen, 2016) – the family members, political party affiliates and businesses and how they helped create the world Van Rey lived in. The criminal files showed how Van Rey mobilised his network after the start of the criminal investigations by calling well-known VVD ministers and former politicians to ask for support. He asked his network to send letters to the regional newspapers in favour of Van Rey and criticising the corruption allegations.[17]

17 Confidential source.

7. Case Findings: The Analysis

7.1 Introduction

In this chapter the characteristics of network deterioration (network corruption) which were found in the literature are applied to the three case studies to get an insight into the turn of events in all three cases. The three cases are all recent corruption cases and in the corresponding official documents and media reports references are made to the role the connections played in the corruption. As such I could be accused of selecting those corruption cases in which it was already known that networks played a role and then proving myself that this was the case. After the literature overview and the presumptions regarding network corruption, I intentionally chose three cases in which I expect to find these features of network deterioration (network corruption), not to test whether the concept of network corruption actually works but to examine if the presumed characteristics and mechanisms come to light. With an open mind and vision I will assess the turn of events in all three cases, how the networks and corruption occur in practice and what features and mechanisms can be distinguished from which I can learn in the rest of this research. The case selection allows an analysis to be carried out on the way in which network corruption functions in concrete cases and to explore the added value of this definition. The concept of network corruption is applied to two national cases (United Kingdom and the Netherlands) and one transnational case (FIFA).

The three cases were presented as large scandals, both in terms of number of individuals involved as well as the size of corruption and other forms of misconduct involved. All three cases involved developed western democracies. The network was the centre of attention and placed in connection with corruption. All three cases have had, and still have, a major impact on society in terms of public distrust towards the organisations involved, the money lost due to the corruption and the violation of democratic rights.

7.1.1 *Case Study 1 International: The FIFA case*

Paragraph 6.2 presented the facts of the FIFA case. Both the facts of the case which were presented in the media and the official US indictment provided important information concerning the role of networks in the emergence of corruption. This paragraph seeks to dive deeper into the case, by assessing to what extent and in what way the features of networks which can bear responsibility for their deterioration (network corruption), as presented in table 1 of Chapter 5, can be found in this real case. I will explore each of the four characteristics and assess their appearances in the FIFA case.

1. Informal collective cooperation with a misuse of professional roles for network interests
The theories from Chapter 4 distinguished the organised from the non-organised or loosely organised collectives. Organisations played a role in all three cases. The question is whether the networks involved are indistinguishable from these organisations, or whether the networks are collective organisations separate from or independent of the organisation(s). Additionally, there is the question of whether their collective action results in corruption. The first feature to check is whether there is a form of *informal collective cooperation* which can be labelled as normal cooperation or whether it is in fact a case of *misuse of professional roles for network interests.*

The indictment mentions how the "aggregate" deprived FIFA, its confederations, and their constituent organisations of their right to the honest and loyal services of the football officials involved. By this reference, the "aggregate" is considered to be a separate actor, other than FIFA the legal entity or corporation. The indictment also mentions how, during a span of 25 years, a network of marketing companies emerged to capitalise on the expanding (US) media market for the sport. While organisations in charge of promoting and governing football were established, these became increasingly intertwined with one another and with the sports marketing companies. This context, according to the indictment, allowed the corruption of the enterprise to flourish.

Another argument for seeing these individuals as an informal collective is that the indictment mentions what happened after the scandal became public. The officials who were suspended or accused were replaced by individuals with the task of reforming. However, they soon were involved in the same abuse they were supposed to eradicate. This is an indication that the power of the collective is so strong that it provided a social context which easily led to the misuse of professional roles to serve the network itself. The network remained in place, even when individuals left. Newcomers soon adapted to its practice. This informal collective consisted of the executive committee members, officials from regional football associations, officials from UEFA, politicians and companies which functioned as intermediaries. The deals between South African President Mbeki and Blatter and the deal involving former French president Sarkozy and Platini are examples of the widespread web in which roles were collectively misused, reaching beyond the FIFA organisation.

The 2015 indictment was addressed to 14 individuals (nine high officials from FIFA, four sports marketing executives and one intermediary). Although it described the alleged criminal offences of each individual, reference was made to the systemic nature of the abuse of their positions ("rampant, systemic, and deep-rooted" corruption). The officials abused their positions of trust, often through an alliance with sports marketing executives, so all could personally gain from the collective misuse of their professional role. All gains (money and highly lucrative contracts) were kept for themselves through the systematic payment of bribes and kickbacks.

Developments concerning Blatter's successor Infantino indicate how professional roles are abused for the interest of the larger network. Infantino used his influence when he gave advice on who should be elected as the new president of UEFA, by sending an 'advisor' to meet with the northern European football associations to tell them that Ceferin should become the next president of UEFA. A few days later, Sweden, Denmark, Norway and Finland announced their support for Ceferin and a couple of months later Ceferin was appointed as UEFA's new president. Newspapers reported Infantino had earlier planned to remove Scala as the head of FIFA's audit and compliance committee to be able to install Ceferin, to whom he is close.

In the FIFA indictment the defendants and their co-conspirators are accused of 'racketeering', which in itself is a direct reference to the level of organisation which was needed to commit the criminal offences and which allowed the corruption to take place. The accused have been divided into three categories which reflect the interdependence of the actions. Joint efforts were necessary to reach the purpose. The actions of football officials acting in a fiduciary capacity within FIFA and its associations were needed to involve FIFA. The sports media and marketing company executives were needed for their willingness to pay for winning contracts. Intermediaries (including businessmen and bankers) had to act in terms of laundering illicit payments. Defendants and co-conspirators showed a form of cooperation ("scheme") in which individual actions are directed towards a common goal. Although some individuals helped to pursue the principal purpose of FIFA and its associations (promoting football), they created a form of co-conspiracy that corrupted the enterprise by engaging in various criminal activities. All categories of individuals were necessary for the joint actions to succeed. However, even if one or more individuals would have left, the collective would have likely succeeded as well. One reason for believing this is that, when the scandal emerged, other defendants and co-conspirators were appointed promising reform. While they were appointed to sort out the wrongdoing, they soon engaged in the same unlawful practices as their predecessors.

2. Shared interest in a generalised form of reciprocity

The *shared interest* features concern the question of what was going through the minds of the network members. This shared interest can be to help one another occasionally or it can imply a *generalised form of reciprocity.*

According to the indictment, the key figures and their co-conspirators are responsible for the corruption of the FIFA enterprise by engaging in various criminal activities in pursuit of personal and commercial gain. They shared the interest that individually and collectively they could enrich the network members. Their shared interest was the continuous exchange of power and money, whereby they all could rise to power. FIFA was misused by some of its executives and employees, to be able to favour the network which they were part of, together with government officials and business-men. Even when the corruption accusation unfolded, Blatter was reappointed as FIFA President in May 2015.

Blatter's strategy was to favour associations in Asia, Africa and Latin America to ensure they supported him. He can be seen as the instigator of making favouring the norm. He oversaw the (various) networks of patronage. Blatter admits that politically motivated collusion took place during the voting process surrounding the bid for hosting the 2018 (Russian Federation) and 2022 (Qatar) World Cups. Many FIFA officials accepted bribes from the ISL marketing company and candidate hosting states in return for votes. Besides the vote buying, votes were "deliberately miscounted." The Spanish and Qatari World Cup Bid Teams traded their votes in the respective 2018 and 2022 bids. The fact that Lord Triesman, Chairman of the English Football Association, admitted that in hindsight his bid team should have reported the four executive committee members right away, but refrained from doing so because the Football Association feared it would jeopardise England's bid, is evidence of the likeliness the FIFA network would return his silence with a return favour at some point in the future or alternatively retaliate if he were to report. By remaining silent, he appeared to trust that someone from the network would do something for him at some time.

All network members wanted to gain from this informal collective cooperation, for themselves, their family and other network members. Other references to this shared interest are Warner's family members gaining from the fraudulent and corrupt practices. FIFA official and former Chilean journalist Mayne-Nicholls Secul also shared the interest in gaining from the network. He was willing to abuse his power in favour of Qatar's bid and in return requested job opportunities in Qatar for three of his family members. The mechanisms of this case are clearly a reflection of the generalised norm of reciprocity: see what you can do for the networks and the networks will contribute to your well-being.

3. Common attitude reflecting the self-consciousness of the network

The features *shared interest* and *common attitude* are difficult to distinguish, because the interest is closely linked to the network's purpose, which can be found by observing the attitude of the collective. The common attitude can coincide with the self-consciousness of its individuals, or it can coincide with *the self-consciousness of the collective.* This latter interpretation of the feature has to be met in order to consider something network corruption. The self-consciousness of the network becomes apparent from the result which can only be realised through the collective organisation, an awareness that the collective needs to be organised into an appropriate organisation with individuals having to take on different role responsibilities.

According to the indictment, the defendants, together with these co-conspirators, "conspired with one another" to use their positions within the 'enterprise' to engage in schemes. "The defendants also participated in the corruption of the enterprise by conspiring with and aiding and abetting their co-conspirators in the abuse of their positions of trust and the violation of their fiduciary duties."

Although the corruption in the FIFA case had been suspected for years, few members of FIFA and its associations voiced their criticism or concern about the corrupt enterprise. One exception is FIFA Secretary General Zen-Ruffinen, who accused Blatter of financial mismanagement and corruption. Not only did Blatter deny the corruption allegations, he acknowledged having ended an investigation into FIFA's finances on the grounds of preserving the confidentiality of the accused members. Both Zen-Ruffinen and Blatter thereby expressed the different role responsibilities for the way FIFA and the associations are organised. They are both aware. Zen-Ruffinen demonstrates the voicing of concerns while Blatter demonstrates continuous loyalty to the enterprise and the way it is organised. Zen- Ruffinen even submitted a dossier to the Swiss authorities on behalf of other Executive Committee members who accuse Blatter of financial mismanagement, conflict of interest and abuse of power. However, it is believed that the enterprise chooses to continue with its current organisations, forcing Zen-Ruffinen to leave FIFA. A similar example which illustrates that FIFA and its associations were aware of the presence of their network was when it became known that Vice President Warner and his family members, by means of an intermediary family enterprise, were involved in a fraud scheme allowing the illegal selling of tickets. The fact that, similar to the Blatter accusations, the network members did not force Blatter or Warner to leave is proof of the network's common attitude to continue with the current cooperation.

In 2012 things appeared to be changing when FIFA imposed a life-time ban on Bin Hammam due to allegations he had bribed 25 CFU members with USD 1 million in total. One of the receivers reported this, 24 others kept silent: proof of a common attitude. Warner had given these envelopes to the 'beneficiaries'. The conscious choice to continue with the corruption instead of voicing criticism towards the FIFA enterprise is evidence of the network members' shared interest. FIFA's decision not to release its own investigation into corruption, instead releasing a (censored) executive summary which it said exonerated the wrongdoings surrounding the bidding processes, is another example of the network organising itself in such a way that the shared interests are served. Garcia resigned when FIFA's appeals committee rejected his claim that the head of the adjudicatory arm, Eckert, had written this summary which did not at all represent the underlying report. The summary concluded that the various incidents which might have occurred did not compromise the integrity of the voting process. This summary is believed to have deliberately breached the anonymity of whistle-blowers. Those in charge of ensuring fairness in FIFA's operation took on their role of erasing criticism, thereby contributing to the common attitude and being part of the same corrupt enterprise.

4. Closed character harming the rights of others

The possible downside of networks, becoming *closed*, is an important feature to consider when assessing network corruption. If the network deprives members outside the group from equal opportunity to access public goods or other benefits, the social capital becomes corruption. Networks which have a closed character can be strong bonds or they can *harm the rights of others.*

The collective abuse by the FIFA officials and sports marketing executives, and the systematic payment of kickbacks and bribes, resulted in various harms. Firstly, the conspiracy deprived FIFA, along with all its related associations and teams and its development programmes, from important financial support and the full value of the media and marketing rights. Secondly, the conspiracy succeeded in keeping highly lucrative contracts for the insiders, thereby shutting out competitors. This practice brought harm to these individual honest competitors but, at the macro level, distorted the market for commercial rights in the football branch. As such, the conduct has far-reaching anti-competitive effects. Thirdly, there is significant reputational harm brought to the victimised institutions, damaging their prospects for attracting conscientious members and leaders.

7.1.2 ***Case Study 2 United Kingdom: NoW phone-hacking scandal***

Paragraph 6.3 presented the facts of the NoW phone-hacking scandal. Both the facts of the case which were presented in the media and the official Leveson Inquiry provided important information concerning the role of networks in the emergence of corruption. This paragraph seeks to dive deeper into the case, by assessing to what extent and in what way the features of networks which can bear responsibility for their deterioration (network corruption), as presented in table 1 of Chapter 5, can be found in this real case. I will explore each of the four characteristics and assess their appearances in the NoW phone-hacking scandal.

1. Informal collective cooperation with a misuse of professional roles for network interests
The Leveson Report explicitly refers to the cosiness of the relationship between the press and the police and to a lesser extent between the press and politicians. The network with Murdoch and Brooks at its centre allegedly became intertwined with the highest levels of government. It is believed that the informal collective fostered the widespread favouring of each other. Leveson simply stated that the connections between the media, the police and the politicians had become "too close". The leading counsel in the Leveson Inquiry, Robert Jay QC, referred to the relationship between the police and the media, and News International in particular, as being, at best, inappropriately close and if not actually corrupt, then very close to it. He linked the nature of this relationship to the fact that the police did not properly investigate phone hacking. In another reference made to the presence of an informal collective cooperation, Mr Jay described the inherent risks engaged when individual members of two powerful institutions (the press and the police) have regular contact. He used the metaphor of rotten apples: not many are needed to

undermine the whole body politic. He pointed out the risk of unhealthy, over-cosy and overly close relations between the press and the police.

Although some police officers and journalists described the exposed network as consisting only of "work-related professional contacts", others clearly thought that close friendships had derived from the extensive networking by individuals such as *The Sun*'s crime reporter Sullivan, who was thought to be both a friend and a professional contact and part of Mr Fedorcio's (MPS) 'inner circle' of favoured journalists. He referred to it as a group of long serving crime reporters who were part of a circle of trusted journalists for Mr Fedorcio. This notion of a favoured grouping or 'inner circle' of journalists appears to be recognised by others of the press reporting on the MPS at the time. Former *Guardian* crime reporter Laville linked this informal group to the length of time certain individuals had been covering crime, having built relationships over many years.

The presence of the social network could also be seen when the plan to introduce the custodial sentence, was followed by a number of significant behind the scenes meetings between the media and politicians. The issue was clearly one which the press had taken to heart, and the nature of the relationship of a number of key players with politicians was such that ready access was available.

The Leveson Report does not go into detail on any specific corruption allegations. However, it concludes that there was a culture of payments at the NoW for information and that this was facilitated and overlooked by management control of financial authorisations. There have been criminal convictions on grounds of bribery and corruption involving journalists and police officers. According to Leveson, the nature of this relationship may explain why the police did not properly investigate phone hacking. This is proof of a collective misuse of professional roles to help the other members of the collective. Phone hacking could only take place with the help of police officers and those police officers had no interest in investigating the corrupt practices and abuse of professional roles within their own police force or the media with whom they cooperated. Another example of abuse of position is the fact that outrageous expense claims by journalists were not debated but laughed at and justified by reference to the fact that it was not the taxpayer who paid for it.

Mr Jay, who cross-examined Cameron and Murdoch, referred to how cultural problems of this nature are usually directed from high up within the organisation, but that this will not always be the case. In his opening statement he wanted to stress that systemic or cultural problems are not always caused by deliberate policy decisions made by those in power. In this regard, he referred to the possibility that the emergence of a certain culture is derived by more subtle and complex forces. This scandal is thereby not only seen as caused by the intentional and rational behaviour of individuals, but is also the outcome of historical trends on what was condoned and not criticised, leading to a slow evolution of complacency resulting in arrogance and short-sightedness. This reference can be seen as considering the scandal to be the outcome of the informal collective cooperation. Regarding the relationship between the media and the police, the Leveson Report quotes Mr Jay, who points to the fact that a situation like the phone-hacking scandal can either be caused by a few rotten apples or, alternatively, small adjustments in the behaviour of a few individuals can turn what is good into what is bad and vice versa.

2. Shared interest in a generalised form of reciprocity

The Leveson Report includes a statement by Lord Blair which is proof of the shared interest the members of the network had. In addition to earlier findings that journalists wanted to be successful in their career, senior police officers wanted to enhance their reputation, for instance to enjoy being in a position to share and disclose confidential information. This shared interest led to a small number of relatively senior officers increasingly becoming too close to journalists. Politicians wanted to be in the picture in a positive way to win voters and support. They also had to be close with journalists to achieve these ends. All members of the social network exchanged information in order to gain authority and become more successful individually and as a collective. The Leveson Report provided an insight into the involvement of the press to influence the political agenda related to press standards and privacy matters. The report also mentions how key figures from the press influenced decisions on acquisitions such as that of the iconic titles. One paragraph discusses in detail the lobbying behind the scenes to influence decision-making concerning the British Sky Broadcasting (BskyB) bid in 2010.[1] This mechanism is a demonstration of the informal collective to maintain freedom of the press and retain the status quo of its members' ownership of the media.

The informal social network in which Murdoch and Brooks were active included senior politicians and journalists and, although the Leveson Inquiry Part 2 has not started, the general impression is that politicians gave journalists scoops (which would help sell more copies) in return for favourable stories about the politicians and their political parties in the newspaper. Through this reciprocal cooperation between individuals, the elite's social network grew and resulted in economic and political benefits for the collective and for its members.

The close relationships between the journalists and police officers were sometimes referred to in the Leveson Report as an "inner circle". Although the aspect of favouring or gaining from the connections could not be proven in all instances, one relationship stands out from the others: the relationship between Fedorcio (chief communications at the MPS) and Wallis (former NoW deputy editor and later director of a PR firm). This long-standing friendship is believed to have influenced the appointment process. No

1 This full takeover would have allowed integration with other entities such as Sky Deutschland and Sky Italia. News Corporation had 39 per cent of the shares at the time. Info available from: Pratley, N. (2011). News Corp needs all of BSkyB. Available from: https://www.theguardian.com/business/2011/jul/11/viewpoint-news-corp-bskyb-takeover (Accessed 04/10/16).

evidence was found which suggests that the process itself, once instituted, was not conducted fairly. However, Wallis had already completed work for the MPS and the fact remains that there was an appearance of bias in selecting the PR firm to be hired. Another example from the Phone Hacking Case illustrates that it was common practice for children of senior NoW journalists to get an internship or work experience within the MPS. The Report describes the communications following Mr Wallis' (then in the position of Executive Editor of the NoW) request to find work within the MPS for his daughter. In the informal communications following his request, reference is made to the things Wallis has done for the police in the past. Such references show the exchange of favours on a network scale. The other report, *Without fear or favour a review of police relationships*, sees "soft corruption", doing favours and treating something or someone much more favourably, as a bigger concern than the "frank corruption" of money passing hands.

One explicit example from the Leveson Report concerns the BskyB bid. Emails sent by Mr Michel, the News Corp head of public affair, to the Culture Secretary's special advisor Mr Smith, showed that News Corp was being given advance notice of key decisions in the Government's scrutiny of its bid to take over BSkyB. Although the Alliance had its PA machinery in place to try and influence the Secretary of State by means of email and formal correspondence, this communication paled in comparison to the behind-the-scenes contact between Mr Michel and Mr Smith. The continuous stream of communication between both men hardly mentioned the bid or the process. It was all about making the connection at the personal level. One important conclusion concerning this practice is made by Leveson, when he refers to the fact that in any case of a judicial review, the risk of judicial bias would not have been discovered because there was great transparency in the way formal documents were exchanged and documented. Leveson sees the main concern to be the hidden problem of voluminous private and unrecorded communications by text and email, which had a great impact in the decision-making but which would never have been discovered. This is proof of network corruption not consisting of clear favours and return favours, but being more implicit and generalised.

Leveson did conclude that in the phone-hacking scandal the evidence did not establish anything resembling deals where News International's support was traded for the expectation of policy favours. It did point out the fact that relationships between the politicians in power, the media (corporations) and the police were often too close. These immensely close relationships did influence policies and decision-making and examples of favourable acquisitions, favourable appointments and favourable laws, policies and regulations are presented without it being clear who influenced them and what was done in return. There is simply the impression that each individual contributed to this practice without being able to isolate individual conduct. Leveson considers the informal contact between representatives of the government and the media in, for instance, the BskyB bid to be illustrative of the bias which creeps into decision-making. The informal communications in the process of this bid reflect a much wider issue about the relationship between the politicians and press.

3. Common attitude reflecting the self-consciousness of the network

The Leveson Report identified that the culture, practices and ethics of the press all had a single focus on legal risk and not on ethical risk and the rights of the individual. A similar conclusion is drawn in regard to the way politicians and the Metropolitan Police Service operated. Within the NoW there was no clear view of who was in charge of monitoring ethics in reporting and nobody seemed to have minded this lack of clarity. The media did have their Code but the systematic failure to hold anyone to account for breaches of the Code made journalists at the NoW believe that compliance was not that important. There are few examples of journalists addressing this issue themselves, one of which concerned Goodman (NoW royal editor) who addressed the unethical methods (phone hacking among others) which were used by himself and his fellow journalists. According to the report, the nature of the relationship between the media and the police may explain why the police did not properly investigate phone hacking. This common attitude was to continue with the corrupt way of working together (paying money in exchange for access to mobile phones and not investigating the allegations following these practices). As such, each party took on their own role to ensure the network was successful in achieving.

A similar reference is made by Leveson when touching upon the relation between the Press Complaints Commission (PCC) and the media that it was supposed to be regulating. Leveson refers to the term "collusion" but thinks this is too strong an accusation. Nevertheless, he did refer to the common attitude of all parties involved, in which everyone played his role to ensure effective checks and balances were absent, all because the connections and interests were too intertwined. For instance, Leveson found that jokes and allegations concerning voicemail interceptions were not taken seriously by the media industry. Even after the first convictions proved that phone hacking had occurred, minimal steps were taken to identify whether phone hacking had occurred or to investigate the extent of these practices. This is proof that the network has a common attitude towards accusations. No serious attempts were made to change the way the media, police and politicians cooperated.

The press would deal with criticism regarding unethical practices by demonstrating unwillingness to engage with those who voiced criticism. In some cases criticism led to intimidation of lawyers, MPs and those investigating the press' conduct. Allegations concerning the close relationship between the media and the police force, as well as the phone hacking, have existed long before the actual investigation into phone hacking started. The media, the police and, to some extent, the politicians, remained loyal to each other. Leveson noticed the existence of strong connections between senior politicians and journalists but also pointed out the necessity of having both working together in a democratic state. The report mentions some instances in which the relationship might have become too close. On the other hand, Leveson also found examples of individuals involved who were aware of their responsibility in ensuring these connections were not going in the wrong direction. For instance, when he became prime minister, Cameron expressed extra caution not to become too close with some individuals personally. An example contrary to his responsibility is the fact that Cameron went to great lengths to arrange face-to-face meetings with Mr Murdoch and other News International executives and editors. This may have played some part in the outcome of him winning the elections, but other factors played a role as well.

4. Closed character harming the rights of others

The Leveson Report quotes police officers and journalists about the aspect of type and nature of the networks. The image that arises is that the true and close connections between journalists and police officers were mainly close because they had evolved over quite some time. Only a few witnesses were of the opinion that close relationships were the result of intensive and conscious networking activities. Some references are made to an "inner circle", referring to some police officers and journalists who were considered to be insiders or favoured or exclusive contacts. This does not automatically lead to the actual favouring of one another, but at least the impression is that these inner circles were not open to others, thereby creating a risk that those who are insiders, albeit indirectly, are at an advantage to the outsiders. The Report mentions that some connections are complex and difficult to discover. What could not be proven is that there was an exclusive inner circle in which NoW and Conservatives were members. Murdoch and their executives dined with politicians from all political parties.

The Report entitled *The Ethical Issues Arising From the Relationship Between Police and Media*, reports that there is continuous contact between the media and police officers and staff at all levels, which is neither recorded nor permitted. This results in improper disclosure of information which is first of all damaging to the public and more particularly to those whose personal information was disclosed. Additionally, the respective organisations (media, MPS) suffered reputational damage, causing public distrust. Although the interactions between journalists and police officers also involved more conventional forms of bribery, it was particularly the close social network surrounding individuals such as Murdoch, Brooks and Coulson that led to infringements of privacy and confidentiality rights and violated the freedom of speech of those outside the network. Several journalists, including former NoW features editor Stenson and Cameron's former communications director and former NoW editor Coulson, were convicted for their part in the UK phone-hacking scandal. The relationship between senior politicians and journalist is more complicated, and the dialogue more sophisticated. According to Leveson, there can be no doubt that within these relationships there have been exchanges of influence on matters of public policy, which are likely to have harmed the public interest.

Another example concerns the communication between the Culture Secretary's office and News Corp concerning the BskyB bid. State Secretary Hunt put off any social arrangements until after the bid. Leveson found examples of his advisor Mr Smith being sensitive and responsive to Mr Michel's tactics. In the Report one example is given of Mr Smith joking with Mr Michel about an opponent of the bid. This is a clear example of breach of confidentiality which is detrimental to third parties, being the other competitors.

Leveson referred to the elements of "trading" and "exclusivity" in the relationships between the politicians and the press, whereby he pointed out the exclusive news and exclusive relationships which led to all sorts of favours not available to others.

7.1.3 ***Case Study 3 The Netherlands: the Dutch city of Roermond***

In paragraph 6.2, the facts of the corruption case concerning the Dutch city of Roermond were summarised. Both the facts of the case which were reported through the media and the official court documents provided important information concerning the role of networks in the emergence of corruption. This paragraph seeks to dive deeper into the case by assessing to what extent and in what way the features of networks which can bear responsibility for their deterioration (network corruption), as presented in table 1 of Chapter 5, can be found in this real case. I will explore each of the four characteristics and assess their appearances in the Roermond case.

1. Informal collective cooperation with a misuse of professional roles for network interests
From the facts of the case study it is clear that Van Rey had built a local municipal network as a countervailing power to the dominance of the former KVP party (now CDA). This social network consists of members of the VVD faction, family members and local entrepreneurs. Additionally, there are links to other VVD politicians at the national level. The court proceedings and media reports illustrate how his family members, political party affiliates and businesses helped create the world Van Rey lived in. On many occasions Van Rey did not distance himself from those with whom he had to do business in his position of senior council officer. The public prosecutors characterised the local government culture to be one of favouritism, in which things were arranged between parties and in which the democratic decision-making process had become a theatre play, where few see through to the fact that it is being performed.

The court proceedings in the Roermond case illustrate the different perceptions of, on the one hand, the public prosecutors and, on the other hand, the judges. The public prosecutors described Van Rey as living in a world of favouritism, bribery and corruption. They hinted at the fact that it wasn't simply a matter of bilateral bribery between concrete individuals. In this world, individuals abused their roles in all sorts of ways that would benefit the individuals involved. The individuals' sense of what is accepted and what is not was lost over time. The court concluded that the decisions which it had to assess in this case gave a strong impression that it is a matter of a 'favour and return favour'- fraud culture, to which favouritism and conflicts of interest were common; a culture of abuse of power and corruption. However, proving corruption is far more complicated because the gifts could not be easily proven.

The public prosecutors in the Roermond case have tried to prove the network by describing the close connections of key figures Offermanns, Van Rey, Van Pol, and Tilman Schreurs. They refer to aspects of culture or custom to favour. Even the earlier Frissen/Sorgdrager report mentions the collective character of the conflicts of interest. The fact that these key figures, their family members and party affiliates all contributed to the culture of favouritism and corruption received no attention from the judges, who isolated individual acts to prove the favour and return favour. If this was not clear, corruption could not be proven. The fact that the joint actions of all individuals had resulted in harm was not subject of the judges' verdict. This reasoning is also reflected in the conviction of Offermanns. The fact that Offermanns was informed by Van Rey about all confidential information on which questions would be asked during his interview and what he should answer, is not seen as one of many actions contributing to collective damage. Thereby the judges do not see any symptom or proof of network corruption in this example. They labelled this practice as isolated breach of the confidentiality agreements applicable to the selection and appointment procedures of high positions in the public sector. The donations made by Van Pol to Van Rey via the company Liba, to pay for the campaigns of Weekers and other VVD candidates, are not seen as bribes by the Court because they were not of real value to Van Rey and although the VVD benefitted from these, Van Rey himself did not benefit directly. It is possible to see these two examples as isolated practices, but they are in fact examples of how the social network sought to ensure its success. The court pointed out the fact that the question whether corruption and some of the other offences were committed had to be answered within a criminal law framework. According to the court, this framework consists of a totally different and much heavier examination than the moral or administrative tests which society, the media and the Dutch governmental sector use to evaluate someone's conduct. Favouritism alone is not enough to prove criminal responsibility for corruption. Senior Council Officers, businessmen, mayors and civil servants all misused their professional roles to serve the network.

2. Shared interest in a generalised form of reciprocity

The Roermond case shows how all individuals involved played a role or had an interest in ensuring that the VVD political party (to which many were a member or affiliate) would gain a strong position in Roermond, in the province of Limburg and at the national level. This shared interest was even directly referred to by the judge when assessing the breach of confidentiality agreements by Van Rey and Offermanns in the selection procedure for the position of mayor of Roermond. The judges saw the striving for a strong VVD presence as proof that it was not a matter of corruption, because then the favour or profit would have been for the individual. The public prosecution tried to convince the judges that Offermanns had already done Van Rey a favour in the past, namely when Offermanns nominated Van Rey in June 2012 as a member of the Provincial Executive of Limburg. However, the judges concluded that there were suspicions but no concrete proof that Van Rey's support for Offermanns' application was a return favour for the support Van Rey received from Offermanns months before.

The shared interest in ensuring that the VVD remained in power can be seen in Van Pol's decision to fund candidates' campaigns via the company Liba, to ensure Van Rey and his family were provided with excellent hospitality, although the judges distinguished between the treats received as a senior council officer and those received as a friend. Weekers' billboard was financed by eight donors, most of whom were entrepreneurs. Equally, the informal collective cooperation had a shared interest to make Van Pol a successful entrepreneur. He won most of the municipal larges projects. Many of the examples of the shared interest provided by investigative journalists and public prosecutors were not part of the indictment. Nevertheless the additional examples of communications and exchanging of favours between network members do show us the shared interest to be successful in political, societal and economic terms.

The Roermond case was first investigated by the Sorgdrager/Frissen investigative commission. At the time there were no allegations concerning criminal conduct. Its conclusion was that it was difficult to distinguish individual acts of conflicts of interest. Van Rey had consistently taken on the appearance of conflicts of interest because of his friendship with project developer Van Pol. Only in two instances was there proof of conflicts of interest. The court later ruled that the trips which Van Rey and Van Pol undertook to watch football matches and to visit real estate fairs abroad, and to which family and friends of Van Rey were also invited, should have made Van Rey realise that they were offered to establish a preferential relationship or to attempt to get him to do something or refrain from doing something in his position as senior council officer. The fact that Van Rey accepted the invitation to join Van Pol in his offer is considered a "gift". This expected return favour was not considered proven by the court when the leaking of confidential information by Van Rey to Offermanns was assessed. This confidential information was not considered a gift. The court distinguished in what capacity trips were made, which parties had been involved and whether the return favour could be found. The generalised reciprocity in the case implies that network favours were done in the confident expectation that the network will do or has done something in return.

3. Common attitude reflecting the self-consciousness of the network

In the Roermond case, the court is convinced that the projects of project developer Van

Pol do stand out from others ordered by the municipality and that Van Rey played a role in this. The court does not elaborate what "standing out" means, but in itself this is not enough to prove that Van Rey directly favoured van Pol in assigning these projects. It substantiated this conclusion by referring to the long project lead times in which there were several moments when decisions had to be made by the municipality, being the entire Municipal Council, the Mayor and the College of Alderpersons. This statement could in fact prove that there was a common attitude within the local municipality to follow Van Rey's proposal. An earlier report by investigative journalists had described Van Rey as being the "mayor" making the strategic plans to get everybody on board. The Sorgdrager/Frissen Report had also referred to a collective responsibility for the conflicts of interest within the municipality. The possibility of a common attitude as such could support the idea of network corruption, whereas the court sees this collective decision-making and corresponding responsibility as proof of absence of corruption.

The court concludes that "small fish" senior council officer Tilman Schreurs should have known that these gifts were given to influence his decision-making as a senior council officer at some point. He was therefore convicted for passive corruption. The court isolated his role, while in other paragraphs it made references to the culture of favouritism and corruption. Although the court considers Tilman Schreurs to have criminal responsibility for passive corruption, he was not sentenced, because the court was not convinced that the acceptance of these gifts led to direct return favours to Van Pol. There is only an appearance of conflicts of interest. The court described this suspect as a "small fish who became part of a massive trial with all consequences that coincide with this". Nevertheless, Tilman Schreurs' support and loyalty to the network was necessary. He openly supported and defended Van Rey.

In the Roermond case, the court confirms that Van Rey, although often considered the main person responsible for the corruption, acted in ways which were either clumsy or irresponsible, stretching the boundaries of what is acceptable, but also showed he cared about the local community and its interests. Some of the gifts accepted or information leaked is considered to be gross misconduct, but the court also refers to aspects of culture or the way in which the local "democracy" had been moulded. The fact that Van Rey had always combined political positions at three levels of government and the fact that he had involved his friend, the project developer, in so many municipal projects had been known to everybody within the VVD and at the local level of Roermond. Van Rey had reported all his trips with Van Pol. As such, many local key figures could have criticised the conduct or tried to reform the way the (local) network functioned. The court points to governmental controls failing; nobody confronted Van Rey with his conduct. The fact that this did not happen could be seen as proof that many were part of his network and helped it to grow over the years. Some civil servants amended official documents because they knew this was necessary to disguise the unfair decision made at the municipality. The Liba firm was needed as an intermediary to finance political campaigns with money from the businesses which benefitted from the social network. This way of acting and arranging is typically linked to role responsibility and self-consciousness of the network.

4. Closed character harming the rights of others

The Roermond case shows a network which became closed to others. The way Van Rey's network functioned made it impossible for other project developers to win municipal contracts. It would also be difficult for non-VVD politicians to become mayor of Roermond because Van Rey and his network played a decisive role in the selection and appointment of the candidates.

In the Roermond case, contrary to the information provided by investigative journalists and the public prosecutors, the breach of confidentiality agreements between Van Rey and Offermanns was not considered symptomatic of a generalised or collective practice or culture, nor was it seen as proof of corruption. The latter was substantiated by the judges by reference to the fact that this way of acting on the part of Van Rey had to do with his desire to ensure the VVD political party (of which both were members) would gain a strong position in the region, without bringing any direct benefits to himself or this party. The fact that this practice could have led to the VVD network gaining political power in the region by not offering equal opportunities to candidates from other political parties is overlooked. Unfair political competition to serve one's own network is one of the characteristics of network corruption. The court did criticise the practice and stated that leaking confidential information to candidates was far beyond what is acceptable. In doing so, the two men violated the integrity norms, which are built on the idea that political office holders serve the general interest and fulfil their tasks in an unbiased and objective manner. Non-network members would not have gotten an honest chance at winning the mayoral position or winning tenders and bids in the municipality of Roermond, despite the availability of integrity rules.

7.2 GENERAL CASE ANALYSIS

The central question of this research is, in what way and to what extent corruption is linked to social networks. The three case studies helped in ascertaining the nature of network corruption. Although the three cases clearly varied in terms of size, type of organisations involved and geographical areas, they shared several features of network deterioration resulting in corruption.

The results in terms of political and economic successes, but also in terms of network corruption, could only be achieved because in all three cases individuals operated as a collective, with an appropriate level of informal organisation and with each individual taking on a different role. The case studies presented a global, national and local network. Despite their great differences, they also share important characteristics. Foremost these networks are homogenous in the sense that they consist of individuals who are very much alike. The network members are key figures from the public and private sectors, most of whom combined several professional positions and many were members or affiliates of a political party or supported politicians. As such they all held key positions within the global, national or local community. The key figures bonded together in closed networks and through as well as within the entity of the network they could use and abuse their power, resulting in corruption. These social networks formed strong informal circles in which the real decisions were made. Although formal institutions were present, in reality democracy and competition were set aside. From the case studies it has become apparent that although there were examples of corrupt behaviour in these networks, the real corruption was caused by the social network.

All three cases show clear examples of collective misuse of professional roles to serve the networks interests. The FIFA case did match all four features of network corruption. The FIFA case presented a social network in which all crimes related to corruption were committed. The abuse was rampant and systemic and only those involved won. The social network exceeded the borders of the FIFA organisations. Individuals such as Blatter, Warner, Blazer, Platini and Infantino abused their professional roles as FIFA and UEFA officials to arrange all sorts of deals, thereby undermining all applicable laws and policies. Of all three cases, this case is most difficult when it comes to drawing the borders of the network. In fact, there was the international network consisting of FIFA officials and businessmen which was connected to the regional networks, which consisted of regional football organisations' officials and politicians. The abuse of professional roles consisted of getting things done purely because one had an official position. This resulted in benefits for network members, who would pay back at some point in time. Nearly all individuals in charge of safeguarding honest voting procedures and integrity within the FIFA organisation abused their role by effectively setting aside all formal procedures. The NoW and the Roermond case also show a widespread misuse of roles. In the NoW case journalists, police officers and politicians used their role to serve the network members, while the journalists in the Roermond case functioned as a watchdog to disclose the abuse of roles by Senior Council officers, businessmen, civil servants and VVD politicians. Here the misuse consists of leaking confidential information and other ways of favouring the network. However, there were also noticeable examples of good behaviour or behaviour which served a wider community or parties outside the network. This is not the case in the FIFA case study, although some individuals expressed their thoughts that football had also benefitted from their decisions.

The informal networks in the three cases all meet the shared interest feature. The individuals cooperated with individuals from other organisations and institutions so that their authority and power would increase. The individuals in the FIFA case were only interested in gaining or remaining in power and making as much money as they possibly could by all means available. This aspect of becoming rich was not the main interest of the two social networks in the NoW and the Roermond case. Although the media outlets wanted to sell as many copies of their tabloids as they possibly could, this was not an interest of the entire network. The journalists, senior police officers and politicians shared the interest of wanting to increase their power and reputation through the collective. Equally, the Roermond case was not about making money, although Van Pol did profit. Here the local and national politicians, their family members and the entrepreneurs such as Van Pol shared the interest of consolidating the power and influence they had in the region. They collectively shared the interest of remaining in key positions, because this meant having a strong say in the decision-making process, which benefitted them all politically and, to a lesser degree, financially. The FIFA case shows examples of generalised reciprocity, but it is not implicit or grown over time as is seen in the other two cases. Most conduct in the FIFA case is in fact crime, whereas the other two cases show a pattern of favouring gradually emerging in corruption. The FIFA network clearly had a shared interest in reaching the top collectively just to be powerful and rich. Although some network members have referred to their responsibility to act in the interest of the football game, none of their collective acting was proof of that. Although the norm of generalised reciprocity is present in the network, this is not a matter of favouring gradually becoming the norm. On the contrary, the social network in this case does not seem to have developed over time; it appears to be a conscious and rational choice to establish this network for the purpose of self-enrichment (goal-directed network). Although this case study's starting point was that of Blatter being accused of corruption, journalists often refer to his predecessor being the initiator of the corrupt enterprise. One obvious example of the self-consciousness of the network is FIFA's head of the adjudicatory arm Eckert, who wrote a summary of a critical report which made FIFA look good on paper, all to preserve the status quo of FIFA's network. In the Roermond case, network members knew about the conduct but also did nothing to correct it. On the contrary, some facilitated the conduct. Civil servants in the city of Roermond automatically revised council meeting minutes and other paper work to make sure all looked good on paper. The network members were self-conscious and aware of the existence of their network.

The common attitude in the FIFA network was to use all means available to protect the network and its members. This resulted in corruption, bribery, fraud, unfair marketing, bid rigging, setting aside internal compliance and even extortion. The corruption in this case concerned corruption by the network and large-scale systemic corruption in the network. It is impossible to make a list which sums up the rights which have been harmed by the manner in which the networks operated. The practice by the FIFA network deprived young boys and girls from the support which they were entitled to, to receive the training they wanted. Honest countries did not get to host the European and World Championship. In NoW the obvious victims were those whose mobile phones were hacked, but one could easily say that those journalists who worked for NoW and had not known about the corrupt practices are victims as well because they lost their jobs due to the bribe paying of their colleagues. In the Roermond case, project developers who were not befriended with Van Rey probably missed their fair chance to win bids or have a fair chance during the mayoral job interview. You could also see citizens of Roermond as victims. Due to the functioning of the network, tax-payers' money had to be used to pay for the overly expensive municipal projects.

In all three cases formal organisations played a role and made the headlines in which the scandals were reported. However, the alleged corruption and large-scale or collective abuse pointed in the direction of another actor: that of the informal collective cooperation by the network. Such cooperation in itself is not wrong, but in these cases there was misuse of professional roles for network interests. FIFA and UEFA officials met with the business men, while doing business on behalf of their respective organisations and in their professional capacity. However, their professional connections became more personal and extended with the involvement of heads of state and politicians. The same can be said for the phone-hacking scandal. Murdoch, Brooks, Coulson, Michel and others became friends with police officers and politicians because of their role in reporting for the newspaper. A small number of relatively senior officers increasingly became too close to journalists, for the enhancement of their reputation. Over the years, these connections became stronger, more informal and personal (emergent network). This elite or 'national network' became a collective which informally worked together, existing besides and across the formal organisations such as News International and the Metropolitan Police Service. Similar to the NoW network, the informal Roermond network also grew over the years. The FIFA network, on the contrary, has been deliberately set up to facilitate corruption. In Roermond, Van Rey had personal reasons for organising a strong network to restrict the power of the KVP party, ruling for decades in his municipality. Van Pol and he grew up together and have been close friends ever since. They made contact with each individual with effective power and influence in the municipality. This network became a community within the municipality of Roermond (emergent network). This social network also had parts of it overridden by more formal networks, including the national network of the VVD political party, and it existed across and besides the official institutions such as the Roermond City Council. The informal collective cooperation of these networks was in fact the wide misuse of professional roles for network interests. Therefore the networks meet the first feature of network corruption.

In both the phone-hacking case and the Roermond case, many individuals have been prosecuted for corruption, but public prosecutors failed to prove the direct return favour in each trial. The favour is made to a network member and does not need to be paid back immediately; it is often a matter of deferred expectations that this person or another network member will do something in return, when the occasion arises. Sorgdrager and Frissen did point out two proven examples in which van Rey clearly had a conflict of interest because of his decision-making being favourable to his friend Van Pol. However, interestingly enough the final report blames more individuals involved for the conflict of interests situation in Roermond. This is a first reference to the more collective nature of the concerns surrounding the decision-making in Roermond.

When Offermanns was convicted of complicity in breaking confidentiality agreements, the court ruled that the public prosecutor had not been able to convincingly establish that Van Rey sought anything in return for the information and, therefore, bribery could not be proven. This illustrates the complexity of proving corruption, when corruption is only seen as bribery in which it is clear what the return favour is or will be. This statement needs to be seen in the bigger context in the public prosecutors' statement that Van Rey was living in a world of favouritism, bribery and corruption. In the NoW case a similar context was named "soft corruption". Criminal law in general, and bribery provisions in specific, cannot deal with generalised reciprocity. The official investigations showed that, based on the current interpretations of bribery, each favour, whether a ticket to a match, a stay at a holiday home, a donation to a political party or the leaking of confidential information, is assessed and evaluated on its own. Although all key figures, their family members and (party) affiliates gained through the network, their individual acts were isolated to prove the way in which they were done in order to obtain a return favour. This has to do with the limitations of the criminal justice system and the fact that it is difficult to attribute responsibility to the level of systems, networks or other collective and coherent contexts. Both the Leveson Report and the Dutch Court expressed awareness of these limitations within a criminal law framework. The latter explicitly referred to favouritism alone not being enough to prove criminal responsibility for corruption. The indictment in the FIFA case was an exception in the sense that it focussed on the patterns within the collective.

There has to be explicit proof of a preferential relation, while the criterion of generalised reciprocity is all about that preferential relation or concrete return favour not being the case. On the contrary, one appears to be favouring another person selflessly, but in reality there is the belief that the network will return your favour at some time. In the FIFA case, bids were not only won by countries by means of vote buying, the implicit power of the involvement of the heads of states also determined the outcome. The informal meetings between News International staff, politicians and civil servants implicitly determined the bid outcomes, policy outcomes and newspaper articles without direct 'quid pro quo'. The informal social network in which Murdoch and Brook were active had among its members top politicians and journalists and the general impression is that politicians would give the journalists a scoop which the journalists could write about in the newspaper (and which made them sell more copies) and in return they would write favourable stories about the politicians and their political parties in their newspaper. Through this reciprocal cooperation between individuals, the elite social network grew and resulted in economic and political benefits for the collective and its individuals. All network members shared the purpose of becoming successful in financial and political terms. They made use of their connections and the implicit generalised reciprocity to achieve this. The network operated as a dynamic system, which meant that even when ruling parties changed from Labour to Conservative, the network adapted and connected with the ruling party's politicians so that it could continue to be successful. The social network is considered to be Britain's elite and as such the individuals identify with this image through self-categorisation. They form a separate entity of those in power across the formal institutions.

In the Roermond case, the former senior council officer Van Rey is the centre of influence who has built a local social network for over 40 years. Over the years, he combined his political positions (on behalf of the VVD political party) with his entrepreneurship. These positions brought along new and valuable connections with key figures from various organisations. Amongst others, these involved local and national VVD politicians, his friend, the largest project developer in Roermond, and his children. The social network proved to be solid and successful. Through these connections his insurance company, his children's consultancy firm and Van Pol Beheer B.V. (real estate investment and project development) were all certain of lucrative business. Van Rey is known for helping anyone in the city of Roermond but in return asked for political support. This is the mutually beneficial way of connecting with others. The fact that he was a VVD senior council officer for 14 years (until he resigned following the corruption allegations) and thereafter won the elections with his own political party LVR, is proof of the advantages this networking has. Through this cooperation between individuals, the local social network in Roermond grew and resulted in economic and political benefits for the collective and its individuals. The loyalty and reciprocity steered the behaviour of the individual network members. The network turned out to be a resilient system, because even when circumstances changed, such as the introduction of local integrity rules, or Van Rey's resignation, the social network remained intact. This also proves the strong purpose the individual members share and support. From their behaviour it becomes clear that their purpose is to ensure the network members remain successful in both business and politics. The identity of the network members was partly shaped by the identity of the social network itself, namely the inner circle of liberal Van Rey, godfather of Roermond and anti-CDA (Christian-democratic political party). This network has become a separate entity and has been referred to as 'The Van Rey Network' by, for instance, journalists, local citizens, local civil servants and other political parties. In this way it has become an informally organised collective.

All three cases show social networks whose members have a common attitude towards the functioning of the network and the outside world. In the FIFA case this means flat-out mafia behaviour, in which each network member acted in a criminal sense to achieve the shared interest of enriching oneself and the network members. The general attitude of the NoW network was to act in line with statutory provisions as much as possible, even if this were to lead to morally unacceptable behaviour. In the Roermond case a common attitude was to follow any ideas and suggestions made by Van Rey. Although everybody has taken note of Van Rey's conflicts of interest, they all showed themselves not to be bothered by it. In all three cases there were signs, at an early stage, that the informal cooperation between individuals was either going in the direction of network corruption or were clear examples of corruption (the FIFA case).

Networks organised themselves in such a way that they would serve the shared interest and fulfil a purpose. They knew that the way the network had organised itself was the reason why the network would gain from it. Only those who explicitly voiced criticism and left the network were no longer part of the network. They created the common attitude together and adhered to it. All networks were successful and got good results out of this common practice. They organised their network in such a way that individuals took on different role responsibilities. While individuals such as Blatter, Blazer, Warner, Murdoch, Brooks and Van Rey can be considered the central figures who were at the centre of all connections and were strategically building this network, other network members took on the roles of facilitators or intermediaries, communicators and supporters. All these roles were needed in different ways, to ensure the network could thrive.

7.3 Sub-Conclusions

This chapter focused on the patterns of influence in networks linked to corruption. By using theories on corruption and networks and translating their interconnectedness into four features, the nature of networks as they are presented in official documents and the media could be assessed. These features coincide with certain risks. The social networks in these cases emerged over time (the NoW and the Roermond case) or were knowingly established (the FIFA case). In all three cases, the social networks led to in-group favouritism and the structural exclusion of others. The individual conduct of network members contributed to the way in which the network functioned and the network reinforced the individual behaviour. The social networks' internal correction mechanism failed because all individuals involved fulfilled their role in such a way that the network would succeed in protecting the shared interests. While the network members gained from their network, the social capital became corrupted.

The cases specify the findings of the theoretical chapters, but they also provide a certain nuancing. Not only did these cases show how the theoretical findings on networks and corruption actually become apparent in practice, but these networks were also linked to various forms of undue influence and could be linked to other crimes besides corruption. Corruption by the network allowed other forms of criminal conduct to thrive, including phone hacking, leaking of confidential information, fraud, violation of public procurement rules, illegal financing of political parties and money laundering (crime and corruption in the network). These acts are all interwoven with the network corruption. The FIFA case matches the features of network corruption, but is also an example of a corrupt organisation and corrupt individuals. Here the network corruption coincided with a corrupt network. Assessing the network does help to understand the underlying mechanisms of corruption, but even without the concept of network corruption, the individuals and the legal entity of the FIFA organisation can be accused of corruption. As such, this is a nuancing of the earlier findings. This is to a lesser degree true of the NoW and Roermond cases. Those two cases met the features of network corruption and using these features helped in understanding the corruption of the collective. However, the corruption in these networks was limited compared to the corruption by these networks. The NoW and Roermond cases did not reveal any corruption networks, networks in which corruption such as bribery was the norm. Notwithstanding that, the case descriptions presented enough proof of network corruption and gave a valuable insight in the mechanisms leading up to the actual network corruption.

The way the four features of network corruption from Chapter 5 are present in the three cases show how they are important for the functioning of the networks and how they can lead to network corruption. Together, the four features of network corruption make it possible to assess networks and their outcome. Assessing the way these characteristics can be seen in real-life cases caused me to conclude that network corruption and corruption networks are related but different phenomena. Network corruption can emerge even if no individual acts of corruption, such as bribery, are noticeable. For instance, in the case of the NoW phone-hacking scandal, if the bribe paying between the journalists and a few police officers had not taken place, the case would still meet the criteria of network corruption because the network operated in such a way that its members were accustomed to acting, doing and thinking in terms of the network's interests (generalised reciprocity) and the informal social network became closed to outsiders.

A similar conclusion can be made concerning the case of the Dutch municipality of Roermond. Examples such as the leaking of confidential information by Van Rey to Offermanns and the way the billboard of Weekers was funded were not considered a form of corruption or bribery. Nevertheless, these actions show a mechanism of network corruption without individual corruption taking place. This leads me to conclude that network corruption foremost concerns corruption by the network which can coincide with corruption in the network, but this is not a prerequisite. The introduction of the concept of network corruption helps to distinguish acceptable and non-acceptable forms of influencing. In this way, the 'grey area' of when conduct is purely a form of interest representation, or when it becomes trading in influence or network corruption, is translated into independent phenomena. The following chapters deal with the question of what this finding means in terms of law and policy making.

8. Networks and Influencing: An Overview

8.1 Introduction

From the previous chapters it has become clear that networks can coincide with all sorts of risks which cause them to head into the direction of network corruption. The case studies show that all sorts of networks exist with diverse forms of influence, both improper and proper influencing. This is precisely why national legislators and international organisations such as the EU have dissenting opinions concerning the criminalisation of trading in influence. On the one hand there is the fear that such criminalisation will make the legal forms of influencing such as interest representation and lobbying illegal. On the other hand, there are enough examples of corruption which took on the form of trading in influence by means of connections. This chapter builds on the theoretical and empirical findings of the previous chapters which required further specification and nuancing of networks and influence. Here the definition of network corruption will be introduced, thereby distinguishing network corruption from other forms of (undue) influence by networks. This will be done by presenting an overview on networks and influence.

8.1.1 *Introducing Network Corruption*

Based on the theoretical framework of networks from Chapter 4, I distinguish four types of networks which are relevant in discussing (undue) influence:

- *a goal-directed network based upon a form of organisation* (legal and/or formal entities such as firms, associations, (semi-) public organisations
- *a goal-directed network based upon an informal open structure* (open network)
- *a goal-directed network based upon an informal closed structure* (closed network)
- *an emergent network based upon an informal closed structure* (closed network)

These four types of networks were chosen because the literature makes a distinction between the more formal (card carrying) organisations and the informal organisations. The formal organisations are by nature moral actors (autonomous). The informal organisations can only be held responsible if the set of specific characteristics are fulfilled. Since the network literature makes a distinction between the more closed (bonding) networks and the open (bridging and linking) networks, I have included both to assess whether this has an effect on the way influence is used and responsibility attributed.

Based on the findings in paragraph 4.3, networks make up social capital for three major purposes:

- *the purpose of helping one another*
- *the purpose of influencing decision-making*
- *the purpose of treating one another in a preferential way*

The first purpose, of helping one another, is related to the intrinsic reward of social interaction (Dasgupta & Serageldin, 2000). The purpose of influencing decision-making is linked to that of interest representation considered to be essential in a well-balanced society, economy and political environment (Warren, 2004). The purpose of preferential treatment is of a more permanent nature and corresponds with the norm of generalised reciprocity described in Chapter 4. Here the individual acts are difficult to distinguish; reciprocity has become the norm.

Overall, the table in this chapter presents a conceptual framework to describe, classify and value networks on the aspect of purpose, the extent to which they observe openness and the extent to which they are formalised. This overview simplifies the features of network corruption and brings these back to two distinguishing features, whereby the variations of different combinations of these features allow us to position network corruption in the jumble of related phenomena.

Table 3 Networks and influence

Purpose **Type of network**	**Helping one another: doing the other a favour**	**Influencing decision-making**	**Preferential treatment**
Goal-directed network with a form of organisation.	Social capital (linking).	Interest representation/ lobbying. The agent who is being influenced is not part of the network.	Trading in influence. The agent who is being influenced is not part of the network.
Goal-directed network with an informal open structure.	Social capital (bridging).	Interest representation/ lobbying. The agent who is being influenced is not part of the network.	Trading in influence. The agent who is being influenced *becomes part* of the network.

Purpose **Type of network**	**Helping one another: doing the other a favour**	**Influencing decision-making**	**Preferential treatment**
Goal-directed network with an informal closed structure.	Social capital (bonding).	Interest representation/ trading in influence. The agent who is being influenced *becomes part* of the network.	**Network corruption.** **Agents *are* part of the network.**
Emergent network with an informal closed structure.	Social capital (bonding).	Interest representation/ trading in influence. The agent who is being influenced *becomes part* of the network.	**Network corruption.** **Agents *are part* of the network.**

Social Capital

As was explained in Chapter 4, networks bring about many positive things. Foremost they form the social capital needed in society. Individuals have a need to belong and to be part of a community. Through these networks individuals become stronger and better informed, and both their well-being and their welfare is likely to flourish thanks to these networks. If individuals in a certain network (occasionally) help each other or do each other a favour, this can be seen as normal networking, creating social capital. This purpose is important in all aspects of society and is related to network values such as loyalty, solidarity and altruism. With this purpose, it does not matter whether it is an (goal-directed) organised collective such as an association or a company or whether it is an (goal-directed or emergent) informal collective with no formal status. Both types of networks are precisely what they are: networks networking. Even if the informal collective becomes closed to outsiders, it remains a network creating social capital by network members helping each other now and then (a bonding network). Independent of the nature of the network, the cooperation which coincides with favouring the network and its members is an appearance of social capital. As was explained in Chapter 4, this does imply that network members are aware of their actions and how these contribute to the bigger or collective outcome. The purpose of these networks can be seen in the way the network members behave. If favouring becomes the norm within the network, leading to decision-makers (agents) deciding in favour of the network, or the norm becomes to treat each other in a preferential way, the social capital will start to deteriorate.

Lobbying

As was explained in Chapter 3, some national governments are afraid to criminalise forms of corruption other than bribery because they are afraid this will endanger freedom of speech or the right to lobby. Equally, there is societal and public concern about the far-reaching effects of lobbying practices and public affairs and the extent to which they undermine the rule of law. Table 3 is a way of distinguishing these phenomena from one another, to shed light on this complex 'grey area' of the appropriateness of influencing decision-making. The influencing of decision-making through interest representation is the essence of democracy. If an (goal-directed) organised network such as an association, company or NGO organises itself in such a way that it can influence a decision-making process, this is a form of interest representation that can best be described as lobbying. The purpose of influencing decision-making is valid and part of a democratic process. I also consider it to be lobbying if the collective is an informal network with an open structure. This openness means that individuals can join or leave the informal network. In this way, it operates in a transparent and democratic fashion, thereby not harming the effective rights of others. It also means that the agent who is being influenced (politician, civil servant, CEO or another person in charge of the decision-making) is susceptible to the interest representation. However, this agent makes balanced decisions and assesses all information on its merits. As such, there is no trading going on between the influencing network and the agent being influenced. Therefore the agent does not become part of these networks. If these networks actively influence decision-making, this is a form of interest representation which is lobbying with the agent remaining outside the network. However, this qualification does not hold for the (goal-directed or emergent) informal networks which become closed and influence decision-making. This closure means that the agent who is being influenced becomes part of the network and no longer decides based on a balanced and well-informed decision-making process. There is a bias from which the network involved benefits and third parties do not get an equal opportunity to be heard. The agent becomes part of the network in this way and the interest representation is no longer a form of lobbying but has become a form of trading in influence.

Lobbying can be done in a decent and an indecent way and correct and incorrect information can be communicated through the channels of the network. International organisations and national policy-makers are increasingly seeking effective instruments to ensure lobbying is done with integrity. Observing the level of openness and purpose of the informal networks is a way to determine and concretise when lobbying is lawful and when it becomes trading in influence or even network corruption.

Trading in Influence

Paragraph 3.3.2 provided an overview of various corruption crimes and their definitions. Particular focus was on trading in influence and the necessity felt by international organisations to ensure national criminal codes have included a provision on trading in influence. The official definition of trading in influence in the Conventions refers to individuals who use their influence in an improper way to impact decision-making by approaching a second person with power and influence on behalf of a third party. This trilateral (or more) relation resembles the phenomenon of lobbying. However, lobbying is generally accepted and trading in influence is not, but capturing their differences is considered burdensome. This overview helps to distinguish both.

The difficulty with trading in influence is that it has several degrees, varying from accepted ways of influencing decision-making to undue influencing. There is the initial degree of trade and reciprocity which is part of politics, e.g. a goal-directed network such as an interest group and the third party such as a politician who is eager to be informed and make use of the available expertise, but still functions as an independent actor. However, the social process could creep up in the direction of network corruption when the trading in influence implies that the third party, such as this same politician, becomes a network member. Trading and reciprocity gradually become the norm, for instance when this politician owes his position to the network.

As was described under the paragraph on lobbying above, trading in influence occurs when an (goal directed or emergent) informal network which is closed to outsiders influences decision-making, thereby including the agent (decision-maker) in the network. Although this implies no transparency and a less democratic form of networking, it only becomes trading in influence when the closed nature of the network is combined with the network influencing decision-making. If the network concerned is a more organised network such as a membership association, firm or NGO which has the purpose of treating its members in a preferential way, thereby reaching out to third party decision-makers of other agents with power, this will be labelled as trading in influence because the favouring and return favouring are taking place. However, the fact that the network itself is rather formalised (membership) means that the agent does not become part of this network. When an informal network serves this purpose of treating members in a preferential way, while keeping its open structure, this is also trading in influence but now the agent becomes part of the network. This type of network incorporates the third-party agent by means of self-categorisation. Contrary to the social capital and lobbying, trading in influence involves the undue advantages of the way in which the network operates because favouring becomes the norm, thereby excluding other parties from getting an equal chance in the decision-making process. If such an informal network is closed, this will result in network corruption, which will be dealt with next.

Network Corruption

The last phenomenon in this table is network corruption, the phenomenon which this research is about. Although it was briefly presented in Chapter 5, it is included in the overview to make clear what the link between networks and corruption is and how social capital becomes deteriorated and corrupted. The previous descriptions of social capital, lobbying and trading in influence were all linked to the type of network and its purpose. Network corruption is the very specific case in which an informal (goal-directed or emergent) network becomes closed to outsiders and treats its members in a preferential way. As was described in Chapter 4, this can be homogenous and inward-looking social networks, but the closure can also take place when these bonding networks have members who function as brokers, thereby gaining extra opportunities for themselves and the network, which are protected by closing the connections to others. So bonding and bridging networks both lead to the deterioration of the network.

The three case studies show the existence of networks based upon an informal structure with varying degrees of openness to others. Equally, the extent to which reciprocity was generalised or specific varied from case to case. Although we tend to look at the respective organisations such as FIFA, the NoW Corporation, political parties, the Metropolitan Police Services or the municipality involved, it is in fact the network across these organisations which caused its outcome to be corruption. At a certain moment the network members act in such a way that their acting is no longer a form of favouring each other but the purpose of the network changes to the preferential treatment (specific or generalised reciprocity). If this development coincides with the thinking in terms of network members and outsiders, it becomes closed. If a network is no longer open for others to join and the norm has become to treat its members in a preferential way, it becomes network corruption. This is distinct from trading in influence, where the informal closed network seeks to influence decision-making but in which the norm has not yet become to favour network members in all instances to the detriment of outsiders. In cases of network corruption, the social network has become an actor besides the individuals acting in it. The theoretical framework regarding corruption and networks as informal autonomous organisations has been used to define network corruption.

Network corruption will be defined as:

> Informal collective cooperation in which professional roles are misused for network interests to such an extent that the dominant norm is that of generalised reciprocity, leading to the exclusion of others, while the members' awareness of their network is reflected in their common attitude.

This definition of network corruption is based on the combined analysis of corruption and network literature and research. It allows the assessment of networks to see when influencing becomes undue influencing.

Table 4 Features of network corruption

1. An informal collective cooperation > misuse of professional roles for network interests
2. Shared interest > generalised reciprocity (previous, present or future favour from the network)
3. Common attitude > self-consciousness of the collective
4. Closed character > exclusion (harming the rights of outsiders)

The features make it possible to assess or test when a network deteriorates. Because of these features, certain mechanisms will start working. The misuse of professional roles for network interests leads to preferential treatment of network members, thereby no longer serving the interests one has to observe when carrying out the profession. As such the actual role in the network takes over the professional role one formally accepted. Part of these networks' social process is that preferential treatment becomes the norm, thereby creating the norm of generalised reciprocity. This implicit norm steers behaviour as a reinforcing power, whereby the network members become wilfully or ethically blind and no longer see that they have a choice to contribute to either the network or third parties. The norm steers their behaviour to such an extent that they collectively act, refrain from acting, decide or think in the interest of the network. As such, the character of the network becomes closed. This common attitude is strengthened because the network members identify themselves more and more with the network. This closed character of the networks leads to the absence of the internal criticism and correction mechanisms, which again reinforces all the other features. These features reinforce one another, thereby resulting in network corruption. In this case, agents are part of the network and together they form an autonomous network organisation.

8.1.2 Network Corruption and Corruption in the Network

When talking about network corruption, I distinguish two aspects. First of all, network corruption is about individuals being so entangled in a network that their individual conduct can influence one another in a way which is unexpected and results in effects which are unpredictable. This is complex collective acting (corruption by the network). Secondly, network corruption is the enabler of other forms of criminal conduct. Phone hacking, violating public procurement rules, vote buying, leaking of confidential information, fraud and intimidation are interwoven with the corruptive acting (corruption in the network). These crimes are interrelated and they all concern abuse of power, reciprocal mechanisms and acts related to the covering up of these acts. This latter aspect has been dealt with in literature, for instance in *The Normalisation of Corruption in Organizations* (Ashforth and Anand, 2003). This was discussed in Chapter 4. However, it is important to underline that the network corruption which is the subject of this research is the corruption emergence caused by networks (emergent networks). Network corruption can be the result of goal-directed informal networks which will be closed, but the norm of preferential treatment and the closure which it can bring about is typical of emergent informal networks. Although related to it, it is not the same as establishing a network for corruption purposes (goal-directed networks). The sub-conclusions of Chapter 7 explained that network corruption can coincide with actual corruption such as bribery in the network but this is not a prerequisite.

In Chapter 4 a distinction was made between corruption in a network and by a network. We do not get a hold on corruption by a network. A large capacity is allocated to law enforcement for the investigations of the FIFA case, the NoW case and the Roermond case. In all three cases, law enforcement officials tried to paint a picture of the connections between the individuals involved. Their main questions were who is connected to whom and what the status of their relationship is. These investigators had a hard time looking for evidence of 'quid pro quo' or what was exchanged by the network members. The network's *modus operandi* was investigated to look for evidence to prove specific criminal offences and crimes. This discrepancy of seeing a social network operate and having to bring it back into individual behaviour is exactly the struggle of policy-makers and law enforcement officials. If individual persons decide to work together in the form of a social network and this network results in corruption, this will be a different form of corruption. This phenomenon is visible in the cases which make the headlines and are brought in connection with corruption but traditionally are not considered corruption. I therefore introduce this new concept of 'network corruption' to capture this phenomenon. With the introduction of the concept of 'network corruption', a phenomenon is named which is visible in practice but until now was not captured in a definition. This is not to say that no labels were given to what was going on in the three cases presented in Chapter 6. On the contrary, the public and also the journalists, scholars and politicians did refer to the 'something else' which was going on in these cases. Something other than the bribery involved. By assessing the formal or informal character combined with the level of openness of the network and its purpose, clarity is offered on how corruption is linked to networks and what features to look for to determine whether the network is acceptable or should be scrutinised because its outcome is trading in influence or 'network corruption'.

Network corruption is neither about individual corrupt behaviour nor about an entire state of being which is corrupt. Network corruption is the phenomenon which captures the collective conduct in a social network which at a certain point changes from social capital into corruption (emergence). Although decision-making is often influenced in unlawful and improper ways, corruption is in fact the violation of the essence of fair decision-making, whereby decision-making is no longer protected by values of legitimacy, transparency and integrity. Furthermore, by introducing 'network corruption', the structure in which corruption develops receives more attention, which means a step in the direction of considering corruption to be a complex collective behaviour, the prevention of which requires alternative approaches.

8.2 Implications of Network Corruption

8.2.1 *The Actual Deterioration of the Networks in the Three Case Studies*

The features of network corruption make it possible to assess when the networks in the three case studies deteriorated. Chapter 7 provided an analysis of each case and an overall analysis of all three cases. In all three cases the context of the network fostered individual and corporate corruption and other crimes and led to corruption by the network. In all three cases a few key figures in senior positions had longstanding friendships which appear to have been the centre of these networks (thereby functioning as the centres of influence).

Case Study 1 International: the FIFA case
The deterioration of the network in the FIFA case is somewhat different from the other two cases, because the systemic corruption within FIFA had existed for decades. FIFA's President Blatter and many of FIFA's executives had for years been accused of vote buying to be elected, to win nominations and to ensure specific countries won the bids for hosting European and World Championships. Hitherto all criticism was banned and those who pointed out the corrupt practices, such as former S-G Zen-Ruffinen, were forced to leave. As such, FIFA functioned as a corrupt corporation in which all those in senior positions abused their power and committed corruption. Things started to change in 2010, when media coverage of the corruption became extensive. Some executives were suspended, but Blatter himself remained in his position.

Nevertheless, FIFA's connections allowed the corporate corruption to take place. The FIFA network consisted of member associations, its affiliated regional federations, national member associations, sports marketing companies, heads of state, former international footballers and its executives' relatives. Buying votes was almost standing practice within FIFA and this norm soon applied to the voting procedures applicable to the wider network, due to the process of socialisation. This process involves making the newcomers aware of the values, norms and conduct, and the need for them to fulfil their roles and to function effectively within the network. Here the abuse of professional roles consisted of allowing the bribe paying, bid rigging, vote buying and political collusion to go on. Those accused in the indictment actively played a role in this practice and traded political or commercial support. Others, like the representative of the United Kingdom's bid team, supported this common attitude of the network, by abusing his professional role by not criticising this practice of which he was aware, and in doing so hoping to gain from it. In this way, certain mechanisms started to work. The misuse of professional roles for network interests led to the preferential treatment of network members, thereby no longer serving the specific interests each individual had to observe in carrying out his profession. As such, the actual role in the network takes over the professional role one formally accepted. This social process within FIFA's network created the norm of generalised reciprocity. This norm steered their behaviour to such an extent that they collectively acted, refrained from acting, decided or thought in the interest of the network. As such, the character of the network became closed; you were either with us or against us. Although FIFA expressed its intention to reclaim tens of millions of dollars that the United States has ordered the convicted criminals to forfeit, it was only a couple of years ago that FIFA's appeals committee rejected Garcia's claim that Eckert, the head of the adjudicatory arm, had fundamentally misrepresented his report on the foul play related to the 2018 and 2022 World Cup bidding processes. This common attitude, seen across the FIFA network and FIFA organisation, is strengthened because the network members identify themselves more and more with the network. This closed character of the network leads to the absence of internal criticism and correction mechanisms, which in itself reinforces all the other features. Although all three cases present examples of intimidation of those who voiced criticism, the experiences that whistle-blowers and investigative journalists had to endure because of their descriptions of FIFA's network bear a lot of similarities with the more formalised networks such as the mafia and their practices.

FIFA's response to current convictions of FIFA's officials does not express a learning effect. Nor have network members, such as politicians, heads of state or businesses involved publicly reflected on their part in the practice. Therefore, it is not strange to consider the network to still be active.

Case Study 2 United Kingdom: News of the World International phone-hacking scandal

Although Leveson chose to investigate the connections between the press and the MPS independently from the connections between the press and the politicians, the conclusions show that the mechanisms observed in these relationships are symptomatic for the overall network of which these three parties and others were members. The network members had a shared interest in enhancing their professional and personal profiles. The relationships had always been close, but certainly the pressure for NoW to sell more copies influenced the newspaper's proprietors, journalists and editors to obtain interesting stories by all means necessary. This led to unlawful practices such as the paying of bribes to police officers, but also meant having more frequent informal communication with politicians and the MPS to receive prior notice of newsworthy events or to receive confidential information. This in itself can be both lawful and unlawful. However, as soon as the majority of communication between the media, the MPS and the politicians became informal, mechanisms started to work which made the network deteriorate.

The relationship building led to unaccountable exchanges in influence and favours. These exchanges varied from the abuse of professional roles when favouring network members' relatives in appointment procedures within the NoW and the MPS organisations to the advancement of media policies which favoured the media interests and the practice of bid rigging. Also the fact that there were no immediate criminal investigations into the phone hacking after the first allegations is proof of abuse of the professional role of the police officers involved who had to investigate their network members. The interest in professional and personal enhancement led to the abuse of professional roles for network interests with rarely a clear favour and return favour. This preferential treatment of network members meant no longer serving the interests one had to observe when carrying out the profession. This is clear from the police officers providing access to voicemails or confidential information and from the NoW staff in charge of observing ethics and the executive management of the media allowing the unusual transactions.

Slowly, this implicit norm of reciprocity steered the behaviour of the network members, thereby allowing the network members to become wilfully blind and no longer see that they have a choice to contribute to either the network or third parties. The norm steered their behaviour to such an extent that they collectively acted, refrained from acting, decided or thought in the interest of the network. As such, the character of the network becomes closed. This common attitude is strengthened because the network members identify themselves more and more with the network. This closed character of the network leads to the absence of internal criticism and correction mechanisms, which again reinforces all the other features. Financial controls failed, ethics procedures were ignored and those within the respective organisations who voiced concerns about certain practices, were themselves discredited and suspended from the organisations and the network. There are two noticeable moments which mark the network's closure. The first is when NoW staff started to make 'in-jokes' about the payments made to the police officers. This is proof of network members being aware of the network's presence and some of the concrete malpractices which took place. This would have been the moment when the network members could halt the deterioration by investigating the practices and the underlying connections between the media, the MPS and politicians. Although the individual bribe paying had already taken place, the network corruption emerged when the abuse of professional roles led to the norm of generalised reciprocity, while the network members became conscious of the existence of the network, making a conscious choice not to address the malpractices and thereby allowing the network to deteriorate and become closed to outsiders.

Likewise, a second moment can be marked which is proof of the network's deterioration. It concerns the conduct of network members in the 2010 BSkyB bid. There was extensive lobbying behind the scenes to influence decision-making concerning the BskyB bid. The Alliance had its solicitors and public relations advisers actively trying to influence the Secretary of State through communication including email and formal correspondence. However, this communication cannot be compared to the extensive informal communication and behind-the-scenes contact between Mr Michel, the News Corp head of public affairs, and staff of the Department for Culture, Media and Sport (DCMS) such as the Secretary of State's special adviser Adam Smith. The bid was barely touched upon and there was no substantive communication about either the substance of the bid or the process. It was all about making the connection on a personal level. On one occasion he joked with Mr Michel about an opponent of the bid. On another, he joined in criticism of Ofcom. This is the moment when the abuse of professional roles leads to the exclusion of third parties. It's the thinking in terms of 'us' and 'them'. He also passed on information about the progress of the bid that would have to be communicated in a much more formal manner. He did not make formal notes of the communications. Legally, no bias would have been discovered in this bid because there was great transparency in the way formal documents were exchanged and documented. The risk of bias was created by communication which was informal and unrecorded, and which contains some mixture of the personal, the political or the presentational. Mr Michel's advice to his principal not to meet with the decision-maker on the grounds of counter-productivity, but that he will privately liaise with his team, is placing the conduct of public policy issues outside the mechanisms of transparency, accountability and public record. At this moment the character of the network changed. This is symptomatic of the relationship between the politicians and the press in this network. The network members abused their professional roles and thereby excluded others. Those who were part of the bid teams should have addressed the informalities exchanged, but because of the closure of the network, the internal correction mechanisms failed.

Both examples explain how the influencing in these networks collectively results in undue influence. They prove that there is an awareness on the part of the network members that the network existed and harmed the rights of outsiders (exclusion). The network in itself influenced all its members who refrained from taking action against the slow process of deterioration.

Case Study 3 The Netherlands: the Dutch city of Roermond

Of all the individuals involved in the network in the Roermond case, only three were prosecuted because of corruption claims. In contrast to the Leveson Inquiry, the judges had to assess the network involved by bringing it back to individuals and their acts and whether there was proof of 'quid pro quo' in each example of preferential treatment. Nevertheless, the court verdicts and the reports by the media show that there were mechanisms at work which turned the network into network corruption. At the centre of the network lay the longstanding friendship between Van Rey and Van Pol. The way in which their professional roles were intertwined with their personal interest is symptomatic of the overall network of which these two men and others were members. Soon after Van Rey and the VVD rose to power in Roermond, the network started to deteriorate. As such, the actual role of Van Rey as 'arranger' or 'informal leader' in the municipality of Roermond took over his professional and limited role as senor council officer. Van Rey wanted to enhance his professional and personal role and contribute to the well-being of the municipality by lowering unemployment and building attractive real estate. This latter aspect played a role in Van Rey's ongoing popularity among Roermond citizens, even after the allegations of corruption. The court took note of his contributions to the municipality when determining the sentence. Nevertheless, Van Rey, assisted by Van Pol, senior council officer Tilman Schreurs, Liba Adviesbureau B.V., local and regional politicians and civil servants established a network from which all network members benefitted, but which deteriorated.

Soon after Van Rey was appointed, this network's social process led to preferential treatment becoming the norm, thereby creating the norm of generalised reciprocity. This implicit norm steered the behaviour as a reinforcing power whereby the network members became wilfully blind and no longer scrutinised the decision-making process. In most cases, the decision-making which favoured Van Pol was directly the result of the strong position of Van Rey in local politics. The Mayor and City Council members and the Municipal Council were formally involved during several stages of the decision-making, but did not form an effective countervailing power. The court is convinced that the projects of project developer Van Pol do stand out from others ordered by the municipality and that Van Rey played a role in this. However, it could not be proven that Van Rey was directly favouring van Pol in assigning these projects.

The mechanisms which led to Van Pol benefitting were more implicit and derived from the network. These projects had a long project lead time with several moments in which decisions had to be made by the municipality and in which not only Van Rey, being the senior council officer, had a say, but the entire Municipal Council, the Mayor and the City Council members. This was a decisive moment, which changed the character of the network. As such, the character of the network became closed. Here the dark side of networks creeps in. This closure is also reflected in the leaking of confidential information to better prepare Offermanns for his interview with the selection committee. A few months before, Offermanns had played a role in Van Rey's nomination as a member of the Provincial Executive of Limburg. Although the judge did not see the reciprocity of this preferential treatment, the conduct is typical of the generalised reciprocity in the networks which become closed due to the abuse of professional roles for network interests. Another such decisive moment was when Van Rey asked Van Pol and another project developer to transfer money via Liba to the election fund of the VVD; he thereby knowingly risked that these project developers would perceive this as establishing preferential treatment from which they would benefit at some time. The Court of Appeal considered it proven that Van Rey used his influence to arrange official decisions during informal talks. This concerns not only the informal talks Van Rey held to ensure Van Pol won the local procurement bids, but also the informal influence he used to arrange the billboard for the other VVD candidate, thereby transferring Van Pol's money to Liba Adviesbureau B.V. Similar to the NoW case, the informal circuit allowed the mechanisms to start working. It was during such informal meetings that the network members could have stopped the deterioration of the network. For instance, Offermanns could have decided to stop Van Rey from providing him the confidential information. State Secretary Weekers could have refrained from offering consultation to Van Rey on taxation issues and, most importantly, the local politicians and civil servants could have taken their role as guardians of local integrity, of local governments, more seriously by asking questions and refraining from amending minutes and deciding in favour of Van Pol in local bids.

The common attitude was strengthened because the network members increasingly identified themselves with the network. This resulted in other network members misusing their professional roles to contribute to the network. There are examples of civil servants amending minutes of council meetings to cover up what was decided informally. Additionally, there are examples of real estate brokers who played a role in high taxation of real estate, from which Van Rey and his friends benefitted, while the municipality paid too much for this real estate. Van Beers, the Mayor of Roermond, allowed Van Rey to chair the local council meetings, thereby providing him with an extra profile and say. Van Beers also attempted to convince the Sorgdrager/Frissen Commission to get rid of the term 'conflict of interest' in their report because that term had such a serious connotation. He served the network interests in this regard, allowing the risk of the network becoming corrupted. As soon as the formal checks and balances started to crumble because of the pressure exerted through the network, the network deteriorated into network corruption. The norm of reciprocity steered the behaviour of the network members to such an extent that they collectively acted, refrained from acting, decided or thought in the interest of the network. This closed character of the network leads to the absence of internal criticism and correction mechanisms, which again reinforces all the other features.

8.2.2 ***Policy Implications***

The introduction of network corruption has implications for the way in which corruption should be approached. While the social capital of social networks is an important fundament of society, the risks of network corruption are overlooked. When (homogenous) individuals bond in a social network, there is a risk that the norm of reciprocity will become dominant and steer the individual behaviour in the direction of corruption. If the network remains somewhat open this can result in trading in influence, but once it becomes closed it can become network corruption. From the point of view of the policymakers and law enforcement officials, designing and applying a policy or model to analyse the network structure in corruption is crucial. For individuals who are members of an informal network, this implies a greater responsibility to be aware of the norm development in their network.

With the recognition of network corruption, the question arises as to who is to be held responsible for the corruption by a network, not only in moral terms but also in legal terms. Can the responsibility of the network be distributed among its members? To answer this question, other forms of collective cooperation and the way they are dealt with in law and policies have to be explored. Various examples of legal instruments aimed at collectivities from national law systems will be presented, after which a particular focus will be on the EU and its established practices of dealing with collectives such as these networks. This will be discussed in Chapter 9.

8.3 Sub-Conclusions

This chapter presented a table on networks and influence, to be able to answer the central question of how both are related. Four different networks (goal-directed networks somewhat organised and goal-directed and emergent informal networks which are open or closed) were linked to three different purposes (helping each other, influencing decision-making and preferential treatment) to assess how the various features would determine the nature of the influencing. This results in four different phenomena: social capital, lobbying, trading in influence and network corruption, whereby a network possessing an informal closed structure with the purpose of preferential treatment is labelled 'network corruption'. Where the networks result in lobbying, trading in influence or network corruption, an additional characteristic is included, namely whether the agent (decision-maker) which the network tries to influence or involve is in fact a network member, is a non-network member or becomes a network member. After this overview, the features of network corruption were used to explore which mechanisms started working and led to the deterioration of the three real-life cases.

Although it remains difficult to point to the exact turning point in these networks, there is some evidence available which indicates the deterioration of the network in each case. The FIFA case concerned a formal organisation in which corruption was the norm and whose members established a network in which preferential treatment became the norm and which was closed to outsiders. Contrary to the other networks, the corruption by the network allowed the corruption in the network to become systemic. As such, the individuals were corrupt, the FIFA organisation was corrupt and the network was corrupt. The network became the corruption itself, but also provided the structure for the individual and organisational corruption. The NoW and Roermond cases differ from the FIFA case in the sense that the informal social networks deteriorated when the network members started to communicate informally, especially when outside agents were involved who started to treat the network and its members in a preferential way and vice versa. The networks slowly deteriorated from social capital to network corruption and in between showed signs of lobbying and trading in influence. The overly close relations led to the closure of these networks, harming the rights of outsiders. These empirical findings at least require a certain nuancing of the earlier theory on networks and corruption. It is not a matter of networks contributing to or becoming either social capital or corruption. Depending on the type of network at stake and the purpose observed in the way the network functions, other forms of (undue) influencing can be observed, such as interest representation/lobbying and trading in influence. In terms of responsibility and the boundary of each network, depending on the type of network and its purpose agents are considered to be part of the moral actor 'network' or considered a connection of the network.

After the previous chapters introduced the concept of network corruption and explained how networks deteriorate in real-life cases, the question which now comes to mind is what the implications of acknowledging network corruption are. In order to be able to present ideas on how to approach networks in anti-corruption policies, Chapter 9 presents ideas on the way forward in practical terms, followed by the main conclusions in Chapter 10.

9. Organising Routes for Development

9.1 Introduction

The previous chapters have described the link between networks and corruption both from a theoretical and empirical perspective. Networks play an important role in our society and present various forms of social capital. Networks present a form of connecting which allows us to help one another, influence decision-making or treat each other in a preferential way. As such, networks can result in due and undue ways of influencing. The new findings on networks and corruption gained from this research automatically lead to the question of how policy-makers and all of us participating in networks should approach networks and networking. This chapter presents some ideas on routes for development in practice. First of all, the EU perspective in terms of policies will be dealt with, after which the legal questions which come up in these policies will be discussed, followed by ideas on how professional ethics can help to create network awareness.

9.2 EU and National Policies

The EU has given anti-corruption greater attention in the last six years. The large-scale EU research project, ANTICORRP, the network of Local Research Correspondents on Corruption (LRCC), the Anti-Corruption Report (ACR) and to a lesser extent the policy coordination by means of the European Semester, are all proof of the seriousness with which the European Commission has approached its corruption agenda. This research on network corruption seeks to contribute to the work which has been done so far by particularly focussing on the link between networks and corruption. The EU has stated that it wants to make use of the already existing anti-corruption instruments from other international organisations such as the United Nations (UN) and the Council of Europe (CoE) and assess what it can contribute to what is already in place. The findings of this research provide reasons why it is useful to make the collectivity of corruption more explicit in policies. In addition to the existing international and European organisations and their anti-corruption conventions, the EU could pay attention and emphasise the role played by networks in the emergence of corruption. This is particularly the case when referring to forms of corruption such as nepotism, political corruption and trading in influence. The EU Lisbon Treaty allowed a stronger EU profile in developing a European criminal policy and the progressive development of a European justice system (Reding, 2011: 11).

This not only includes the prevention and combating of crime by means of cooperation between police and judicial authorities, but criminal laws may also be adjusted where necessary.[1] This legitimises exploring EU policy development regarding network corruption.

9.2.1 *The EU Leading by Example*

9.2.2.1 Model Integrity System: Greater Coherence and Attention to Informal Processes

In terms of corruption prevention, current assessment models could be amended to include network awareness. The European Commission refers to the gaps in the national anti-corruption legal frameworks and calls for instance for better whistle-blower protection and clearer rules on the financing of political parties. Such a framework should not become a 'tick-box' or 'check-list' which can be used by the EU and its member states to check whether the various legal provisions which regulate individual behaviour are in place. It is necessary to explain how independent legal instruments (such as the public procurement rules, the revolving-door rules, the rules on lobbying, the criminalisation of corruption and the various integrity policies) seek to prevent network corruption, meaning the collective and not only the individual act of corruption. Bid rigging, revolving-door constructions and unfair forms of lobbying do not only concern an individual seeking influence but are manifestations of the network. Current integrity system models such as the NIS allow assessment of the formal anti-corruption and integrity systems, but seem to suffer from loopholes when it comes to assessing the informal processes of networks. The models fall short in recognising network corruption.

It is important for the knowledge on social networks and corruption to be incorporated in the model anti-corruption systems and integrity systems such as, the National Integrity System (NIS) and Local Integrity System (LIS). This means that there could be an element included which allows for an easy overview on the way social networks occur across the formal system (1). Additionally, the assessment of policy instruments could include integrity of networks (beyond the border of organisations) (2). Also, the foundation of networks could be assessed by translating norms from law and policies into norms for networks (3). Social networks could get a special status and corresponding responsibilities in these anti-corruption systems (4). These elements are a step in the direction of addressing network corruption.

The EU institutions could lead by example, by showing the coherence in their anti-corruption/integrity system. This is a necessity for changing national policy-makers' thinking and it would improve the EU's legitimacy in that its standard is not only imposed on member states but equally applies to EU institutions. Equally, the EU and its

1 Art. 3 (2) TEU and Art. 67 (3) TFEU.

institutions should show their awareness of how networks are present in and across their own organisations. Of particular importance are greater transparency and justifications regarding the appointments of European Commissioners and EU civil servants and the lobbying which takes place at the institutions. The policies to prevent network corruption have to be coordinated with the entire set of policies which relate to corruption. Through the instrument of mainstreaming network corruption issues are brought right into the core of all policy work, so that they are central to all activities such as legislation, policy development, research, dialogue, resource allocation, implementation and monitoring of programmes and projects.

9.2.2 EU Instruments on Collective Wrongdoing

In addition to these soft policies, the EU could explore whether collective phenomena, such as network corruption, could become collective crimes. The topic of collective behaviour is not new to the EU. On the contrary, the EU has made laws and policies aimed at the eradication of organised crime and the collective actions distorting fair competition. Both are examples of policies in which harm or damage is not attributed to individuals only. Here the collective cooperation is to blame for the outcome. The *2008 Council Framework Decision on the fight against organised crime* is the EU's main instrument against organised crime and it criminalises offences linked to participation in a criminal organisation. It seeks to harmonise the laws of EU member states on the criminalisation of these offences and lays down penalties for them (Council of the European Union, 2008). This decision mentions two types of conduct, of which EU member states must recognise at least one as an offence. The first offence is that of active participation in an organisation's criminal activities, with the knowledge of its aim or of its intention to commit crimes (art. 2a). The second offence is an agreement on the perpetration of crimes without necessarily taking part in committing them (art. 2b). Here paragraph 2 of article 1 refers to 'structured association' as "an association that is not randomly formed for the immediate commission of an offence, nor does it need to have formally defined roles for its members, continuity of its membership, or a developed structure." Although this still implies individual responsibility for the functioning of the criminal organisation (association), it is an attempt to address in criminal law the collective cooperation of individuals which results in serious harm.

One's involvement in such a criminal organisation is considered to be a fact when one has the intent (*mens rea*) and the knowledge of either the aim and general activity of the criminal organisation or its intention to commit the offences in question and knowing that his/her participation will contribute to the achievement of the organisation's criminal activities and the active involvement in the organisation's criminal activities (*actus reus*). This can vary from including the provision of information or material means to the recruitment of new members or the financing of activities. Alternatively, this membership is considered if an individual agrees with one or more persons that an activity should be pursued even if that person does not take part in the actual execution of the activity.

Another example of the EU's attempt to punish collective wrongdoing concerns the notion of participation which has received the EU's attention in relation to competition law (Keiler, 2011: 191). An undertaking is already liable for anti-competitive behaviour (article 101 paragraph 1 TFEU) if "(...) the undertaking concerned attended meetings at which anti-competitive agreements were concluded, without manifesting its opposition to such meeting (...)." The criterion of participation is already fulfilled if:

> "the undertaking intended, through its own conduct, to contribute to the common objectives pursued by the participants as a whole and that it was aware of the substantive conduct planned or implemented by other undertakings in pursuance of those objectives, or that it could have reasonably foreseen the conduct and that it was ready to accept the attendant risk. In that regard, where an undertaking tacitly approves an unlawful initiative, without publicly distancing itself from the content of that initiative or reporting it to the administrative authorities, the effect of its behaviour is to encourage the continuation of the infringement and to compromise its discovery. It thereby engages in a passive form of participation in the infringement which is therefore capable of rendering that undertaking liable in the context of a single agreement." (ECLI:EU:T:2008:256, paragraph 130).[2]

Earlier, the European Commission already found that the undertaking was responsible for the participation in anti-competitive activities because it organised meetings which it attended and in which it participated, as well as collecting and supplying data, acting as a moderator between participants and encouraging the finding of compromises, in exchange for a remuneration. Here participation is already established if an undertaking contributed to anti-competitive behaviour in a passive role. In this way the EU law seeks to protect the collective good of a well-functioning internal market.

Both examples show that EU lawmakers and the European Court of Justice (ECJ) do recognise criminal liability of individuals for forms of collective criminal conduct, thereby referring to the different roles fulfilled by the natural and legal persons involved. These instruments are not suitable for dealing with network corruption but are a first step in acknowledging collective behaviour in law and policies.

---

2 AC-Treuhand appealed the judgment before the CJEU on four grounds aiming at the annulment of the decision or the annulment or reduction of the fine. The Court rejected all of them in ECLI:EU:C:2015:717.

9.2.3 *National Policy-Makers*

This research provides an EU perspective on network corruption and considers it crucial for the EU to lead by example in establishing one solid EU policy on fighting corruption in which the coherency of all its policies and instruments is clearly reflected. The EU also needs to lead by example by addressing any risks of network corruption in its own institutions. A clear demonstration of how its own representatives, officials and civil servants seek to prevent their networks from deteriorating is not only a means to prevent network corruption in itself, but also strengthens the support among the wider EU public for the current and future EU anti-corruption policy.

Equally, the national policy-makers need to demonstrate the coherence of all policies aimed at preventing justified influencing becoming a form of unjustified influencing. There needs to be a thorough understanding in society about the common purpose of the large number of policies which have been initiated. For instance, rules on whistle-blowing, revolving door, financing of political parties, public procurement and the criminalisation of corruption are all elements of a larger plan to fight corruption and to uphold important norms in society. Policy-makers need to clarify responsibility across institutions, and not let the responsibility be watered out by grey zone legislation and the presence of informal networks. The importance of efficient enforcement of the laws that are in place should be underlined, regulating not only corruption and trading in influence, but also conflict of interest and organised crime and the protection of whistle-blowers. This is also about creating awareness regarding norms: what is not strictly illegal is not necessarily okay.

9.3 LEGAL ASPECTS

9.3.1 *Collective Responsibility in Legal Terms*

The previous paragraph presented how EU policy development can incorporate or think through the findings of this research on networks and corruption. Two of the main policy instruments concern harmonisation instruments aimed at ensuring that for certain crimes all member states have criminal provisions in place. Harmonisation of criminal law is difficult and may Member States still have to a large extent sovereignty over their national criminal law. Criminalising membership of a criminal organisation is one thing, but policies which seek to address the responsibility of networks will certainly have far-reaching legal implications. Collective responsibility in legal terms is something which has to be further explored when organising routes for developments on networks and corruption. Chapter 4 dealt with the philosophical debates on collective responsibility and provided an introduction to the examination of whether collective responsibility is ever appropriate or applicable in law. The discussion on group responsibility in (criminal) law is an ongoing one. Legal scholars have foremost discussed group responsibility for collective harm in connection to large-scale collective atrocities such as genocide and acts against humanity. Ongoing violations of international humanitarian law have led to a legal exploration of the extent to which the basic principle of individual responsibility accommodates liability for the acts of others.

9.3.1.1 Starting Point of Collective Responsibility in Law

The starting point for collective responsibility under international criminal law was the Charter of the International Military Tribunal at Nuremberg, where the idea of criminalising membership of organisations responsible for acts against humanity was laid down (Hale & Cline, 2014: 272-273). The United Nations War Crimes Commission (UNWCC) believed it would have been impossible for prosecutors to prove the guilt of each individual criminal charged with a war crime committed during World War II. The crimes committed by large groups would have placed an unmanageable burden on the public prosecutors who had to ensure there was hard and convincing evidence for each individual's act in the totality of the war crimes committed (Hale & Cline, 2014: 273). Many of the accused would escape justice due to the fact that specific evidence of individual complicity could not be obtained. Representatives of UNWCC realised they were "facing a novel question with regard to associations of criminals and whether membership in such an association was prima facie evidence to justify placing an individual's name on the list." (Hale & Cline, 2014: 274). Dr. Ecer (the UNWCC's Czech representative) influenced legal reasoning within the international community when stating that "(…) *in some circumstances, the mens rea is proven by the criminal act itself.*" (Hale & Cline, 2014: 276). His line of reasoning, analogous to English criminal law, was that once the act of joining an association of criminals was established, the "presumption of guilt" should be reversed so that the burden of proof lies with the accused, hereby eliminating the need to provide evidence on the defendant's specific role in the underlying crime (Hale & Cline, 2014: 276-277). In this manner, individual members may still be prosecuted for committing a specific crime in addition to membership in an association, which can aggravate their punishment.

The majority of the UNWCC approved the idea that "when a group was identified as having a criminal purpose or activity, each member could be punished simply for being a member of the group." (Hale & Cline, 2014: 280). The Commission saw justification for collective responsibility as a form of liability "in the criminal nature itself of the organisations, as proved by facts establishing beyond doubt that they had actually and systematically perpetrated innumerable crimes." (Hale & Cline, 2014: 281). Although there is no universal agreement on the scope and interpretation of collective responsibility, partly due to the national sovereignty in criminal law enactment, but mostly due to the principles of presumption of innocence and due process of law, it remains an issue which is debated widely and which has been used in the court proceedings of the War Tribunals (Hale & Cline, 2014).

9.3.1.2 Collective Responsibility in the Netherlands Today

Since World War II, collective responsibility has been on and off the table of lawmakers. A 2012 initiative by a Dutch MP, to include a form of collective responsibility for acts of violence in the public space put this topic on the Dutch table again (House of Representatives, 2012). The proposed amendment to the Dutch Criminal Code sought to hold a group criminally liable if it has been involved in riots or acts of violence in the public space. An example of such a collective act of violence took place when Dutch football fans of Feyenoord caused permanent damage to a 500-year-old fountain in Rome, before a Europa League match against AS Roma on 20 February 2015. In addition, 18 people were injured. Police fired teargas to clear hundreds of fans and many individuals were arrested for causing injury, resisting arrest and insulting public officials. More than 40 of these hooligans were convicted, most of them sentenced to community service, though one was sentenced to a prison term of one and a half years for serious assault (Nagtegaal, 2015). No one could be held responsible for the damage done to the Roman fountain, because it was not possible to distinguish which of the individuals did this. The Dutch government and a foundation set up ad hoc by Dutch citizens living in Italy paid money for its repair.

Another 'Dutch case' concerns a criminal complaint against the tobacco industry (Sick of Smoking, n.d. a). Lawyers in 17 countries are following Dutch lawyers, the Dutch cancer association KWF and lung cancer patients who are pioneers in suing four tobacco producers for attempted murder or aggravated assault. According to them, the tobacco industry consciously and deliberately addicts people to their product, with fatal and life-threating consequences (Sick of Smoking, n.d. b). One of the lawyers explains that they fight against a power bigger than the state, against an industry that has penetrated every pore of society with creative but wrongful tactics. The industry adds all sorts of chemicals to cigarettes, which not only lead to addiction but also lead to depressive feelings if not consumed. Another tactic is to aim for children to start smoking to compensate for the adult smokers who die early. It remains to be seen whether or not the claim will be successful, but this case shows how a civil society tries to hold a collective or industry responsible for their collective conduct. The four well-known tobacco producers are being sued without distinguishing who (individually) did what against whom. It's a matter of their joint action or collective way of working.

In some countries, freedom of association can be restricted if the association creates the structure and culture from which criminal behaviour emerges. One such example is the civil and/or administrative laws which forbid certain biker associations. Here it must be a case of the structural crime of the association; the fact that some of its members are involved in criminal activities is not enough proof of any criminal association. Associations can be formal or informal. In Germany, biker associations can be dismantled and their property taken from them if the association is responsible for such structural crime (Pelgrim & Meeus, 2017). In the Netherlands, the Minister of Security and Justice is drafting a bill which should make it easier to use instruments like administrative or civil law instead of criminal law to prohibit associations linked to crime without having to use the complex criminal procedures (Pelgrim & Meeus, 2017). Using administrative law to deal with associations believed to be responsible for crimes is quite new and therefore little information is available on its effect. Nevertheless, it is further proof that our society is considering ways to deal with collectives and collective outcomes more effectively. There is an eye for the effect that associations, networks and other loosely organised collectives can bring about.

Dutch public prosecutors increasingly attempt to use civil law to ban motorcycle clubs known for their involvement in crime. On 20 December 2017, Bandidos Motorcycle Club was officially banned in the Netherlands because of its permanent culture of lawlessness, both in words and actions. The court stated that even informal associations can be seen as legal entities when the facts and circumstances together express the fact that the individuals' connections show some form of organisation. Thereby the Court referred to a list of members' names, the regular meetings the members held and evidence on paper that some of the members were key figures who had a greater say in the decision-making (ECLI:NL:RBMNE:2017:6241). As such, this instrument to prohibit a collective can equally be used for formal and informal associations.

When thinking about the collective behaviour of groups resulting in damage and the support for legal collective responsibility, it mostly concerns examples of violence and crimes against humanity as described in the following subparagraphs. However, there are various other examples of serious societal or global damage caused by informal collectives, such as damage caused to the environment (global warming, loss of biodiversity) or damage caused to the financial/economic system, or harm to societal health (obesity). Although responsibility in a moral and legal sense starts with the search for who is to blame, this search will soon result in singling out individuals and their contribution to the collective harm. For instance, car owners are to blame for their cars' emissions and the effect they have on global warming, while national governments are blamed for not granting more subsidies for green and sustainable initiatives. Equally, obese individuals will be held responsible for choosing to eat too much unhealthy food and exercising too little, while food manufacturers will be blamed for putting too much sugar, salt and fat in their products. These examples of complex collective acting and responsibility have a lot in common with the emergence of network corruption.

9.3.2 *Crime as a Cooperative Enterprise*

9.3.2.1 Two Legal Systems on Participation

The adding up of individual acts and placing responsibility with the individual does not help in understanding how the collective outcome came about. Legal scholars have explored the possibilities to attribute criminal responsibility to collectives. Most national criminal codes only acknowledge individual responsibility based on intention or guilt. The criminal laws are largely built on the idea that only human beings can carry out criminal conduct. In this way, complicity and participation in criminal law are brought back to the level of the individual. The criminal responsibility of corporations can be seen as a derivative of conduct by individuals such as the director or leader of the organisation (functional perpetrator) (Keiler, 2011: 180-181). According to Keiler (2011: 196), organised and white-collar crime, such as corruption, poses problems for traditional models on participation. "Traditionally, the description of all criminal offences is built on the concept of the sole perpetrator. (....) However, in contemporary society crime has increasingly become a co-operative enterprise." (Keiler, 2011: 174). Although several people can cooperate in such a way that it results in a crime such as corruption, the criminal law systems are such that the proper scope of liability has to be determined based on an individual's criminal act or his participation in a criminal offence. Whether it concerns an armed robbery or corruption, there is a continuum of involvement in a criminal offence, varying from providing aid or assistance to planning, facilitating and orchestrating the offence (Keiler, 2011: 174).

Criminal law systems draw a distinction between those who actually commit the offence and those who contribute to it in another way (accomplices). Criminal law has different approaches to the participation in crime, but the expression of complicity in (national) law is unsatisfactory. Traditionally, criminal law systems can be divided into those who apply the Unitarian concept of participation and those who recognise the differentiated concept of participation (Keiler, 2011: 175-178). The *Unitarian system* treats all contributions to a criminal act equally, but a distinction is made between the various forms of responsibility at the sentencing stage of court proceedings. Here, all those involved are deemed to be perpetrators. All participants are deemed to fulfil the criterion of *actus reus* regardless of their factual contribution to the crime. This holistic view of the committed crime leads to a sort of collective responsibility for the criminal offence (Keiler, 2011: 177). All individuals qualitatively participated in an equal way in the criminal offence but quantitatively their involvement differed. Their liability is independent of that of the principal offender. There is a minority of EU member states (Ireland, France and Austria) in which accomplices and perpetrators are liable for the same offence, with the possibility to make a distinction between them in the sentencing part (Pereira, 2015: 233).

The *differentiated system* distinguishes between the different forms of participation in terms of nature or degree of responsibility. The level of responsibility is translated into different degrees, whereby a distinction is made between the perpetrator and the accessories (the instigator/the accomplice) (Keiler, 2011: 176). Here the central question is who can be seen as the 'central character' in a criminal offence, the perpetrator from whom the liability of all other participants can be derived (Keiler, 2011: 178).

The interpretation of the criteria for membership in criminal organisations and the distinction in law systems show that there are different ways to assess complicity and participation. This distinction is not only useful in a theoretical sense, it helps in exploring how to approach *mens rea* and *actus reus* in network organisations. The criminal nature of a network and the different roles fulfilled by individuals allowing the collective to function in the way it did, can all be reference points to attribute responsibility and liability in cases of network corruption.

Ex-post evaluation is used to prove the link between the individual (agent) and the (criminal) outcome. According to Keiler (2011: 194), every person who had a "substantial responsibility" for the criminal outcome is liable without having to prove *actus reus*. This would imply that role fulfilment is assessed to determine role responsibility and thereby individual liability. For network corruption this would imply that its network members' role in contributing to the realisation of the network corruption is assessed. This is different than trying to prove the causality between what an individual did (the act) and how it led to the network corruption. Independent of the Unitarian or differentiated law system, the fact that (in retrospect) an individual had and accepted a role responsibility in the network which helped the network to organise itself the way it did, and which resulted in corruption, implies a collective responsibility.

9.3.2.2 RICO

One exceptional example of how collective harm caused by informal collective cooperation can be addressed in law is the US Racketeer Influenced and Corrupt Organisations Act (RICO). This act was briefly referred to in the FIFA case in paragraph 6.2. RICO does do justice to the serious nature of corruption caused by a form of (loosely) organised collective. RICO seeks to prove and prohibit a pattern of crimes conducted through an "enterprise", which the act defines as "any individual, partnership, corporation, association, or other legal entity, and any union or group of individuals associated in fact although not a legal entity." (United States Department of Justice, 2009). This act seeks to address the economic roots and organisational infrastructure of ongoing criminal activities. RICO is a comprehensive legal instrument which has far-reaching implications and creates offences and penalties above and beyond those prescribed for specific individual criminal offences for those involved in an ongoing illegal enterprise that engages in racketeering. Besides the criminal actions, RICO allows the government and private plaintiffs to start civil proceedings. This can result in government seizing and confiscating what it considers to be the profits of crime or requesting the court to order the forfeiture of assets, to impose sanctions or to provide injunctive relief against an individual or organisation involved in a "pattern of racketeering." This can result in: forcing a defendant to forfeit any interest in property, restricting a defendant from engaging in certain future activities or investments, or dissolving or reorganising an enterprise (United States Department of Justice, 2009). When someone is indicted under RICO, the US attorneys have the option of seeking a pre-trial restraining order or injunction to seize a defendant's assets temporarily to prevent the transfer of potentially forfeitable property, as well as require the defendant to put up a performance bond. Despite its harsh provisions, a RICO-related charge is considered easy to prove in court, as it focuses on *patterns of behaviour* as opposed to criminal acts (Moran, 1986: 144).

The RICO Act should not be thought of as a way to punish the commission of isolated criminal acts. Rather, the law establishes severe consequences for those who engage in a pattern of wrongdoing as a member of a criminal enterprise. Liability for a RICO violation requires that a person be involved in an enterprise that operates through a pattern of racketeering activity. On several occasions there were RICO claims made against informal organisations, which raised the question of what qualifies as an enterprise. The US Supreme Court determined that an enterprise can be any group with members who are associated in a relationship in order to achieve a common purpose, provided the relationship lasts long enough to allow them to pursue that purpose. In the terminology of RICO law, such groups are known as "association-in-fact" enterprises (HG Legal Sources, n.d.). The statute does not define "pattern", but in the literature and in RICO cases a pattern is described as "consisting of two or more predicate acts which are related to the enterprise and to each other, as part of a single scheme which causes injury." (Moran, 1986: 158). According to the Supreme Court, to qualify as a pattern the criminal activities must be related and continuous (the "relationship plus continuity" test) (H.J. Inc. v. Northwestern Bell Telephone Co., 1989). Relatedness will be established if the crimes have similar characteristics such as the same perpetrators, victims and methods of commission. Continuity will be established if the crimes occurred over a substantial period of time. Although this explanation of the Supreme Court provided some guidance, many state racketeering laws contain complete and more precise "pattern" definitions (American Bar Association, 2016).

9.3.3 *Incentives to Report Network Corruption*

The previous subparagraph dealt with the exploration of how collective harm caused by networks can be addressed in criminal law. This is an important 'route' to consider, because of the international anti-corruption conventions and the current states parties' reservations to criminalise trading in influence. Notwithstanding that, the alternative route of acknowledging network corruption in civil and administrative law needs consideration. A first way to apply civil law in network corruption cases is to explore whether disciplinary measures can be taken against employees who have contributed to the network corruption. A second way is to allow redress for damage to private or public interests caused by network corruption. Makinwa (2013) argued how private law has potential because it creates a plurality of points at which the sanctioning process for corruption can be initiated and/or enforced. E.g. third parties affected by unfair competition as a result of network corruption can have a legal standing to bring a claim. Søreide's research on business corruption (2008) reveals that firms rarely react to corruption, even when this resulted in them losing important contracts or other interesting business opportunities. "They rarely lodge complaints against the tender procedures, they do not seek legal redress by initiating a court action, and they seldom ask their home country to intervene at a diplomatic level. Furthermore, they do not make liability claims for lost tender expenses, and they do not make their suspicions public in other ways" (Søreide, 2008: 408). This often is not due to lack of proof but because of concerns regarding future business cooperation (Søreide, 2008: 408). Although this research is related to business corruption, by analogy the findings related to determinants of when executives will speak out about competitors' involvement in corruption are to be considered when third parties are affected by network corruption. The chances such form of 'whistleblowing' would work, increase if (local) institutions respond to their allegations and reports in a constructive way which would imply an impartial and thorough investigation of the allegation and subsequent prosecution of the alleged offender(s). As such it is important that it is likely that the prosecution of firms and individuals involved in the network corruption will be successful. If this is combined with effective legal sanctions which gives the reporting party a cost advantage (debarment from future tenders or a penalty in the form of a fine) this could be a strong incentive to report unfair competition (Søreide, 2008: 415-416).

Another instruments which can be interesting when considering routes for development to prevent network corruption, is to explore whether network members who are aware of the network's deterioration can report this in any way. Many EU Member States offer some form of leniency, reward or immunity to someone who was involved in anti-competitive activities such as bid rigging, price-fixing or who was member of a cartel. Although network corruption can emerge even if no individual criminal conduct took place, the closure of the network and the generalised reciprocity do violate principles of fair competition, equal treatment and other democratic rights. In the case studies presented in this research, network members who took on the role of criticaster could be identified. If the network corruption emerged and more so when this also created the context for corruption and other abuses, criticasters could self-report or blow the whistle about this corruption. Luz & Spagnalo (2017) clarify which changes are required to stimulate wrongdoers to blow the whistle in multiple offense situations, and in particular in cases where collusion and corruption occur together in public procurement markets. They argue that all countries should consider creating leniency policies to fight corruption, and coordinating them with anti-competition leniency policies. The absence of formal leniency programs for corruption, besides hindering anti-corruption enforcement, reduces wrongdoers' incentives to report or blow the whistle. Nor would they collaborate in cases against corruption when they risk criminal prosecution for the corruption offense (Luz & Spagnalo, 2017: 764-765). Luz & Spagnalo do argue that such policies need to be designed in a careful way not to stimulate opportunistic behaviour. They also introduce the option of a "one stop point" where individuals or companies can report all crimes simultaneously, given that they have enough information and evidence, before they are granted leniency. This policy strategy would work in cases of network corruption linked to crimes. Alternatively, network corruption has negative implications on society which can, if made concrete, lead to a claim based on damage to the public interest.

Another legal response to network corruption can be in the form of administrative law. Rose-Ackerman (2016) argues that corruption which is not caused by the individual "bad apple" has to be understood and addressed by focussing on the administrative structure in which it emerged. This requires consideration because if the focus is too much on the criminal law, officials might become scared to be involved in networking. According to Rose-Ackerman (2016) lasting change can be achieved if, criminal prosecutions are coupled with reforms in public administration that are consistent with the good governance principles of administrative law. For instance principles like 'transparency' and public disclosure of information should include information about networks and networking. Additionally, current integrity instruments such as codes of conduct should entail provisions which help to raise awareness on the dark side of networks. In line with civil law, disciplinary actions should apply to civil servants and public office holders which are responsible for network corruption. In line with the criminal fines and private remedies the grounds for allowing administrative fines could be extended to network corruption.

9.4 Professional Ethics

9.4.1 *The Importance of Forward-Looking Ethics*

The findings of this research should not only be translated in terms of EU policy recommendations and law amendments; after all it is about networks consisting of individuals. When we talk about individuals and the way they organise themselves, their network awareness is essential. This calls for the need to pay attention to professional ethics. Asking questions about norm development and one's contribution to the effect a network can bring about is a call for the application of prospective ethics. We tend to judge an action in a *retrospective* (backward-looking) way. If we want to analyse the responsibility of networks, we need to consider three aspects when developing a concept of responsibility. Firstly, it should not only be connected to acting. Secondly, it should not be based upon a causal manner of perceiving responsibility. Thirdly, it should not solely be used retrospectively to assign responsibility. If there is something wrong, we want to know whose fault this was. Which act led to the harmful situation and who performed that act? A forward-looking (or *prospective*) ethical approach might look at the goal and function of a network and the roles network members have in that network and the way in which they contribute to goal achievement. That is, what is one's role within the larger whole? (Wempe, 2016: 201). How can network members find the courage to address their collective responsibility? In this situation we can distinguish concrete actions by concrete individuals, but only to a certain point. If no one addresses the norm development and closure of the network, they fail as a collective. In that case, we may hold the network responsible for failing to organise itself in a non-corrupt way. We might even distinguish between the responsibilities of the different partners in the network.

Accepting the responsibility of such a network implies the presence of role responsibilities. In particular, specific members of the network should have responsibilities for stimulating conditions that foster the honest and fair functioning of the network. This concerns the responsibility of the network, which will be distributed among the network members. Agents can be aware of their role and knowingly accept it, but in emergent networks agents may be unaware of the role they play. One of the key characteristics of an autonomous network organisation is that of self-consciousness which is reflected in individuals taking on different roles. Role and role responsibility need to be understood from both an ethical and legal perspective. Based on the empirical findings, I suggest acknowledging *six roles* in networks for the sake of understanding how networks emerge and to clarify individual responsibility in the collective. One of the main characteristics of autonomous network organisations is that of the self-consciousness or the awareness of the network members that there is a network. This awareness can be seen in the fact that the network is turned into an appropriate organisation. These roles are non-limitative and based on the findings of the cases studies. The roles which can be distinguished are the following: orchestrator, strategist, facilitator, intermediary, supporter and criticiser.

1. The *orchestrator* is the agent who guides and supports the network's activities and its continuation. He/she is often the initiator of the network and is connected to most of the network members. This role can be compared to that of centre of influence, as discussed in Chapter 4. The responsibility of the orchestrator is to maintain oversight of norm development in the network. He/she has initiated the network to obtain a certain objective and has links to most of its members. The orchestrator creates the sense of community by building trust between its members. He/she has a great responsibility to keep an eye on the functioning of the network in the larger community. He/she has to lead by

example and actively refers to the collective achievements in his/her statements. The main responsibility of the orchestrator is to establish trust in the network to boost co-operation.

2. The *strategist* is the agent who defines network objectives, sets out the strategy to achieve these objectives and knows how the network can adapt to changing circumstances. The responsibility of the strategist is not so much related to the soft aspects of the network, but to the hard objectives and how to achieve these. He/she has a responsibility to keep an eye on whether the objectives and the strategies are ethical and how both influence the norm development within the network. He/she is also responsible for monitoring changes in law, polices and societal norms and how this has to be observed in the network's strategies.

3. The *facilitator* is the agent that makes an action or process easy or easier by providing assistance or guidance to the network members, either directly or indirectly. The responsibility of the facilitator is to help and guide network members. In doing so, the facilitator has to assess the ethical dimension of the assistance or guidance. He/she is responsible for refraining from providing assistance if the individual help in itself amounts to unethical conduct.

4. The *intermediary* is the agent who acts as a link between people in and outside the (core) network in order to try and bring about an agreement foremost by passing on information. Both the facilitator and the intermediary take on the responsibility of solving issues and building bridges necessary to achieve the objectives set by the strategists. Although there is clear hierarchy in the network, they consider themselves to be at the service of the orchestrator and strategist. The responsibility of the intermediary is connecting the (sub-) network to the larger network. As such, he/she is responsible for exchanging and reproducing information in such a way that it is fair and objective and does not harm the network or its outsiders.

5. The *supporter* is the agent who is actively interested in and wishes success for the network without having an active role; he/she is foremost expressing solidarity and is rather indifferent about the morality of the network. The responsibility of the supporter is small, because he/she is not actively shaping the network, nor is he/she in the position to oversee the network in its entirety. However, he/she is responsible for evaluating the statements and conduct of the orchestrator and the observations of the criticiser to determine whether to continue in his/her support. The supporter must have an eye on the way the network is led, and there is a possibility that he/she becomes a criticiser.

6. The *criticiser* is the agent who is actively interested in and wishes success for the network but not at all costs. The criticiser scrutinises the conduct of the network and its members and asks questions which seek to evaluate the morality of the network. The responsibility of the criticiser is to challenge the network and its members on the aspect of ethical behaviour. This entails asking critical questions and addressing the way the network and its members behave. These responsibilities can stimulate the networks and ensure they achieve their goals and it means that prospective ethics need to be firmly anchored in networks.

A network needs to organise itself in such a way that these roles are fulfilled by its members. This can result in social capital, but it can also lead to network corruption. Each individual takes on a role and these different roles imply different sorts of responsibilities within the network.

9.4.2 *How to Keep an Eye on Exogenous Norms*

Professional ethics not only entails reflecting on one's role in the network, but also requires awareness of the conflicting norms: norms within the networks conflicting with societal norms. If a network becomes isolated from a wider societal context in such a way that the norms develop independently from the societal norms, this poses a risk for corruption. Norm development at the network level develops slowly, over a long period of time with some noticeable leaps. It is first of all important for network members to reflect on this norm development and whether the network norms still respect the hypernorms. The *orchestrator* and *strategist*, and to a lesser extent the *criticiser*, have oversight of this norm development and have to address it if the norm becomes generalised reciprocity. Integrative Social Contract Theory (ISCT) builds on the idea that endogenous network norms meet the hypernorms. Societal or hypernorms are to be found in the laws (treaties, constitutions, statutory laws). They can also be found in traditional organisations such as corporations or municipalities (self-regulation, ethics programmes). However, norms in society develop faster than laws can been enacted.

In order to ensure that the norms of a social network respect the hypernorms, the orchestrator, the strategist and, to a lesser extent, the criticiser should particularly keep an eye on norm development in society. This includes keeping an eye on jurisprudence and verdicts by disciplinary tribunals, but it also means monitoring the opinions voiced by the public through the new media. More than ever are we able to know how norms are developing through the possibilities the Internet offers. For instance, although tax evasion by wealthy people and multinationals is legally facilitated by national governments and trust offices serve as the intermediaries, public opinion on whether it is acceptable and ethical has changed rapidly. Although other types of networks played a role in these tax evasion constructions, it is also an example of a collective cooperation which, if we look at the individual conduct, is lawful, but its collective outcomes are now considered to be violating norms of equal treatment and transparency.

9.4.3 *Reflection*

Acknowledging network corruption implies that network members have to adapt to the new reality where networks can be held responsible. This implies a different sort of awareness. Questions which network members need to ask themselves are: In what networks am I participating? In which capacity am I taking part in this network? When is my way of acting and communicating contributing to the development of norms in the networks to which I am a member? What is my role in this network? How do I contribute to this network and how do I contribute to the major overriding ideal societal goal? These are all critical questions which require a person to stop and think for a minute. The scope of the reflection differs from one role to another, but the responsibility to critically assess one's own role and how it contributes to the functioning of the network is the same. Individuals, networks, organisations, associations – all need to organise moments of reflection.

Although reflecting is something considered important when evaluating our behaviour, some aspects require special attention in the context of networks. One is that we need to recognise our own and our collective biases. We are all framed by what we hear, read or have experienced and contribute to framing ourselves. This is of particular importance in the network context. As was described in Chapter 4, individuals associate and connect with like-minded people. In this manner we are inclined to be strengthened by these others in our beliefs and thoughts. We need to be aware of our own subjectivity. This can be altered if we pause and take time to reflect and recognise our own cognitive bias which has developed over time. Why do we act in a certain way, how have customs in our social networks developed, why do we trust network members and are we still welcoming individuals who think and act differently? If we challenge our own biases, we start to reason in a logical and rational way instead of continuing to think and act as we have always done. In the case of unexpected events, quick and intuitive reasoning is okay and useful, but otherwise we have to try to use logical and rational reasoning.

Additionally, we need to recognise the defining moments in networks. According to Badaracco (1998), these moments force individuals to take a close look at their fundamental values and to prioritise these. In the network corruption cases, individuals retrospectively think they should have acted differently in specific situations. Recognising defining moments in networks can be difficult if we are under time pressure or stress or if we feel insecure; this limits our capacity to think critically. If we believe that we might be in a decisive situation soon, we should prepare ourselves, discuss it with others and put our thoughts on paper. If confronted immediately, we should dare to pause or ask for extra time, to be able to oversee and think through all aspects of the situation in which we are to decide or act.

We also need to practise our ability to distinguish facts from assumptions. In particular, the informal and unrecorded information between network members stimulated the preferential treatment. Network members should be aware that such information can be subjective or based on assumptions. It is also important to practise our understanding of causal links and correlations. Too often we think in terms of causal links, while many phenomena such as network corruption can only be explained when recognising that it was caused by various factors such as collective cooperation. This requires the skill to see our own position or role and the bigger social system or network we act in. The case studies have shown that often individuals were acting with good intentions, and retrospectively did not see the wrongfulness of their behaviour because there was no causal link between their actions and the damaging consequences. If we learn to see how our own conduct contributes to collective action, we might be more aware and decide to act differently.

Another thing to reflect on is the mechanism by which like attracts like. If we surround ourselves with people who have features that are similar to ours, we run the risk of creating an individual and collective tunnel vision. Although the importance of organising checks and balances, countervailing powers and criticism is stressed in many integrity models and anti-corruption frameworks, we as human beings organise ourselves in homogenous networks. This limits our ability to approach an issue in various ways and with various perspectives. Try to invite others to discuss dilemmas, to make sure a situation is seen from different perspectives.

When reflecting, it is important to distinguish specific from general interests. Specific, individual interests and self-interests play a role in our day-to-day activities and we as human beings are designed to protect ourselves, which is in fact the fundamental feeling which leads to our desire to be part of networks. However, striving for one's own interests is not wrong per se but interests should optimally be aligned. Also, we need to accustom ourselves to asking more questions and accepting more questions. Critical thinking cannot take place without asking questions to ourselves and to others which touch upon the motive for or the reason behind our decisions and acts.

9.5 Sub-Conclusions

When organising routes for development for policies on network corruption, the EU can take the lead in initiating EU policies on this issue. By doing so, the EU can contribute to existing anti-corruption policies. The EU has an important role in setting the standard and leading by example. This means an innovation of the instruments it uses to assess member states' anti-corruption frameworks by incorporating a tool which allows for an easy overview of the way social networks occur across the formal system. The scope of policy instruments should go beyond the boundary of organisations and the societal norms should be translated into norms for networks.

There are promising examples of EU policies and laws seeking to deal with responsibility and liability for crime caused by collectives such as networks. Such instruments lead to all sorts of legal questions. Most EU Member States have criminal provisions in place which criminalise the membership in a criminal organisation. In reality, public prosecutors are hesitant to use this in cases of network corruption. This is because the level of organisation is still perceived difficult to prove. The way in which our network society develops, illustrates the importance of innovating our criminal law to meet the requirements of today and the future. One way would be to incorporate into criminal law a provision on network corruption. However, most national lawmakers are fiercely against the recognition of collective crimes. One way to solve this and to do justice to the serious and collective nature of network corruption is to allow the *mens rea* and *actus reus* criteria to be fulfilled if a pattern of criminal behaviour of an association of people can be recognised. Hereby *mens rea* is the element of criminal responsibility referring to a person's awareness of the fact that his or her conduct is criminal. *Actus reus*, is the element known as the physical act of a crime. The EU could consider whether some elements of the US RICO Act can be used in future attempts to harmonise anti-corruption criminal law. By focussing on the patterns of behaviour instead of the individual conduct, network corruption can be a crime for which one can be held responsible based on the role one had and accepted. As such, the role of criticaster is important, because this role could coincide with reporting the network corruption. Addressing network corruption in policy strategies should also imply that there are greater incentives for members of networks which form network corruption to 'blow the whistle' when the network becomes closed and in which reciprocity becomes the norm.

One way to assess the 'association', 'enterprise' or 'organisation' of network corruption and the role each individual took on, is to organise one criminal trial for all involved. If prosecutors seek to prove the network corruption, it is essential that multiple defendants are heard during one network corruption court trial. The court case following the Dutch corruption scandal in Roermond dealt with three of the suspects during one court proceeding and although the judges still looked at individual acts, it can be seen as a step in the direction of dealing with the networks and the collective responsibility during one trial, to discover the roles and patterns.

To conclude, accepting the concept of network corruption requires new approaches to anti-corruption. Prevention and repression are both needed and international organisations and national legislators need to acknowledge that corruption can be caused by networks, in addition to individuals and organisations. The EU can initiate policies aimed at innovation of (criminal) law but the findings of this research highlight the importance of professional ethics. Rather than knowing how to act when a specifically predesigned ethical dilemma comes up, the skill to reflect is more future-proof and context-independent. It is essential to use both ethics and law when approaching networks in anti-corruption. The prospective ethics can help in developing an eye for the goal and function of a network, the roles network members have in that network and the way in which they contribute to achievement of that goal. Without the skill to reflect on one's own role in and contribution to networks, every anti-corruption instrument will be ineffective. Ideally, we want employees and civil servants to be aware of their role and role responsibilities before they become a professional. Professional ethics should be given greater attention in organisations and in education.

10. Conclusions

10.1 Introduction

The main purpose of this research was to increase our understanding of the link between networks and corruption.[1] First by exploring whether and how the bodies of knowledge on corruption and on networks referred to this linkage and secondly, by assessing whether the findings from network and corruption literature helped to discover the mechanisms in those corruption cases linked to networks. In addition, the research aimed to contribute to the development of more effective anti-corruption policies in general and more specific within the EU. In order to contribute to both purposes a set of characteristics has been developed, based on the findings in the corruption and network literature, through which networks can be assessed on the aspect of deterioration. This set of characteristics was used in the empirical part of the research: the three case studies. The case study of FIFA concerned a transnational network, the case concerning the News of the World (NoW) concerned a national network and the case about the Dutch municipality of Roermond was in fact a local network with some ties to the national level. The case study analysis helped to understand the specific network deterioration in real life but also led to a certain nuancing of the concept of network corruption. Following this exploration, Chapter 9 presented how networks and network responsibility could be incorporated in (EU) anti-corruption polices, law and professional ethics. This final chapter presents the overall conclusion of the research. It begins with the reasons for the research, the central question and the methods used. The theoretical concepts and the major findings of the empirical research are discussed. Then the practical implications and routes for development are summarised. Lastly the opportunities but also the limitations of this research are discussed and suggestions for future research presented.

10.2 From 'Quid Pro Quo' to 'Generalised Reciprocity'

When I first started to do research into the National Integrity Assessment (NIS) Netherlands in 2011, I also wanted to report on the complexity of the concept of trading in influence and explore when lobbying becomes trading in influence and/or corruption (Slingerland *et al.*, 2012). The key figures whom I interviewed and the supervisory committee of the NIS project deemed it impossible to distinguish these phenomena or to be able to point to the exact moment when influencing becomes undue influencing.

---

1 For sake of clarity and readability, I choose to minimise the number of literature references in this concluding chapter.

Although it would surely be difficult to point out the dividing line between influencing and undue influencing, this does not imply that it is impossible to conclude that someone's conduct surely crossed the border of lawful influencing. A difficulty in evaluating whether the influencing is in fact corruption is that we tend to approach it by looking at individual conduct. This is problematic because the 'quid pro quo' or reciprocity can be difficult to spot with this limited view. However, if we incorporate the network structure in this assessment of influencing, patterns of behaviour become visible which show that there is an implicit 'quid pro quo' in the norm of reciprocity which steers the behaviour of network members, raising questions about the corrupt nature of the network.

In several major corruption cases in western societies, public prosecutors failed to convince the judiciary of corrupt practices, due to the limited scope of the concept of corruption in criminal law. When the facts of the cases which are part of this research became public, the overall reaction was that these practices had to be halted and the organisations and individuals involved had to be punished. This search for the 'evildoer' is common in our legal and ethical reasoning; however, as these cases have demonstrated, this approach is not adequate in attributing responsibility for the corruption caused by networks (e.g., Anechiarico, 2016; Heywood, 1997; Johnston, 2005; Wempe, 2010; Ashforth & Anand, 2003). This narrow perspective on responsibility is also present in the criminal investigations and prosecutions in these cases: public prosecutors aiming to prove the collective nature of the corruption, but judges having to establish individual corrupt acts. This led me to research the link between social networks and corruption, thereby formulating the following question:

In what way and to what extent is corruption linked to the functioning of social networks, and what does this entail for our knowledge of corruption and networks and the policies to eradicate corruption?

The research has shown that those features which allow networks to achieve positive purposes can also have a downside leading to the deterioration of networks. Various disciplines have studied the phenomenon of corruption, making the available theory and research on corruption quite extensive. The dominant position upheld in this voluminous body of knowledge on corruption either sees corruption as an individual act of abusing one's professional role or entrusted power in return for private gain, or considers corruption to be an entire state of being of an organisation or country (e.g., OECD, 2008; Klitgaard, 1997; Pinto *et al.*, 2008). References to such 'endemic' or 'systemic' corruption are common, by which scholars refer to the wide practice of corruption within the context of an organisation or country. Some scholars have explored the forms of corruption which are broader than the individual act and broader than the immediate and obvious method of influencing (e.g., Anechiarico & Jacobs, 1996; Warren, 2004). This literature describes corruption without the clear favour and return favour. There is corruption literature which indicates that social systems (networks) and individuals are mutually reinforcing and causing corruption (e.g., Nielsen, 2003; Uribe, 2014; Ashforth & Anand, 2003. This literature is still limited and does not provide an in-depth analysis of the way in which networks can be linked to corruption. Having assessed the corruption definitions and typologies and assessing their connections to networks, I've come to define corruption as: *allowing improper interests to influence decision-making at the expense of the general interest.* As such, I choose to get rid of the explicit reference to 'quid pro quo' or 'in return for', which is the main character of corruption. The result of the decision-making which has been influenced by undue interests is the core aspect of the corruption and not the actual exchange of interests. In this way, I do not see corruption as something which can only be attributed to an individual. Here corruption is the outcome or result of a (social) process. Instead of assessing the nature of individual actions, this definition seeks to look at the outcome of a process before labelling something 'corruption'. Because the corruption literature is still rather limited in its references to networks, the research of network literature was required.

10.3 The Downside of Networks

The literature on networks is equally as extensive as the literature on corruption. Most literature and research deal with the link between social networks and social capital (e.g., Owens & Young, 2008; Putnam, 2000; Granovetter, 1973; Brass *et al*, 2004). However, there is little information available on the link between networks and corruption. In most literature, networks are considered to make up the important social organisation needed in society. We all associate with others, form groups and thereby help each other. This psychological mechanism has been important in history because group formation meant a better chance of survival. Network formation is a way of striving for one's own interest by informally cooperating with like-minded people. Network formation can be done consciously with a certain purpose in mind (goal-directed networks) or happen naturally and grow organically over a certain period (emergent networks) (e.g. Provan *et al.*, 2007). Networks are dynamic and adapt to the circumstances. Networks influence the beliefs, behaviour and thinking of their members, which reinforces their contribution to and actions within the social network. Due to these social processes, network members start to identify with the network and in their acting do what is best for the network. The principle of reciprocity is a key characteristic of networks, steering the behaviour of network members to achieve the network's purpose: to help one another, to influence decision-making or treat one another in a preferential way (e.g., Putnam, 2000; Fukuyama, 2001; Granovetter, 1973). Although this principle is necessary to achieve the purposes of networks, its downside receives far less attention in network literature.

From a communitarian perspective, society foremost needs more citizens who are willing to scrutinise political decision-making by organising themselves in networks. Communitarians consider networks to have evolved over time and to form communities which restore loyalty, solidarity and goodwill in society, contributing to a strong moral awareness. Such networks can threaten to sanction members who deviate from the network's practices but offer certainty and stability if they conform to it (e.g., Etzioni, 2015; Sandel, 2009). Communitarian thinking underlines the importance of human interdependence and the strength of social relations which reinforce individuals and vice versa. Contrary to the communitarian approach, contract thinkers emphasise that networks are communities which can freely decide which norms to adopt by means of a micro-social contract which observes the societal hypernorm (e.g., Donaldson & Dunfee, 1999a). Both approaches help in understanding how norms develop within networks (social process or conscious choice), but they do not provide a solution to norm development or creation within networks which lead to the deterioration of the network. Nonetheless, these approaches have helped to understand the issue which scholars of network theory continue to debate, which is whether unethical behaviour can be explained by looking at the social structure of the network or the individual rational actor with his own beliefs and thinking. This research builds on the idea that both the social structure of the network and the individuals establishing or joining the social networks need to be characterised and understood, to be able to see how they mutually reinforce one another and can result in network corruption.

Individuals associate with like-minded people to serve the individual and collective interests by helping each other through this form of cooperation (e.g., Brass *et al.*, 2004; Putnam, 2000). This specific form of reciprocity ('I'll do this for you and you will do something for me') is a basic way of exchanging favours. It is inherently part of social interaction and politics. Social processes within networks of homogenous individuals (bonding networks) contribute to the development of the norm of generalised reciprocity ('I'll do this for you without expecting anything specific back from you, in the confident expectation that someone else will do something for me down the road'). This form of generalised reciprocity is of value in our society because not every single exchange needs to be balanced (e.g., Putnam, 2000). It is complemented by investments in internal relations, thereby strengthening the social network's collective identity, with which individuals identify. Individual beliefs in loyalty, solidarity and reciprocity have led to this general norm which in turn influences the individual network members in the way they think and act. In this manner, network members are more successful at getting jobs, winning projects and simply being successful. The bonding networks are generally inward-looking and with a high degree of personal contact, a shared history and common purpose (Putnam, 2000). This also makes these networks more at risk of becoming corrupt, because the generalised reciprocity interacts with the other features leading to the closure of the networks towards others. Nevertheless, network theory also indicates that those network members who function as a broker, and connect (through weak ties) the closed bonding networks across the structural holes with other networks, are the most successful. These 'bridging connections' give these brokers (centres of influence) an advantage. The broker has more diverse contacts and as such is more likely to be a candidate for involvement in new opportunities (e.g., Stam, 2010; Burt, 2000; Szreter & Woolcock, 2004). Additionally, this position brings together otherwise disconnected contacts, which gives this individual a disproportionate say in whose interests are served when the contacts come together. Closure can be necessary to realise the value found in these holes. As such, the bonding or closed networks gain from the opportunities obtained by bridging or broker connections but equally make the risk of the network's deterioration greater because of their exclusion of non-networks members, and this is what links networks to corruption. Informal collective cooperation such as networking is valued and widely seen as something which is very valuable and existential for us human beings and the society we live in. The downside or pitfalls of networks are grossly overlooked.

10.4 Attributing Responsibility to Networks

Even if we do observe the deterioration of networks, we still face the difficulties of having to attribute responsibility to networks. The prevailing notions of responsibility no longer work regarding issues which are caused by collective acting, such as climate change, the obesity crisis, the financial crisis, the harm caused by certain motorcycle associations and network corruption. In these examples it is difficult to distinguish a knowing and willing action by individuals, foremost because there is no direct or causal link between the individual behaviour and the damage caused (e.g. Wempe, 2010; May, 1987; French, 1984). It was the collective acting in which interdependent factors mutually reinforced each other with corruption as the outcome. In recent decades the debate about collective responsibility has developed and led to the recognition of responsibility of organised collectives such as organisations and countries (e.g., Copp, 1979; French, 1984). The networks which are part of this research do not meet the criteria of organised collectives, but they are by no means a mere coincidence. They may be goal-directed networks or emergent networks; in either case they bear features of some form of loose organisation which creates a basis for responsibility attribution (e.g., McGary, 1986; May, 1987; Wempe, 2010).

10.5 The Four Features of Network Corruption

After this analysis of corruption and network theory and research, I was left with eight features (three from the corruption literature and five from the network literature) which together would form a raw sketch of those networks which can bear responsibility for their deterioration into corruption. I extracted three corruption features from the analysis of corruption definitions and typologies in chapter 3. These are three features of corruption linked to networks. They are: (1) collective misuse of professional roles for network interests, (2) generalised reciprocity and (3) harming the rights of outsiders. I extracted five network features from the network literature, which jointly can be seen as features of informal networks which can bear responsibility for their deterioration. They are: (1) informal structure, (2) shared interest, (3) common attitude, (4) self-consciousness and (5) closed character.

One by one I compared them and searched for overlapping features or features which needed to be complemented by a second meaning to better distinguish the original interpretation given to the feature. I started off with the feature of 'an informal structure' and linked it to the feature 'misuse of professional roles for network interests' to clarify the singularity and wrongfulness of this structure or cooperation as opposed to the common way of 'cooperating'. Thereafter, I combined the autonomous network organisation's feature of 'shared interest' with the corruption feature of 'generalised reciprocity' (previous, present or future favour from the network) to distinguish the normal network interest in helping one another from the absolute norm which has influenced the network's shared interest over time. I continued with the autonomous network organisation's feature of 'common attitude' and, with the knowledge gained on self-categorisation, I linked it to the 'self-consciousness of the collective' to distinguish those networks whose identity coordinates the behaviour and role of their members from the networks in which individuals cooperate but foremost remain individuals with their separate and unique identities (self-consciousness of the individuals). I concluded by combining the feature of autonomous network organisation, i.e. 'closed character', with the network feature 'harming the rights of outsiders' because the closure is the reason third parties are harmed (insiders vs. outsiders), and by distinguishing this meaning of the closed character from networks which can be just strong bonds.

These four features help to see the mechanisms leading to networks deteriorating. Although the exact turning point for network deterioration is hard to discover, these features interplay in such a way that certain mechanisms will start working and these mechanisms can be observed. The misuse of professional roles for network interests leads to preferential treatment of network members, thereby no longer serving the interests one has to observe when carrying out the profession. As such the actual role in the network takes over the professional role one formally accepted. Part of these networks' social process is that preferential treatment becomes the norm, thereby creating the norm of generalised reciprocity. This implicit norm steers behaviour as a reinforcing power, whereby the network members become wilfully blind and no longer see that they have a choice to contribute to either the network or third parties. (Heffernan, 2011). The norm steers their behaviour to such an extent that they collectively act, refrain from acting, decide or think in the interest of the network. As such, the character of the network becomes closed, thereby harming the rights of outsiders. This common attitude is strengthened because the network members increasingly identify themselves with the network. This closed character of the network leads to the absence of the internal criticism and correction mechanisms, which again reinforces all the other features. These features reinforce one another, thereby deteriorating into network corruption. I define the concept of network corruption as:

Informal collective cooperation in which professional roles are misused for network interests to such an extent that the dominant norm is that of generalised reciprocity, leading to the exclusion of others, while the members' awareness of their network is reflected in their common attitude.

The literature on corruption shows that there is a multitude of corruption definitions available, varying among disciplines and perspectives (micro, meso, macro or state of being to process). This research is conceptual and explorative in nature, seeking to grasp a societal phenomenon by introducing the concept of network corruption (Eisenhardt, 1989; Freeman *et al.*,2017). The concept of network corruption adds another dimension to the corruption phenomenon, indicating that it is necessary to broaden the definition of corruption to a network definition, to acknowledge that it is in fact the collective of a network that contributes to the emergence of corruption. References to trading in influence and political corruption are a first step in thinking in terms of corruption as a collective or as a network. Acknowledging the existence of network corruption provides a solution to corruption which is the result of the combined actions of a social network.

10.6 Network Corruption Specifications and Nuances in the Case Studies

Despite their differences, the FIFA case, the NoW case and the Roermond case have in common that the real damage or corruption was the result of the complex collective behaviour of the informal networks. In all three cases, the basis of the social network was formed by longstanding friendships between a few individuals who formed small bonds. In the FIFA case, the goal-directed network was established by FIFA's president at the time, Blatter, and a few other key figures, whereby the FIFA organisation was the corrupt formal organisation in which corruption was endemic, but which soon led to the emergence of the wider informal global or transnational network (e.g. US Department of Justice, 2015). The bonding network had bridging connections, and this wider network bears all the features of network corruption. The NoW case is about the emergent network which developed over time and which was hugely influenced by the pressure felt by the NoW organisation to sell more copies of their newspapers (e.g. Honourable Lord Justice Leveson, 2012). This network was smaller than that of FIFA and although bribery, intimidation and other crimes also took place within this network, corruption was not the norm as was the case within FIFA. The NoW case meets all the features of network corruption, and makes perfectly clear how normal networking can deteriorate when the network's members start to abuse their professional roles for the network's interest and the network's norm becomes that of generalised reciprocity, leading to the closure of the network (e.g. ECLI:NL:RBROT:2016:5272). In all three cases the deterioration mechanism really started to work when network members decided to continue their professional communication in an informal, unrecorded way. The Roermond case has a lot of similarities with the NoW case, although there are examples of individual network members acting corrupt, it was the deterioration of the network as a whole which resulted in network corruption.

Using the characteristics of network corruption in the three case studies has led to the findings that informal social networks can deteriorate and become network corruption. This network corruption can emerge even if there are no individual corrupt acts such as bribery. The networks become closed and the norm becomes to treat all networks members in a preferential way without there being any concrete return favour. The result meets the definition of corruption which I introduced in Chapter 3. I define corruption as *allowing improper interests to influence decision-making at the expense of the general interest.* The concept of network corruption is related to the phenomenon of corrupt networks, and as the case studies showed, these sometimes go hand in hand. The FIFA case illustrated that the corrupt network was present (and thus individual corruption was as well) and while the network grew it also led to and resulted in network corruption.

10.7 VARIOUS FORMS OF NETWORKS AND INFLUENCE

This research offered a table of networks and influence, whereby four types of networks were distinguished which could serve three different purposes that would lead to either proper forms of influence (social capital and lobbying) or improper forms of influence (trading in influence and network corruption), whereby trading in influence in essence can start as the normal trading inherent to politics, but gradually move in the direction of the deterioration of the network. The first network is the 'goal-directed network with a form of organisation' such as card-carrying membership associations or companies, which has the purpose of helping one another, it is in fact linking social capital. If such a network actively tries to influence decision-making, this would be a form of interest representation or lobbying, whereby the agent who is being influenced would not be part of the network. If the purpose were to change to preferential treatment, it would be a matter of trading in influence, whereby the agent who is being influenced becomes part of the network. The second network is the 'goal-directed network with an informal open structure', for example platforms and interest representation groups, which has the purpose of helping one another, it is in fact bridging social capital. If such a network actively tries to influence decision-making, this would be a form of interest representation or lobbying, whereby the agent who is being influenced would not be part of the network. If the purpose were to change to the preferential treatment, it would be a matter of trading in influence, whereby the agent who is being influenced becomes part of the network. The third and fourth networks are the 'goal-directed network with an informal closed structure' and the 'emergent network with an informal closed structure', such as individuals and representatives of powerful organisations, which have the purpose of helping one another, this is in fact bonding social capital. If such a network actively tries to influence decision-making, this would be a form of interest representation which should be labelled as trading in influence, whereby the agent who is being influenced becomes part of the network. If the purpose were to change to the preferential treatment, it would be a matter of network corruption. As such, these phenomena are related, though they do not form a gradual difference but rather a fundamental one with their own unique properties.

10.8 Organising Routes for Development

This brings me to the question of how this knowledge of corruption and networks can contribute to policies to eradicate corruption. The focus of this research has been on the EU and its anti-corruption policies. With corruption being a major concern to the EU because of its serious threat to the internal market and the rule of law, and because corruption scandals undermine public trust in the EU itself, it is important that the EU leads by example, by setting EU anti-corruption standards for EU member states while actively expressing how its institutions and representatives prevent their networks from becoming corrupt. The EU is determined to ensure it understands the phenomenon of corruption and wants to add something to what is already done in terms of anti-corruption by other international organisations (European Commission, 2011a; 2014c; ANTICORRP, n.d. b), first by introducing the Anti-Corruption report (ACR) and the EU corruption research project ANTICORRP and now by mainstreaming anti-corruption in its economic policy dialogues in the European Semester. Although the EU wants to take action against political corruption and high-profile corruption, the existing assessment tools it uses and those which it has developed itself are deficient in addressing network corruption. The NIS and LIS model and, to some extent, the EU ACR present an inventory of the national anti-corruption frameworks (all institutions and policies by law and in practice). What are missing in these models are coherency and an understanding of the network structure of corruption. (e.g., Huberts & Six, 2012; Slingerland, Six & Huberts, 2012). This form of corruption is the blind spot in current anti-corruption and integrity systems. This means that there should be an element included which allows for an easy overview of the way social networks function across the formal institutions and system.

Additionally, the current policy instruments which seek to prevent undue forms of influence, such as the rules on the financing of political parties, the rules on asset declarations, rules on conflict of interest and lobbying should be presented, used and interpreted with the network structure in mind. As such, the assessment of undue influencing should not be limited by screening individual acts, for instance an individual donation to a political party or the incompatibility of functions for a top official. To the contrary, it implies that the information from these policy instruments should be integrated to get a real overview of the existing networks. Not only for monitoring purposes, but also to create network awareness and network responsibility among individuals. The network approach also implies that the normal and totally accepted individual acts can collectively cause network corruption. Therefore the distinction in such instruments between accepted or non-accepted activities should be less strict and be supplemented with questions helping to stimulate an individual's awareness of his network. Only when these policy instruments are linked to networks can network awareness develop among policy-makers, politicians, public prosecutors and network members etc. who otherwise would continue to compare individual acts to these instruments, while their reflection should be on the nature of the network and their role in it.

A next step would be to look at the member states' civil, administrative and criminal law and consider how legal instruments can help to prevent or redress network corruption (e.g. Hale & Cline, 2014; Keiler, 2011; Makinwa, 2013). One way would be to ensure whistleblower policy strategies which include incentives and legal safeguards for network members who want to report network corruption. Another way would be to request member states to criminalise this form of corruption. This research presented ways to innovate criminal law in such way that the collective responsibility can be established. For instance, by combining the court proceedings of networks members to allow an assessment by the judges on the mechanisms leading up to the network corruption and each individual's role in it. This was done to some extent in the Roermond case. Another way is to extend the possibilities of participation beyond anti-competition law or by introducing a law similar to the US' Racketeer Influenced and Corrupt Organisations Act (RICO), in which a pattern of behaviour resulting in corruption is enough to prove criminality instead of having to prove individual criminal acts (e.g., Moran, 1986). Other means are also available. The risk of network deterioration should be mentioned in codes of conduct and there should be strong incentives for individuals or companies to report network corruption, varying from solid leniency programmes for those who were part of the network corruption to economic benefits of reporting network corruption by others e.g. individuals and organisations who are the victim of the network corruption. Additionally disciplinary measures should also apply in cases in which employees, civil servants or officials have proven not to take action against the closure of the network and its norm development to treat network members in a preferential way. There are recent examples of Dutch civil law actions against collectives such as the civil law ban in the case of the Motorcycle Club Bandidos which indicate that there ways in which the law can deal with informal collectives and their responsibility (ECLI:NL:RBMNE:2017:6241).

Additionally, the topic of networks should get far more attention in professional ethics as part of anti-corruption polices than it now does. Being able to reflect is a precondition for anti-corruption rules and standards to have effect. Reflection is not restricted to the boundaries of an organisation. If the EU manages to design policies which allow for reflection and assessment of our roles and participation in networks, we will be challenged to look beyond the micro- and meso-level to see how we can contribute and solve societal problems in collectives such as networks. This research presented four features to distinguish whether a network has become deteriorated. This retrospective approach is a step in the direction of acknowledging that social networks have a moral status of their own. The introduction of collective responsibility for social networks has an ever bigger potential if we consider the prospective ethical dimension. This means that responsibility is not determined once there is a realisation that damage was done; on the contrary, the prospective ethics underlines the importance of asking questions and reflecting on the roles that one has in networks and the way in which a person or an organisation is able to solve societal problems (e.g. Wempe, 2011).

Incorporating professional (prospective) ethics in anti-corruption policies and assessment models is an important step in dealing with and preventing network corruption. If we acknowledge networks as autonomous organisations, we should hold the collective responsible in its own right or translate this responsibility into responsibilities of the individual network members. It is important to localise responsibility, not only to talk in terms of liability but, more importantly, to try to prevent future cases of network corruption and to address them as soon as they are about to happen. The feature of 'self-consciousness' is important in this regard, because it is concerned with role responsibilities within networks. Understanding the network part of this research implies looking for the role each individual played in the network instead of assessing whether his or her individual actions were corrupt or not. Understanding the link between networks and corruption implies that we assess roles and role responsibilities in a network. I recognise six roles in networks for the sake of understanding how networks emerge and to clarify individual responsibility in the collective.

The *orchestrator* is the agent who guides and supports the network's activities and its continuation. Orchestrators are the initiators of the network and are connected to most of the network members. They are the centre of influence. Their main responsibility is to establish trust in the network to boost cooperation. The *strategist* is the agent who defines network objectives and sets out the strategy to achieve these objectives and knows how the network can adapt when circumstances change. The *facilitator* is the agent that makes an action or process easy or easier by providing assistance or guidance, either directly or indirectly, to the network members. The *intermediary* is the agent who acts as a link between people in and outside the (core) network and arranges agreements by transferring information. Both the facilitator and the intermediary to function as a broker, which is necessary to achieve the objectives set by the strategists. Depending on the type of network and the purpose of the network, the agents they connect with can become part of the network themselves. The *supporter* is the agent who is actively interested in and wishes success for the network without having an active role; he/she is foremost expressing solidarity. The *criticiser* is the agent who is actively interested in and wishes success for the network but not at all costs. A network needs to organise itself in such a way that these roles are fulfilled by its members. This can result in social capital, but it can also lead to network corruption. Each individual takes on a role and these different roles coincide with different responsibilities. This is important to be able to assign responsibility retrospectively, but it also offers an alternative preventive approach.

This research showed that acknowledging network corruption can help in understanding the many examples of corruption which were not caused by individual acts of persons or organisations and which could therefore not be addressed accordingly. Current theories on corruption are deficient in describing the collective nature of corruption caused by networks, while network theory is deficient in describing what the pitfalls of networks can be. Corruption is linked to the functioning of social networks in many ways. Networks can form a context in which the norm is to act in a corrupt manner, leading to systemic corruption such as bribery. Corruption can also be linked to networks in which the norm is that of generalised reciprocity without individual corruption but which become closed to outsiders, thereby resulting in corruption. This is a form of 'network corruption' which can stand on its own, but which can also be the structure through which a corruption network and individual corruption come into being. The present research has described the emergence of this phenomenon and what this entails for our knowledge of corruption and networks and the policies to eradicate corruption. The research hopes to create a greater awareness among the public, decision-makers, political parties and law enforcement authorities of the processes that take place within networks which contribute to the changing character of networks in the direction of corruption.

10.9 SUGGESTIONS FOR FUTURE RESEARCH

With the finalisation of this research, I automatically think back at the time when I first spoke with my fellow corruption researchers about the idea of exploring networks and corruption. Looking back, I do feel proud about the end result of this research. The link between networks and the emergence of corruption is a fascinating topic and I do consider the concept of network corruption to contribute to the scientific, political and societal discussions about when due influencing becomes undue influencing. Linking corruption to the context of networks had not been explored adequately in theory, the introduction of network corruption complements and innovates current scientific ideas on corruption and is another concrete step which helps us sharpen our thinking of what corruption is and how it comes into existence. Several disciplines were used because methodological holism was considered essential when exploring this phenomenon. This way the exploration could go beyond the boundaries of monodisciplinary research and networks and corruption were analysed from different perspectives. This is the added value of the research: not a simple or one dimensional view on corruption emergence. Notwithstanding that, this variation of disciplines also meant that none of the disciplines could be used and presented in-depth. This resulted in two theoretical chapters in which the most important sources from literature were presented but which nevertheless meant that not the entire body of knowledge on corruption or networks from all disciplines was described.

The empirical part of the research illustrates and clarifies how networks can deteriorate even when there is no individual corruption taking place. The three cases have all had a great impact on our society and made visible how most legal instruments lack in addressing corruption adequately. These cases were relevant but also they were only three out of the many corruption cases available. This is one of the limitations of the research. Had I been able to use more case studies, the link between the network context and the corruption (network corruption, corrupt networks, corrupt organisations and individual corruption) would probably been more explicit and specific. Equally, the link between other types of networks, exact turning points and other related crimes could have been tested and specified more into detail. Therefore I'm very anxious to find out what would have become visible concerning networks and corruption in other case studies. For future research, a strong recommendation is use the concept of network corruption to analyse many more cases. Also further research into examples of networks which are healthy and do no deteriorate could help in understanding how to organise a network. Among the subjects which could be included in follow-up studies could also be those in our society who do not belong to any one of the important networks.

10.10 Some Final Words

The last word has not been spoken about 'network corruption'. Nor has this scientifically challenging concept yet been overly researched. We might not even be able to capture the full complexity of networks and corruption, but we can certainly deepen our insight into their link. This can be achieved by taking a theoretically and methodological broader approach, as done in this research.

We should move further and acknowledge that corruption is more than bribery. If we explore the topic of network corruption further we might get a clearer sight at what we as a society accept as ways of influencing and what we consider to be undue forms of influencing. This requires that we all are able to assess our own acting in a larger societal context, varying from how we contribute to the street where we live, the organisation we work for and the networks we're a member of. Only in this way, we can assure that our awareness of collective acting and collective responsibility is sustainably sharpened.

Literature

Books, chapters of books and articles

Abraham, J. (2002). The pharmaceutical industry as a political player. *The Lancelet.* Vol. 360, Issue 9344, 9, pp. 1498-1502.

Adler, P.S. & Kwon, S.W. (2009). *Social Capital: The Good, the Bad and the Ugly.* Marshall Research Paper Series Working Paper MKT 03-09. USC Marshall School of Business. Reprint of Adler, P.S. and Kwon, S.W. (2000). Social Capital: The Good, the Bad and the Ugly. In E.L. Lesser (ed.). Knowledge and Social Capital. Woburn: Butterworth-Heinemann.

Alatas, S. H. (1968). *The Sociology of Corruption: The Nature, Function, Causes and Prevention of Corruption.* Singapore: Donald Moore Press.

Alter, C. & Hage, J. (1993). *Organizations working together.* Newbury Park, CA: Sage.

Andvig, J.C. & Moene, K.O. (1990). How Corruption May Corrupt. *Journal of Economic Behavior and Organization,* 1990 (13), 63-76.

Anechiarico, F. (2010). Protecting integrity at the local level: the role of anticorruption and public management networks. *Crime, Law and Social Change.* February 2010, Volume 53, Issue 1: pp. 79–95.

Anechiarico, F. & Jacobs, J.B. (1996). *The Pursuit of Absolute Integrity. How Corruption Control Makes Government Ineffective.* Chicago and London: Chicago University Press.

Ashforth, B.E. & Anand, V. (2003). The Normalization of Corruption in Organizations. *Research in Organizational Behavior* 2003, Volume 25: pp. 1-52.

Avineri, S. & De-Shalit, A. (1992). *Communitarianism and Individualism.* Oxford: Oxford University Press.

Badaracco, J.L. (1998). Defining Moments: When Managers Must Choose between Right and Wrong. January 1, 1998 / First Quarter 1998 / Issue 10. Available from: https://www.strategy-business.com/article/9523?gko=3e58d (Accessed 29/08/18).

Baker, W.E. & Faulkner, R.R. (1993). The Social Organization of Conspiracy: Illegal Networks in the Heavy Electrical Equipment Industry. *American Sociological Review*, Vol. 58, No. 6 (Dec., 1993): pp. 837-860.

Baumeister, R.F. & Leary, M.R. (1995). The Need to Belong: Desire for Interpersonal Attachments as a Fundamental Human Motivation. *Psychological Bulletin* 1995, Vol. 117. No. 3: pp. 506.

Bell, D. (2016). Communitarianism. *The Stanford Encyclopedia of Philosophy* (Summer 2016 Edition), E.N. Zalta (ed.). Available from: https://plato.stanford.edu/archives/sum2016/entries/communitarianism/ (Accessed 29/08/18).

Bhaskar, R. (2000). *The possibility of naturalism.* London: Routledge.

Brass, D.J., Butterfield, K.D. & Skaggs, B.C. (1998). Relationships and unethical behaviour: a social network perspective. *Academy of Management Review* 1998, Vol. 23, No. 1: pp. 14-31.

Brass, D.J., Galaskiewicz, J., Greve, H.R. & Tsai, W. (2004). Taking stock of networks and organizations: a multilevel perspective. *Academy of Management Journal* 2004, Vol. 47, No. 6: pp. 795-817.

Brown, A.J. *et al.* (2005). *Chaos or Coherence? Strengths, Opportunities and Challenges for Australia's Integrity Systems.* National Integrity Systems Assessment (NISA) Final Report. Key Centre for Ethics Law Justice & Governance, Griffith University and Transparency International Australia.

Burt, R.S. (2000). The Network Structure of Social Capital. *Research in Organizational Behaviour*, Volume 22: pp. 345-423.

Carpenter, D. (2013). Detecting and Measuring Capture. In D. Carpenter & D. Moss (Eds.), *Preventing Regulatory Capture: Special Interest Influence and How to Limit it* (pp. 57-68). Cambridge: Cambridge University Press.

Carroll, A.B. (1999). Corporate Social Responsibility. *Business and Society* 1999, 38 No.3: pp. 268-295.

Carr, I. (2007). Fighting Corruption Through Regional and International Conventions: A Satisfactory Solution? *European Journal of Crime, Criminal Law and Criminal Justice* (2007): pp. 121-153.

Cartier Bresson J. (1997). Corruption Networks, Transaction Security and Illegal Social Exchange. *Political Studies.* Volume 45, Issue 3: pp. 463-476.

Chugh, D. (2012). *The Psychology of Corruption. The Motivations behind and Conditioning of Corruption in India.* Young Psychologist 2012, National Paper Presentation Competition, Christ University, Bangalore, India.

Cooper, D.E. (1968). Collective Responsibility (A Defense). In: May, L. & Hoffman, S. (eds.) (1991). *Collective Responsibility: Five Decades of Debate in Theoretical and Applied Ethics.* Savage: Rowman & Littlefield Publishers, Inc.

Copp, D. (1979). Collective Actions and Secondary Actions. *American Philosophical Quarterly* 16 (3): pp. 177-186.

Corlett, J.A. (2001). Collective Moral Responsibility. *Journal of Social Philosophy* 2001, 32: pp. 573-584.

Council of Europe's Group of States against Corruption (GRECO) (2014). *Third Evaluation Round Addendum to the Second Compliance Report on Spain "Incriminations (ETS 173 and 191, GPC 2)" and "Transparency of Party Funding".* Strasbourg: GRECO.

Dasgupta, P. & Serageldin, I. (2000). *Social Capital: A Multifaceted Perspective.* Washington: The World Bank.

Davis, J.B. (2014). Social Capital and Social Identity. *Social Capital and Economics: Social Values, Power, and Identity.* A. Christoforou & J. Davis (eds.), London: Routledge, 2014.

Della Porta, F. (1997). The Vicious Circles of Corruption in Italy. In: Della Porta, D. & Méni, Y. (1997). *Democracy and Corruption in Europe.* London/Washington: Pinter. pp. 35-49.

Della Porta, D. & Vannucci, A. (1999). *Corrupt Exchanges. Actors, Resources, and Mechanisms of Political Corruption.* New York: Walter de Gruyter Inc.

Della Porta, D. & Vannucci, A. (2005). *Corruption as a Normative System.* Presentation at the International Conference on Corruption control in Political Life and the Quality of Democracy: A Comparative Perspective Europe – Latin America CIES - ISCTE, 19-20 May 2005.

Dohmen, J. (1996). *De Vriendenrepubliek. Limburgse kringen.* Nijmegen: Uitgeverij SUN. Available from: http://www.vriendenrepubliek.nl/images/de_vriendenrepubliek.pdf (Accessed 29/08/18).

Donaldson, T. (1982). *Corporations and Morality.* New York: Prentice Hall, Englewood Cliffs.

Donaldson, T. (1989). *The Ethics of International Business.* New York: Oxford University Press.

Donaldson, T. & Dunfee, T. (1994): Toward a unified conception of business ethics: Integrative Social Contracts Theory. *The Academy of Management Review*, Vol. 19, No. 2 (Apr. 1994): pp. 252-284.

Donaldson, T. & Dunfee, T. (1999 a): When Ethics Travel: The Promise and Peril of Global Business Ethics. *California Management Review*, Vol. 41, No. 4 (Summer 1999): pp. 45-63.

Donaldson, T. & Dunfee, T. (1999 b): *Ties that Bind. A Social Contracts Approach to Business Ethics.* Cambridge, MA: Harvard Business Press.

Duyne Van, P.C. (2001). Will Caligula go transparent? Corruption in acts & attitudes. *Forum on Crime and Society.* Vol. 1, No. 2: pp. 73-89.

Eisenhardt, K. M. (1989). Theories from case Study Research. *The Academy of Management Review,* Volume 14, No. 4: pp. 532-550.

Emirbayer, M. & Goodwin, J. (1994). Network Analysis, Culture, and the Problem of Agency. *American Journal of Sociology.* Vol. 99, No. 6 (May 1994), pp. 1411-1454.

Encyclopedia Brittanica (2018). State Capture. Available from: https://www.britannica.com/topic/state-capture (Accessed 01/01/19)

Etzioni, A. (1993). *The Spirit of Community. Rights, Responsibilities, and the Communitarian Agenda*. New York: Crown Publishers, Inc.

Etzioni, A. (2015). Communitarianism. *The Encyclopedia of Political Thought*. M.T. Gibbons. Published 2015 by John Wiley & Sons, Ltd.

European Council (2010). *The Stockholm Programme – An Open And Secure Europe Serving and Protecting Citizens.* (2010/C 115/01). Official Journal of the European Union.

European Commission (2011a). *Communication from the Commission to the European Parliament, The Council and the European Economic and Social Committee. Fighting Corruption in the EU.* Available from: https://eur-lex.europa.eu/legal-content/EN/ALL/?uri=CELEX%3A52011DC0308 (Accessed 29/08/18).

European Commission (2011b). *Establishing an EU Anti-corruption reporting mechanism for periodic assessment ("EU Anti-corruption Report").* Available from: http://ec.europa.eu/dgs/home-affairs/what-we-do/policies/pdf/com_decision_2011_3673_final_en.pdf (Accessed 29/08/18).

European Commission (2014a). *Businesses' Attitudes Towards Corruption in the EU.* Available from: http://ec.europa.eu/public_opinion/flash/fl_374_en.pdf (Accessed 29/08/18).

European Commission. (2014b). Press Release. *Eurobarometer: Corruption on the rise?*

Available from: http://europa.eu/rapid/press-release_IP-12-135_en.htm (Accessed 29/08/18).

European Commission. (2014c). *EU Anti-Corruption Report.* 3 February 2014. Available from: http://ec.europa.eu/dgs/home-affairs/e-library/documents/policies/organized-crime-and-human-trafficking/corruption/docs/acr_2014_en.pdf (Accessed 29/08/18).

European Commission. (2014d). *Annex United Kingdom to the EU Anti-Corruption Report.* 3 February 2014. Available from: http://ec.europa.eu/dgs/home-affairs/what-we-do/policies/organized-crime-and-human-trafficking/corruption/anti-corruption-report/docs/2014_acr_united_kingdom_chapter_en.pdf (Accessed 29/08/18).

European Commission (2017). 2017 *European Semester: Country-specific recommendations.* Available from: https://ec.europa.eu/info/sites/info/files/2017-european-semester-c

ountry-specific-recommendations-commission-recommendations-communication.pdf (Accessed 29/08/18).

European Parliament (2018). *Transparency register: who is lobbying the EU? (infographic).* 9 January 2018. Available from: http://www.europarl.europa.eu/news/en/headlines/eu-affairs/20180108STO91215/transparency-register-who-is-lobbying-the-eu-infographic (Accessed 29/08/18).

Fort, T.L. (2000): A Review of Donaldson and Dunfee's Ties That Bind: A Social Contracts Approach to Business Ethics. *Journal of Business Ethics* (2000, 28): pp. 383-387.

Freeman, R.E., Kujala, J. Sachs, S. & Stutz C. (2017). Stakeholder Engagement: Practicing the Ideas of Stakeholder Theory. In: R. E. Freeman, J. K. S. Sachs (Eds.), *Stakeholder Engagement: Clinical Research Cases, Issues in Business Ethics.* Volume 46.

French, P.A., (1984). *Collective and Corporate Responsibility.* New York: Columbia University Press.

Frissen, P.H.A., Sorgdrager, W., Ferket, J. & Schulz, J.M. (2012). *De schijn en de feiten. Een onderzoek naar mogelijke belangenverstrengeling in de gemeente Roermond.* The Hague: Uitgeverij.

Fukuyama, F. (2001). Social capital, civil society and development. *Third World Quarterly.* 2001. Vol. 22, No 1: pp. 7-20.

Goossen, H. & Sniekers, T. (2014). *El Rey. Van jager tot prooi.* Media Groep Limburg.

Graaf de, G. (2005). De corrupte functionaris, zijn omkoper en hun relatie. *Justitiële verkenningen*, jrg. 31, nr. 7, 2005: pp. 49-63.

Granovetter, M.S. (1973). The Strength of Weak Ties. *American Journal of Sociology.* Volume 78, Issue 6: pp. 1360-1380.

Granovetter, M.S. (1992). Problems of Explanation in Economic Sociology. In: Nohria, N & Eccles, R. (eds). *Networks and Organizations: Structure, Form and Action.* Boston: Harvard Business School Press. pp. 25-56.

Haines, R. & Leonard, L. (2007). Individual characteristics and ethical decision-making in an IT context. *Industrial Management and Data Systems.* 7 (1): pp. 5-20.

Hale, K. & Cline, D. (2014). Holding Collectives Accountable. The UNWCC's Undervalued Role in Developing Collective Responsibility, Yesterday and Today. Criminal Law Forum: *The Official Journal of the Society for the Reform of Criminal Law*. v25 n1-2 (201406): pp. 261-290.

Heffernan, M. (2011). *Willful Blindness*. New York: Walker Publishing Company.

Heidenheimer, A.J. & Johnston, M. (Eds.) (2002). *Political Corruption. Concepts and Contexts*. 3rd edition. New Brunswick and London: Transaction.

Herxheimer, A. (2003). Relationships between the pharmaceutical industry and patient organisations. *British Medical Journal*. International edition 326: pp. 1208-1210.

Heywood, P.M. (1997). Political Corruption: Problems and Perspectives. *Political Studies*. XLV: pp. 417-435.

Heywood, P.M. (2015). Introduction. Scale and focus in the study of Corruption. In: Heywood, P.M. *Routledge Handbook of Political Corruption*: pp. 1-13.

Hirschman, A.O. (1970). *Exit, Voice, and Loyalty: Responses to Decline in Firms, Organizations, and States*. Cambridge, MA: Harvard University Press.

Hodgson, G.M. & Jiang, S. (2007). The Economics of Corruption and the Corruption of Economics: An Institutionalist Perspective. *Journal of Economic Issues*. Vol. XLI No. 4 December 2007: pp. 1043-1061.

Hoekstra, A. (2016). Institutionalizing Integrity Management. Challenges and solutions in times of financial crises and austerity measures. In: A. Lawton, Z. Van Der Wal & L. Huberts (Eds.), *Ethics in Public Policy and Management*. Edition: 1, Chapter: 9, Publisher: Routledge: pp. 147-164.

Höffling, C. (2002). *Korruption als sociale Beziehung*. Wiesbaden: Springer Fachmedien.

Huberts, L.W.J.C. (2014). *The Integrity of Governance. What It Is, What We Know, What Is Done, and Where to Go*. Palgrave Macmillan UK.

Huberts, L.W.J.C., Lasthuizen, K.M. & Peeters, C.F.W. (2006). Measuring corruption: Exploring the iceberg. In C. Sampford, A. Shacklock, C. Connors & F. Galtung (Eds.), *Measuring corruption* (Law, Ethics and Governance) UK: Ashgate Publishing: pp. 265-293.

Huberts, L.W.J.C., F. Anechiarico & F.E. Six (2008). 'Local integrity systems'. In L.W.J.C. Huberts, F. Anechiarico and F.E. Six (eds) *Local Integrity Systems: World cities fighting corruption and safeguarding integrity.* The Hague: BJu Publishers: pp. 3-17.

Huberts, L.W.J.C. & Six, F. (2012). Local Integrity Systems. Toward a Framework for Comparative Analysis and Assessment. *Public Integrity.* Vol. 14, issue 2: pp. 151-172.

Huberts, L.W.J.C., Pijl, D. & Steen, A. (1999). Integriteit en corruptie. In C.J.C.F. Fijnaut, E.R. Muller & U. Rosenthal (Eds.), *Politie. Studies over haar werking en organisatie.* Alphen aan den Rijn: Samsom: pp. 445-472.

Hulten van, M. (2010). *Influence Marketing. Paper based on all input received for the Saxion-Tiri/Pien Conference on 8 and 9 April 2010*, SAXION, Deventer, the Netherlands.

Hulten van, M. (2011). *Corruptie. Handel in macht en invloed.* Den Haag: Sdu Uitgevers.

Jennings, A. (2011). Investigating corruption in corporate sport: The IOC and FIFA. *International Review for the Sociology of Sport.* 46(4): pp. 387-398.

Jennings, A. (2015). *FIFA Imperium. De Voetbalmaffia van Sepp Blatter.* Amsterdam: Uitgeverij Thomas Rap.

Johnston, M. (2005). *Syndromes of corruption: Wealth, Power, and Democracy.* Cambridge University Press.

Kaptein, M. & Wempe, J. (2002). The *Balanced Company. A Theory of Corporate Integrity.* Oxford University Press.

Keiler, J. (2011). Towards a European Concept of Participation in Crime. In A. Klip (2011). (ed.). *Substantive Criminal Law of the European Union.* Antwerp, Apeldoorn, Portland: Maklu Publishers: pp. 173-196.

Kincaid, H. (2014). Dead Ends and Live Issues in the Individualism-Holism Debate. Chapter 8 in J. Zahle and F. Collin (eds.). *Rethinking the Individualism-Holism Debate.* Springer International Publishing Switzerland.

Klitgaard, R. (1988). *Controlling Corruption.* Berkeley and Los Angeles: University of California Press.

Klüver, H. (2013). *Lobbying in the European Union: Interest Groups, Lobbying Coalitions, and Policy Change.* Oxford Scholarship Online.

Knoke, D. & Yang, S. (2008). *Social Network Analysis.* 2nd ed. Quantitative Applications in the Social Sciences; 154. Thousand Oaks: Sage Publications.

Kolthoff, E. & Khonraad, S. (2016). Ondermijnende aspecten van georganiseerde criminaliteit en de rol van de bovenwereld. *Tijdschrift voor Criminologie.* v58 n2 (201606): pp.76-90.

Lauchs, M., Keast, R. & Yousefpour, N. (2011). Corrupt Police Networks: Uncovering hidden relationship patterns, functions and roles. *Policing and Society: An International Journal of Research and Policy,* Vol. 21, No. 1: pp. 110-127.

Lessig, L. (2010). Democracy After Citizens United. *Boston Review.* Available from: http://bostonreview.net/lessig-democracy-after-citizens-united (Accessed 02/01/19).

Leveson Inquiry. (2012). *An Inquiry into the Culture, Practices and Ethics of the Press.* Executive Summary.

Lewis, H.D. (1948a). Collective Responsibility (A Critique). In: May, L. & Hoffman, S. (eds.) (1991). *Collective Responsibility: Five Decades of Debate in Theoretical and Applied Ethics.* Savage: Rowman & Littlefield Publishers, Inc.

Lewis, H.D. (1948b). Collective Responsibility. *Philosophy.* 24: pp. 3-18.

Leys, C. (1965). What is the Problem About Corruption?. *The Journal of Modern African Studies.* Cambridge University Press. Vol. 3, No. 2 August 1965: pp. 215-230.

Luz, R.D. & Spagnalo, G. (2017). Leniency, Collusion, Corruption, and Whistleblowing. *Journal of Competition Law & Economics,* 13(4), 729-766.

Macauley, R. (n.d.). *Fighting Corruption. Incriminations. Thematic Review of GRECO's Third Evaluation Round.* GRECO: Strasbourg.

Makinwa, A. O. (2013). *Private Remedies for Corruption: Towards an International Framework.* Eleven International Publishing.

May, L. (1987). *The Morality of Groups*, University of Notre Dame Press.

McGary, H. (1986). Morality and collective liability. *Journal of Value Inquiry*. Vol. 20 No. 2, 1986: pp. 157-165.

Meadows, D.H. (2011). *Thinking in Systems.* A Primer. London: Earthscan Ltd.

Miller, S. (2011). Corruption. *The Stanford Encyclopedia of Philosophy* (Spring 2011 Edition), E.N. Zalta (ed.). Available from: https://plato.stanford.edu/archives/spr2011/entries/corruption/ (Accessed 28/08/18).

Mitchell, J.C. (1969). *Social networks in urban situations: Analyses of personal relationships in Central African towns.* Manchester (UK): Manchester University Press.

Moran, D.J. (1986). The Meaning of Pattern in Rico. *Chicago-Kent Law review.*Vol.62. Issue 2. Article 2: pp. 139-159.

Nielsen, R.P. (2003). Corruption Networks and Implications for Ethical Corruption reform. *Journal of Business Ethics.* Vol. 42 Issue 2: pp. 125-149.

Nye, J.S. (1967). Corruption and Political Development: A Cost-Benefit Analysis. *American Political Science Review* 61 (2): pp. 417-427.

Organisation for Economic Co-operation and Development (OECD) (2007). *Human Capital: How what you know shapes your life. A Bigger Picture.* Chapter 6. Available from: https://www.oecd.org/insights/37966934.pdf (Accessed 28/08/18).

Organisation for Economic Co-operation and Development (OECD) (2008). *Corruption. A Glossary of International Standards in Criminal Law.* Paris: OECD.

Owens, L.A. & Young, P. (2008) You're hired! The power of networking. *Journal of Vocational Rehabilitation* 29 (2008) IOS Press: pp. 23-28

Oxford Reference (n.d.). Regulatory Capture. Available from: http://www.oxfordreference.com/view/10.1093/oi/authority.20110803100411608 (Accessed 01/01/19).

Palazzo, G., Krings, F. & Hoffrage, U. (2012). Ethical blindness. *Journal of Business Ethics.* Vol. 109 Issue 3: pp. 323-338.

Pearson, D.E. (1995). Community and Sociology. *Society.* July 1995, Volume 32, Issue 5: pp. 44-50.

Pellegrini, L. (2011). Economic Analysis of Corruption. Chapter 2 of *Corruption, Development and the Environment.* Springer.

Pereira, R.M. (2015). *Environmental criminal liability and enforcement in European and international law.* Koninklijke Brill NV: Leiden, the Netherlands.

Pinto, K., Leana, C.R. & Pil, F.K. (2008). Corrupt Organizations or Organizations of Corrupt Individuals? Two Types of Organizational-Level Corruption. *Academy of Management Review.* 2008, Vol. 33 No. 3: pp. 686-709.

Posadas, A. (2000). Combating Corruption under International Law. *Duke Journal of Comparative & International Law*: pp. 345-414.

Posner, R. (2013). The Concept of Regulatory Capture. In D. Carpenter & D. Moss (Eds.), *Preventing Regulatory Capture: Special Interest Influence and How to Limit it* Cambridge: Cambridge University Press: pp. 49-56.

Provan, K.G, Fish, A. & Sydow, J. (2007). Interorganizational Networks at the Network Level: A Review of the Empirical Literature on Whole Networks. *Journal of Management* 2007; 33: pp. 479-516.

Provan, K.G. & Lemaire, R.H. (2012). Core Concepts and Key Ideas for Understanding Public Sector Organizational Networks: Using Research to Inform Scholarship and Practice. *Public Administration Review.* September/October 2012: pp. 638-648.

Putnam, R.D. (2000). *Bowling Alone: The Collapse and Revival of American Community.* New York: Simon & Schuster.

Rawls, J. (1999). *A Theory of Justice.* The Revised edition. The Belknap press of Harvard University Press Cambridge, Massachusetts.

Reding, V. (2011). On Substantive Criminal Law of the European Union. In A. Klip (2011). (ed.). *Substantive Criminal Law of the European Union.* Antwerp, Apeldoorn, Portland: Maklu Publishers: pp. 11-13.

Rose-Ackerman, S. (2016). Corruption and Government. *The Regulatory Review.* Opinion 26 April 2016. Available from: https://www.theregreview.org/2016/04/27/rose-ackerman-corruption-and-government/ (Accessed 28/08/18).

Rothstein, B. & Torsello, D. (2013). *Is Corruption Understood Differently in Different Cultures?* Anthropology meets Political Science. Working Paper Series 2013:5. Gothenburg: The Quality of Government Institute.

Sandel, M.J. (2009). *Justice; What's the Right Thing to Do?* New York: Farar, Straus and Giroux.

Sandel, M.J. (2012). *Niet alles is te koop. De morele grenzen van marktwerking.* Uitgeverij Ten Have.

Slingerland, W. (2016). Norms for networks: a contractarian approach to corruption. Chapter 8 In J.D. Rendtorff (Eds): *Perspectives on Philosophy of Management and Business Ethics Ethical Economy,* Vol. 51. Springer.

Slingerland, W., Eijkelhof, F., Hulten Van, M., Popovych, O. & Wempe, J. (2012a). *Country survey, 'National integrity system assessment Netherlands'.* The Hague: Transparency International Netherlands.

Slingerland, W., Six, F & Huberts, L.W.J.C. (2012). Integriteitssystemen en hun werking. In J.H.J. van de Heuvel & L.W.J.C. Huberts. *Integriteit en integriteitsbeleid in Nederland.* Deventer: Kluwer.

Smiley, M. (2017). Collective Responsibility. *The Stanford Encyclopedia of Philosophy* (Summer 2017 Edition), Edward N. Zalta (ed.). Available from: https://plato.stanford.edu/archives/sum2017/entries/collective-responsibility/ (Accessed 29/08/18).

Søreide, T. (2002). *Corruption in public procurement. Causes, consequences and cures.*

Report R 2002: 1. Chr. Michelsen Institute Development Studies and Human Rights. Bergen: Norway.

Søreide, T. (2008). Beaten by Bribery: Why Not Blow the Whistle? *Journal of Institutional and Theoretical Economics.* JITE 164 (2008), pp. 407-428.

Søreide, T. (2014). *Drivers of Corruption. A brief Review.* World Bank Group. Washington.

Stam, W. (2010). Industry Event Participation and Network Brokerage among Entrepreneurial Ventures. *Journal of Management Studies.* Volume 47, Issue 4: pp. 597-774.

Sutherland, E. H. (1949). *White Collar Crime.* New York: Dryden Press.

Szreter S, W. & Woolcock, M. (2004). Health by association? Social capital, social theory, and the political economy of public health. *International Journal of Epidemiology.* 2004; 33: pp. 650-67.

The Right Honourable Lord Justice Leveson. (2012). *An Inquiry into the Culture, Practices and Ethics of the Press Report. Volume I.* London: The Stationery Office. Available from: https://assets.publishing.service.gov.uk/government/uploads/system/uploads/attachment_data/file/270939/0780_i.pdf (Accessed 28/08/18).

The Right Honourable Lord Justice Leveson. (2012). *An Inquiry into the Culture, Practices and Ethics of the Press Report. Volume II.* London: The Stationery Office. Available from: https://assets.publishing.service.gov.uk/government/uploads/system/uploads/attachment_data/file/270941/0780_ii.pdf (Accessed 28/08/18).

The Right Honourable Lord Justice Leveson. (2012). *An Inquiry into the Culture, Practices and Ethics of the Press Report. Volume III.* London: Volume III. The Stationery Office. Available from: https://assets.publishing.service.gov.uk/government/uploads/system/uploads/attachment_data/file/270942/0780_iii.pdf (Accessed 28/08/18).

The Right Honourable Lord Justice Leveson. (2012). *An Inquiry into the Culture, Practices and Ethics of the Press Report. Volume IV.* London: The Stationery Office. Available from: https://assets.publishing.service.gov.uk/government/uploads/system/uploads/attachment_data/file/270943/0780_iv.pdf (Accessed 28/08/18).

Tops, P. & Tromp, J. (2016). *De Achterkant van Nederland. Hoe onder- en bovenwereld verstrengeld raken.* Amsterdam: Balans.

Trevino, L.K. & Youngblood, S.A. (1990). Bad Apples in Bad Barrels: A Causal Analysis of Ethical Decision-Making Behavior. *Journal of Applied Psychology*. 1990. Vol. 75. No. 4: pp. 378-385.

Turner, J. C., Hogg, M. A., Oakes, P. J., Reicher, S. D., & Wetherell, M. S. (1987). *Rediscovering the Social Group: A Self-Categorization Theory*. Oxford and New York: Blackwell.

United Nations Committee on the Elimination of Racial Discrimination (2015). *Concluding observations on the nineteenth to twenty-first periodic reports of the Netherlands*. Available from: http://tbinternet.ohchr.org/Treaties/CERD/Shared%20Documents/NLD/CERD_C_NLD_CO_19-21_21519_E.pdf (Accessed 28/08/18).

United Nations Office on Drugs and Crime (2004). The Global Programme Against Corruption. *UN Anti-Corruption Toolkit* (3rd edition). Vienna: UNODC.

Uribe, C.A. (2014). The Dark Side of Social Capital Re-examined from a Policy Analysis Perspective: Networks of Trust and Corruption. *Journal of Comparative Policy Analysis: Research and Practice*. Volume 16, Issue 2, 2014: pp.175-189.

Van den Heuvel, G.A.A.J. (1998). *Collusie tussen Overheid en Bedrijf - een vergeten hoofdstuk uit de organisatiecriminologie*. Rede bij de aanvaarding van het ambt van hoogleraar in de Criminologie aan de Universiteit Maastricht op vrijdag 23 januari 1998. Available from:

https://cris.maastrichtuniversity.nl/portal/files/1423722/guid-2f4d2ea7-241c-4d83-b2be-3f7e348966c0-ASSET1.0 (Accessed 02/01/19).

Warburton, J. (2013). Corruption as a social process from dyads to networks, in: Larmour, P. & Wolanin, N. *Corruption and Anti-Corruption*: pp. 221-237.

Warren, M.E. (2004). What Does Corruption Mean in a Democracy? *American Journal of Political Science*, Vol. 48, No. 2 (Apr., 2004): pp. 328-343.

Welten, R. (2012). *'Gij zult maatschappelijk verantwoord ondernemen!' Een pleidooi voor een doorleefde bedrijfsethiek*. Lectorale rede January 2012. Deventer: Saxion.

Wempe, J. (2009). Industry and Chain responsibilities and Integrative Social Contracts Theory. *Journal of Business Ethics*, (2009, 88): pp. 751-764.

Wempe, J. (2010). Chain Responsibility and the Collaborative Enterprise, in: Tencati, A. and Zsolnai, L. (ed.), *The Collaborative Enterprise. Creating Values for a Sustainable World.* Oxford: Peter Lang Academic Publishers: pp. 267-288.

Wempe, J. (2011). From task to role responsibility: towards a prospective business ethics, in: Tencati, A., and Perrini, F., *Business ethics and corporate sustainability. Studies in Trans Atlantic Business Ethics series*, ch. 3.

Wempe, J. (2016). *Morele moed van ondernemingen. De contouren van een prospectieve ethiek.* Inaugurele rede 13 May 2016. Vrije Universiteit van Amsterdam. Available from: http://www.feweb.vu.nl/nl/Images/Oratie-Wempe-Uitgesproken_tekst_tcm257-767275.pdf (Accessed 28/08/18).

Wempe, J. & Slingerland, W. (2016). My brother's keeper: a new phase in the debate on corporate responsibility. Chapter 7 In J.D. Rendtorff (ed.): *Perspectives on Philosophy of Management and Business Ethics Ethical Economy*, Vol. 51. Springer.

Werhane, P. H. (1985). *Persons, Rights and Corporations.* Englewood Cliffs, N.J.: Prentice-Hall.

Wuthnow, R. (2002). Bridging the Privileged and the Marginalized? Chapter 2 In: Putnam R.D. (ed.). *Democracies in Flux. The Evolution of Social Capital in Contemporary Society*. Oxford University Press Inc.

Yin, R. K. (2003). *Case study research: Design and methods* (3rd ed.). Thousand Oaks, California: Sage.

Youd, K. (2014). The Winter's Tale of Corruption: The 2022 FIFA World CUP in Qatar, the Impending Shift to Winter, and Potential Legal Actions against FIFA. *Northwestern Journal of International Law & Business.* Volume 35 Issue 1 Fall: pp. 16-7197.

Zahle, J. (2016). Methodological Holism in the Social Sciences. *The Stanford Encyclopedia of Philosophy (Summer 2016 Edition)*, Edward N. Zalta (ed.). Available from: https://plato.stanford.edu/entries/holism-social/ (Accessed 28/08/18).

Zimbardo, P. (2008a). *The Lucifer Effect: How Good People Turn Evil.* Ebury Publishing.

Zimbardo, P. (2008b). *The psychology of evil.* Ted Talk February 2008. Available from: http://www.ted.com/talks/philip_zimbardo_on_the_psychology_of_evil (Accessed 28/08/18)

Newspapers and web documents

American Bar Association (2016). *Pleading a "Pattern of Racketeering Activity" under State and Federal Statutes by Bendana, A.M. 14 March 2016.* Available from: http://apps.americanbar.org/litigation/committees/businesstorts/articles/winter2016-0316-pleading-pattern-of-racketeering-activity-under-state-and-federal-statutes.html (Accessed 28/08/18).

Anechiarico, F. (2016). Political Corruption. *Roundtable Discussion and Public Forum on Political Corruption.* Museum of Political Corruption Albany, New York April 4, 2016. Available from: https://www.youtube.com/watch?v=IYpouX8TMz0 (Accessed 20/10/16).

ANTICORRP (n.d. a). *Anti-Corruption Evidence: From Research to Policy-Making.* Available from: http://anticorrp.eu/news/anti-corruption-evidence-from-research-to-policy-making/ (Accessed 28/08/18).

ANTICORRP (n.d. b). *Welcome to the ANTICORRP Project.* Available from: http://anticorrp.eu/ (Accessed 28/08/18).

AP News. (2017). *The Latest: FIFA says it will seek restitution in bribe case.* AP News 22 December 2017. Available from: https://www.apnews.com/1565e1391c0c42b29e51c4c84d5504f2/The-Latest:-FIFA-says-it-will-seek-restitution-in-bribe-case (Accessed 28/08/18).

BBC (2013). *Fifa's report into ISL scandal is just window dressing.* 30 April 2013. Available from: http://www.bbc.com/sport/football/22355455 (Accessed 26/07/16).

BBC (2014). *Andy Coulson freed from prison.* 21 November 2014. Available from: http://www.bbc.com/news/uk-30142722 (Accessed 08/12/17).

BBC (2015a). *Phone hacking: CPS calls end to prosecutions.* 11 December 2015. Available from: http://www.bbc.com/news/uk-35070715 (Accessed 08/12/17).

BBC (2015b). *Fifa corruption crisis: Key questions answered.* 21 December 2015. Available from: http://www.bbc.com/news/world-europe-32897066 (Accessed 20/07/16).

BBC (2015c) *Fifa World Cup: Key official banned for seven years.* 6 July 2015. Available from: http://www.bbc.com/sport/football/33416906 (Accessed 27/07/16).

BBC (2015d). *News of World features editor sentenced over hacking.* 6 July 2015. Available from: http://www.bbc.com/news/uk-29205846 (Accessed 21/11/15).

BBC (2015e). *Triesman claims four Fifa members sought 2018 bribes.* 10 May 2011. Available from: http:/news.bbc.co.uk/sport2/hi/football/9481461.stm (Accessed 26/07/16).

BBC. (2016). *Leveson Inquiry: Labour demands part two goes ahead.* 9 February 2016. Available from: http://www.bbc.com/news/uk-35530347 (Accessed 04/04/16).

BBC Panorama (2010). *FIFA's Dirty Secrets.*

Binnenlands Bestuur (2019). *Rechter vraagt om minder starre houding Van Rey en OM.* Available from: https://www.binnenlandsbestuur.nl/bestuur-en-organisatie/nieuws/rechter-vraagt-om-minder-starre-houding-van-rey.9605616.lynkx (Accessed 21/02/19).

Berglund, N. (2015). *Ex-Yara bosses sentenced to jail.* News in English.no. 7 July 2015/ Available from: http://www.newsinenglish.no/2015/07/07/ex-yara-bosses-sentenced-to-jail/ (Accessed 20/11/15).

Café Weltschmerz (2016). '*De Limburger probeert me al jaren kapot te maken*'; Ton Lankreijer en Jos van Rey. 29 July 2016. Available from: https://www.youtube.com/watch?v=hkKNELb57rM&feature=youtu.be (Accessed 28/08/18).

Cambridge Dictionary (n.d.). *Collusion.* Available from: https://dictionary.cambridge.org/dictionary/english/collusion (Accessed 27/12/18)

Conn, D. (2017a). Sepp Blatter after the fall: 'Why the hell should I bear all the blame?' *The Guardian.* 19 June 2017.Available from: https://www.theguardian.com/football/2017/jun/19/sepp-blatter-fifa-president-corruption- (Accessed 22/11/17).

Conn, D. (2017b). How the FBI won 'the World Cup of fraud' as Fifa scandal arrives in court. *The Guardian.* 6 November 2017. Available from: https://www.theguardian.com/football/2017/nov/06/fifa-scandal-fbi-new-york-trial-chuck-blazer-sepp-blatter (Accessed 21/11/17).

Corporate Europe Observatory (n.d.). *Lobbycracy.* Available from: https://corporateeurope.org/tags/lobbycracy (Accessed dd. 28/08/18).

Council of Europe (n.d. a). *Details of Treaty No.173 Criminal Law Convention on Corruption.* Available from: http://www.coe.int/en/web/conventions/full-list/-/conventions/treaty/173 (Accessed 28/08/18).

Council of Europe (n.d. b). *What is GRECO?* Available from: https://www.coe.int/en/web/greco/about-greco/what-is-greco (Accessed 02/01/18).

Council of Europe (n.d. c). *The Fight against Corruption: A Priority for the Council of Europe.* Available from: https://www.coe.int/en/web/greco/about-greco/priority-for-the-coe (Accessed 20/02/18).

De Limburger (2016). *Live blog proces Van Rey.* 10 May 2016. Available from: http://www.limburger.nl/cnt/dmf20160510_00020314/live-blog-proces-van-rey (Accessed 25/10/16).

De Stentor (2016). *Twee jaar cel geëist tegen VVD'er Jos van Rey.* 10 May 2016. Available from: http://www.destentor.nl/algemeen/binnenland/twee-jaar-cel-ge%C3%ABist-tegen-vvd-er-jos-van-rey-1.6000855 (Accessed 25/10/16).

Eriksson, A. (2016). EU commission presents 'realistic' lobbying rules. eu*observer* 28 September 2016. Available from: https://euobserver.com/institutional/135280 (Accessed 27/10/17).

Feenstra, W & Misérus, F. (2016). *FIFA president Infantino violated code of ethics with voting advice.* 20 July 2016. Available from: http://www.volkskrant.nl/sport/fifa-president-infantino-violated-code-of-ethics-with-voting-advice~a4342795/ (Accessed 27/07/16).

Feuer A. (2017). Why Are Corruption Cases Crumbling? Some Blame the Supreme Court. New York Times 17 November 2017. Available from: https://www.nytimes.com/2017/11/17/nyregion/menendez-seabrook-corruption-cases-crumbling-.html (Accessed 06/03/18).

FIFA (n.d. a). *Associations.* Available from: http://www.fifa.com/associations/ (Accessed 20/07/16).

FIFA (n.d. b). *Who We Are.* Available from: http://www.fifa.com/about-fifa/who-we-are/index.html (Accessed 19/07/16).

FIFA (2015a). *Independent Ethics Committee bans Joseph S. Blatter and Michel Platini.* 21 December 2015. http://www.fifa.com/governance/news/y=2015/m=12/news=independent-ethics-committee-bans-joseph-s-blatter-and-michel-platini-2747411.html (Accessed 27/07/16).

FIFA (2015b). *FIFA Financial Report 2014.* Available from: http://www.fifa.com/mm/document/affederation/administration/02/56/80/39/fr2014weben_neutral.pdf (Accessed 20/07/16).

Goossens, H. & Sniekers. T. *De Limburger* 7 January 2016. Wat heeft Van Rey kunnen wijzigen in het eindrapport? Available from: http://www.limburger.nl/cnt/dmf20160107_00005633/wat-heeft-van-rey-kunnen-wijzigen-in-het-eindrapport (Accessed 10/06/16).

Gibson, O. (2014a). Fifa dismissal of Michael Garcia's World Cup appeal is Orwellian farce. . *The Guardian* 16 December 2014. Available from: https://www.theguardian.com/football/2014/dec/16/fifa-michael-garcia-world-cup-appeal-farce (Accessed 10/06/16).

Gibson, O. (2014b). Michael Garcia quits Fifa ethics committee over handling of report. *The Guardian* 17 December 2014. Available from: https://www.theguardian.com/football/2014/dec/17/michael-garcia-resigns-fifa-ethics-committee (Accessed 10/06/16).

Gibson, O. (2015). Fifa's secretary general Jérôme Valcke under new pressure over $10m 'bribe'. *The Guardian.* June 2015.Available from: https://www.theguardian.com/football/2015/jun/02/fifa-jerome-valcke-under-pressure-10m-bribe (Accessed 26/07/16).

Greenslade, R. (2015). Will Leveson part two take place? I very much doubt it. *The Guardian.* 11 December 2015. Available from: http://www.theguardian.com/media/greenslade/2015/dec/11/will-leveson-part-two-take-place-i-very-much-doubt-it (Accessed 04/04/16).

Hanning, J. & Bell, M. (2011). Rebekah, Dave, and the Chipping Norton set: Where power in Britain lies. *The Independent.* 10 July 2011. Available from: http://www.independent.co.uk/news/media/press/rebekah-dave-and-the-chipping-norton-set-where-power-in-britain-lies-2309790.html (Accessed 10/09/15).

Harwell, D. (2015). Nike becomes suspected player in alleged $150 million FIFA bribery scandal. *The Washington Post.* 27 May 2015. Available from: https://www.washingtonpost.com/news/wonk/wp/2015/05/27/meet-the-unscrupulous-executives-who-conspired-with-fifa-officials-to-funnel-150-million-in-bribes/ (Accessed 02/04/16).

International Chamber of Commerce. (n.d.). *Commission on Corporate Responsibility and Anti-corruption.* Available from: http://www.iccwbo.org/about-icc/policy-commissions/corporate-responsibility-anti-corruption/ (Accessed 01/04/16).

Klitgaard, R. (1997). *International Cooperation Against Corruption.* November 1997. Internet Centre for Corruption Research. Available from: http://www.icgg.org/downloads/contribution02_klitgaard.pdf (Accessed 13/01/15).

Kreling, T. (2015). Lagere celstraf voor ex-VVD'er Hooijmaijers. *De Volkskrant* 7 April 2015. Available from: http://www.volkskrant.nl/binnenland/lagere-celstraf-voor-ex-vvd-er-hooijmaijers~a3945895/ (Accessed 10/01/16).

Leveson Inquiry. (n.d.). *About the Inquiry.* Available from: http://webarchive.nationalarchives.gov.uk/20140122145147/http://www.levesoninquiry.org.uk/about/ (Accessed 01/04/16).

1Limburg (2015, 19 January 2015). '*Vooronderzoek naar Van Rey duurt helemaal niet lang*'. Available from: http://www.1limburg.nl/vooronderzoek-naar-van-rey-duurt-helemaal-niet-lang (Accessed 05/08/15).

Longman, R. & Ruiz, R.R. (2017). Chuck Blazer, Central Figure in FIFA Scandal, Dies at 72. *New York Times*, 13 July 2017. Available from: https://www.nytimes.com/2017/07/13/sports/soccer/chuck-blazer-central-figure-in-fifa-scandal-dies-at-72.html (Accessed 25/10/17).

Lyall, S. & Becker, J. (2011). A Tenacious Rise to the Top in the Brutal Men's World of Tabloids. *New York Times.* 7 July 2011. Available from: http://www.nytimes.com/2011/07/08/world/europe/08profile.html?_r=0 (Accessed 10/09/15).

Meijer, R. (2017). Nieuwsuur: Justitie manipuleerde herhaaldelijk onderzoek om wenselijke resultaten te krijgen. *De Volkskrant* 7 December 2017. Available from: https://www.volkskrant.nl/politiek/nieuwsuur-justitie-manipuleerde-herhaaldelijk-onderzoek-om-wenselijke-resultaten-te-krijgen~a4543733/ (Accessed 02/01/18).

Nagtegaal, B. (2015). Cel en taakstraffen voor Feyenoordrellen in Rome. *NRC Handelsblad*. 11 December 2015. Available from: http://www.nrc.nl/nieuws/2015/12/11/cel-en-taakstraffen-voor-feyenoordrellen-in-rome (Accessed 21/05/16).

NOS (2014). *Van Rey in integriteitscommissie*. 23 April 2014. Available from: http://nos.nl/artikel/639429-van-rey-in-integriteitscommissie.html (Accessed 25/10/16).

NOS (2016). *De zaak-Van Rey: van krantenartikel tot corruptiezaak*. 4 April 2016. Available from: http://nos.nl/artikel/2097046-de-zaak-van-rey-van-krantenartikel-tot-corruptiezaak.html (Accessed 25/10/16).

Nieuwsuur (17 December 2012). *Schijn van belangenverstrengeling?* Available from: http://www.uitzendinggemist.net/aflevering/172100/Nieuwsuur.html# (Accessed 28/07/16).

O'Caroll, L. (2015). Andy Coulson wanted me to be fall guy for hacking, Clive Goodman tells court. *The Guardian* 21 May 2015. Available from: https://www.theguardian.com/uk-news/2015/may/21/andy-coulson-clive-goodman-phone-hacking-fall-guy-court (Accessed 04/08/16).

O'Carroll L. & Wintour P. (2014). Andy Coulson guilty over phone hacking as Rebekah Brooks walks free. *The Guardian*. 24 June 2014. Available from: http://www.theguardian.com/uk-news/2014/jun/24/andy-coulson-rebekah-brooks-phone-hacking-trial (Accessed 28/03/16)

OECD (2014). *Bribery in international business*. Available from: http://www.oecd.org/corruption/anti-bribery/ (Accessed06/01/14).

Oxford Dictionaries (n.d.). *Old Boy's Network*. Available from: https://en.oxforddictionaries.com/definition/old_boy_network (Accessed 17/02/18).

Parlement (n.d.). *Mr.Drs. F.H.H. (Frans) Weekers*. Available from: http://www.parlement.com/id/vg09llkaxzrs/f_h_h_frans_weekers (Accessed 31/07/16).

Pelgrim, C. & Meeus, J. (2017). De minister wil een sheriff-ster om motorbendes te verbieden. *NRC Handelsblad* 31 May 2017. Available from: https://www.nrc.nl/nieuws/2017/05/31/de-minister-wil-een-sherrif-ster-om-motorbendes-te-verbieden-10798965-a1561137 (Accessed 27/12/17).

Plougmann, L. (n.d.). *The basics of anti-corruption.* U4 Anti-Corruption Centre. Available from: http://www.u4.no/articles/the-basics-of-anti-corruption/ (Accessed 25/11/15).

Pratley, N. (2011). News Corp needs all of BSkyB. *The Guardian.* 11 July 2011. Available from: https://www.theguardian.com/business/2011/jul/11/viewpoint-news-corp-bskyb-takeover (Accessed 20/02/18).

Rawlinson, K. (2016). Former NoW editor Andy Coulson sets up PR firm. *The Guardian.* 21 January 2016. Available from: https://www.theguardian.com/media/2016/jan/21/former-now-editor-andy-coulson-sets-up-pr-firm (Accessed 23/09/16).

Rayner, G. (2012). Leveson Inquiry: Jeremy Hunt asked News Corp for advice on phone hacking, new emails show. *The Telegraph* 11 May 2012. Available from: http://www.telegraph.co.uk/news/uknews/leveson-inquiry/9260316/Leveson-Inquiry-Jeremy-Hunt-asked-News-Corp-for-advice-on-phone-hacking-new-emails-show.html (Accessed 04/10/16).

Roermond. (2016). *Bevolkingscijfers per 1 januari 2016.* Available from: https://www.roermond.nl/organisatie/BS/PuZa/bevolkingscijfers_01012016.pdf (Accessed 28/07/16).

Ruiz, R.R. (2017). 2 Top Soccer Officials Found Guilty in FIFA Case. *New York Times* 22 December 2017. Available from: https://www.nytimes.com/2017/12/22/sports/soccer/fifa-trial.html (Accessed 27/12/17).

Sick of Smoking (n.d. a). *The Dutch Complaint against the Tobacco Industry.* Available from: https://sickofsmoking.nl/en/rechtzaken/the-complaint-against-tobacco-industry/ (Accessed 30/10/17).

Sick of Smoking (n.d. b). Lawyers in 17 countries are following Dutch lawyers' lead in suing the tobacco industry for attempted murder or aggravated assault. Anti-smoking organizations and lawyers from 15 countries gathered in Geneva recently to discuss the Dutch approach to the, until now, unique case, AD reports. Available from: https://sickofsmoking.nl/en/rechtzaken/the-complaint-against-tobacco-industry/ (Accessed 30/10/17).

Slingerland, W. & Wempe, J. (27 June 2013). De sleutelrol van politieke partijen in het Integriteitsysteem (The Key Role of Political Parties in the Integrity System). *Civis Mundi.* Available from: http://www.civismundi.nl/?p=artikel&aid=2118 (Accessed 15/07/15).

Steen van der, P. (2017). Jaar voorwaardelijk voor Van Rey in hoger beroep. *NRC Handelsblad.* 20 December 2017. Available from: https://www.nrc.nl/nieuws/2017/12/20/voorwaardelijke-celstraffen-voor-van-rey-en-van-pol-a1585624 (Accessed 28/12/17).

Tharoor, I. (2015). It's not corruption that keeps FIFA's Sepp Blatter in power. It's history. *The Washington Post.* 29 May 2015. Available from: https://www.washingtonpost.com/news/worldviews/wp/2015/05/29/its-not-corruption-that-keeps-fifas-sepp-blatter-in-power-its-history/ (Accessed 10/06/16).

The Alliance for Lobbying Transparency and Ethics Regulation (ALTER-EU), Public debate on lessons from a #Lobbycracy 'Transformation for Transparency and Rules for Revolving Door'(dd. 2 April 2013). Available from: https://www.alter-eu.org/documents/2013/04/lessons-from-a-lobbycracy (Accessed 25/09/17).

The Critical Thinking Community (n.d.). *The Socratic Method.* Available from: http://www.criticalthinking.org/pages/socratic-teaching/606 (Accessed 10/06/2016).

The Guardian (2014a). Qatar World Cup bid whistleblower fears for her family's safety. 20 November 2014. Available from: https://www.theguardian.com/football/2014/nov/20/qatar-world-cup-bid-whistleblower (Accessed 20/02/18)

The Guardian (2014b). Ex-NoW journalist Dan Evans gets suspended sentence over hacking. 24 July 2014. Available from: http://www.theguardian.com/uk-news/2014/jul/24/ex-now-journalist-dan-evans-suspended-sentence-hacking (Accessed 25/11/15)

The Guardian (2014c). Available from: Rise and fall of Mohamed bin Hammam – timeline. 1 June 2014. https://www.theguardian.com/football/2014/jun/01/mohamed-bin-hammam-timeline (Accessed 26/07/16).

The Guardian (2015). Former Fifa vice-president Reynald Temarii banned for eight years. 13 May 2015. Available from: https://www.theguardian.com/football/2015/may/13/fifa-reynald-temarii-banned-eight-years-ethics (Accessed 26/07/16).

The New York Times. (2015). The Rise and Fall of Sepp Blatter. 21 December 2015. Available from: http://www.nytimes.com/interactive/2015/05/27/sports/soccer/sepp-blatter-fifa-timeline.html (Accessed 26/07/17).

The Sunday Times. (2015). 'Please, this is very secret' – the explosive claims of bribery and vote-rigging that Fifa decided to kick into the long grass. 7 June 2015. Available from;

http://www.thesundaytimes.co.uk/sto/news/focus/article1565648.ece (Accessed 27/07/16).

The Guardian (2016). A cosy consultation which will pander to the press. 2 December 2016. Available from: https://www.theguardian.com/media/2016/dec/02/a-cosy-consultation-which-will-pander-to-the-press (Accessed 17/02/17).

Transparency International. (n.d. a) *Politics and Government*. Available from: http://www.transparency.org/topic/detail/politics_and_government (Accessed 03/09/15).

Transparency International. (n.d. b). *Anti-Corruption Glossary*. Available from: https://www.transparency.org/glossary (Accessed 03/09/15).

Transparency International. (n.d. c). *National Integrity System Assessment*. Available from: http://www.transparency.org/whatwedo/nis (Accessed 27/11/15).

Transparency International EU: "Lobbycracy has the potential to degrade and destroy democracy" @javorbenedek in the @Europarl_EN #lobbying" (dd. 3 September 2015)

Van der Steen, P. & Dohmen, J. (2016). De zaak-Van Rey: daar kan je zo een 'House of Cards' van maken. *NRC Handelsblad* 11 May 2016. Available from: https://www.nrc.nl/nieuws/2016/05/11/de-zaak-van-rey-daar-kan-je-zo-een-house-of-card-1619987-a1341593 (Accessed 25/10/16).

Volkskrant (2016). Offermanns geen kandidaat meer voor burgemeesterschap Roermond. 22 October 2016. Available from: http://www.volkskrant.nl/binnenland/offermanns-geen-kandidaat-meer-voor-burgemeesterschap-roermond~a3335643/ (Accessed 25/10/16).

Whoriskey, P. (2012). As drug industry's influence over research grows, so does the potential for bias. *The Washington Post*. 24 November 2012. Available from: https://www.washingtonpost.com/business/economy/as-drug-industrys-influence-over-research-grows-so-does-the-potential-for-bias/2012/11/24/bb64d596-1264-11e2-be82-c3411b7680a9_story.html (Accessed 28/03/16).

Xuecun, M. (2015). Beware of China's Safety Record. *New York Times*. 25 November 2015. Available from: http://www.nytimes.com/2015/11/26/opinion/beware-of-chinas-safety-record.html (Accessed 30/03/16).

Zapotosky, M. (2017). *The Washington Post.* 13 July 2017. The Bob McDonnell effect: The bar is getting higher to prosecute public corruption cases. Available from: https://www.washingtonpost.com/world/national-security/the-bob-mcdonnell-effect-the-bar-is-getting-higher-to-prosecute-public-corruption-cases/2017/07/13/5ac5745c-67e6-11e7-9928-22d00a47778f_story.html?utm_term=.825565a449b7 (Accessed 27/12/17).

Legal Sources

Council of Europe (1999a) Criminal Law Convention on Corruption (ETS No.173.) Available from: http://conventions.coe.int/Treaty/en/Treaties/Html/173.htm (Accessed 22/11/15).

Council of Europe (1999b) Civil Law Convention on Corruption (ETS No.174.) Available from: http://conventions.coe.int/Treaty/en/Treaties/Html/174.htm (Accessed 22/11/15).

Council of Europe (2009). *Explanatory Report to the Criminal Law Convention on Corruption (ETS No. 173).*

Crown Prosecution Service (2015). *Statement from the Crown Prosecution Service: No further action to be taken in Operations Weeting or Golding.* 11 December 2015. Available from: http://www.cps.gov.uk/news/latest_news/no_further_action_to_be_taken_in_operations_weeting_or_golding/ (Accessed 07/04/16).

Department for Culture, Media & Sport, Home Office and The Rt Hon Karen Bradley MP. (2016). Press release. *Government seeks views on press regulation issues.* 1 November 2016. Available from: https://www.gov.uk/government/news/government-seeks-views-on-press-regulation-issues (Accessed 17/02/17).

European Commission. (n.d. a). The European Semester: why and how. Available from: https://ec.europa.eu/info/strategy/european-semester/framework/european-semester-why-and-how_en (Accessed 22/07/17).

European Commission. (n.d. b). Corruption. Available from: http://ec.europa.eu/dgs/home-affairs/what-we-do/policies/organized-crime-and-human-trafficking/corruption/index_en.htm (Accessed 21/11/15).

European Commission. (n.d. c). Anti-corruption experience sharing programme. Available from: https://ec.europa.eu/home-affairs/what-we-do/policies/organized-crime-and-human-trafficking/corruption/experience-sharing-programme_en (Accessed 20/10/17).

European Commission Directorate-General Migration and Home Affairs. (2017). Ref. Ares(2017)2943272 - 13/06/2017.

HG Legal Sources. (n.d.) RICO Law. Available from: https://www.hg.org/rico-law.html (Accessed 20/10/17).

House of Representatives (2012). *Voorstel van wet van het lid Helder tot verruiming van groepsaansprakelijkheid in het Wetboek van Strafrecht in geval van openlijke geweldpleging*. Kamerstukken II 2011/12, 33 234, nr. 2.

Openbaar Ministerie. (2015). *Transacties met omkopers oud-gedeputeerde Hooijmaijers*. 13 March 2015. Available from: https://www.om.nl/vasteonderdelen/zoeken/@88614/transacties-omkopers/ (Accessed 10/01/16).

Maurice, E. (2015). *Romanian anti-corruption protests bring down PM*. euobserver. 4 November 2015. Available from: https://euobserver.com/beyond-brussels/130949 (Accessed 21/11/15).

OECD. (1999). *OECD Convention on Combating Bribery of Foreign Public Officials in International Business Transactions*. Available from: http://www.oecd.org/corruption/oecdantibriberyconvention.htm (Accessed 06/01/14)

United Nations Office on Drugs and Crime. (n.d.). *United Nations Convention against Corruption*. Available from: https://www.unodc.org/unodc/en/corruption/uncac.html (Accessed 20/02/18).

United Nations Office on Drugs and Crime. (2004). *United Nations Convention against Corruption*. Available from: https://www.unodc.org/documents/brussels/UN_Convention_Against_Corruption.pdf (Accessed 16/01/16).

United Nations Office on Drugs and Crime. (2006). Legislative Guide for the Implementation of the United Nations Convention against Corruption. Available from: https://www.unodc.org/pdf/corruption/CoC_LegislativeGuide.pdf (Accessed 20/02/16).

United States Department of Justice. (n.d.).*The Foreign Corrupt Practices Act of 1977* (15 U.S.C. §§ 78dd-1, et seq.). Available from: https://www.justice.gov/criminal-fraud/statutes-regulations (Accessed 01/04/16).

United States Department of Justice. (2009). *Criminal RICO: 18 U.S.C. §§ 1961-1968. A Manual for Federal Prosecutors.* Fifth Revised Edition. Available from: https://www.justice.gov/sites/default/files/usam/legacy/2014/10/17/rico.pdf.

United States Department of Justice. (2015). *Nine FIFA Officials and Five Corporate Executives Indicted for Racketeering Conspiracy and Corruption.* 27 May 2015. Available from: https://www.justice.gov/opa/pr/nine-fifa-officials-and-five-corporate-executives-in dicted-racketeering-conspiracy-and (Accessed 20/07/16).

United States District Court Eastern District of New York v. Webb et al. (2015). Indictment 15 CR 0252 (RJD) (RML). 20 May 2015.

Securities and Exchange Commission (SEC). (2011). *SEC Charges Johnson & Johnson With Foreign Bribery.* Available from: https://www.sec.gov/news/press/2011/2011-87. htm (Accessed 30/03/16).

The Council of the European Union (2008). *Council Framework Decision 2008/841/JHA of 24 October 2008 on the fight against organised crime.* Available from: http://eur-lex. europa.eu/legal-content/EN/TXT/?uri=celex:32008F0841.

US Department of Justice (2015). *Nine FIFA Officials and Five Corporate Executives Indicted for Racketeering Conspiracy and Corruption.* 27 May 2015. Available from: https:// www.justice.gov/opa/pr/nine-fifa-officials-and-five-corporate-executives-indicted-racket eering-conspiracy-and (Accessed 02/04/16).

World Bank (n.d.). State Capture. Available from: www1.worldbank.org/publicsector/.../ STATE%20CAPTURE1.doc (Accessed 01/01/19).

Case Law

EU Court of Justice (Second Chamber), 22 November, 2015, ECLI:EU:C:2015:717.

EU Court of First Instance (Third Chamber, extended composition), 8 July, 2008, ECLI: EU:T:2008:256.

Gerechtshof Den Haag, 12 March 2015, ECLI:NL:GHDHA:2015:533.

Hof Amsterdam, 7 April 2015, ECLI:NL:GHAMS:2015: 1212.

Hof Amsterdam, 7 April 2015, ECLI:NL:GHAMS:2015:1231.

Hof Amsterdam, 7 April 2015, ECLI:NL:GHAMS:2015:1232.

Hof Den Haag, 20 December 2017, ECLI:NL:GHDHA:2017:3702.

Rechtbank Limburg, 13 November 2015, ECLI:NL:RBLIM:2015:9622.

Rechtbank Midden-Nederland, 20 December 2017, ECLI:NL:RBMNE:2017:6241.

Rechtbank Rotterdam, 12 July 2016, ECLI:NL:RBROT:2016:5272.

Rechtbank Rotterdam, 12 July 2016, ECLI:NL:RBROT:2016:5277.

Rechtbank Rotterdam, 12 July 2016, ECLI:NL:RBROT:2016:5280.

Supreme Court, 26 June 1989. H.J. Inc. *et al.* v. Northwestern Bell Telephone Co. *et al.*, 492 U.S. 229. No. 87-1252.